Is That an Old Camera?

100 View Camera Photos of the North Country

Is That an Old Camera?

100 View Camera Photos of the North Country

by

Allen Anway
&
Ruth Anway

Groundglass Press
Superior, Wisconsin

Groundglass Press
1219 North 21st Street
Superior WI 54880

Is That an Old Camera
100 View Camera Photos of the North Country

Printed in the United States of America

Library of Congress Control Number: 2014952984

ISBN: 978-0-9778500-6-8

TABLE OF CONTENTS

Introduction

In the mid-1960s I was a physics graduate student at the University of Chicago, married to Dorothy and with baby Carol. One day while walking the quadrangles, I spied a gentleman taking a picture of a campus building with a 4×5 camera on a tripod. 4×5 means the nominal cut film size is 4 inches by 5 inches, far larger than the typical 35mm film commonly used then. Thus I first met university photographer, David Windsor. By his acquaintance I became introduced to View Camera Photography, a life changing experience for me.

David joined our informal group who ate lunch together at the university. One day I asked him to tell me the steps to make a Kodak Dye Transfer print. From memory he told me each one of about 20 difficult steps to accomplish this. I then realized that I was in the presence of a walking photographic encyclopedia, a person I called upon for photographic answers for the rest of my life.

Later at the university, an acquaintance sold me a 5×7 Burke & James Grover monorail view camera with 12 inch f/4.5 Carl Meyer Anastigmat lens at a friend's price. So I purchased 5×7 black and white film (cheap film) and proceeded to take pictures. Walking to the Lake Michigan shore with Dorothy, Carol, and camera was so arduous that we placed the heavy camera in the stroller and carried the lighter baby.

With the weight and size of a view camera a serious disadvantage, why would one pursue this kind of photography? There are three advantages: (a) large size of film allows sharper pictures compared with small film sizes, (b) keeping the camera back vertical makes vertical lines—as in architecture—vertical and parallel, and (c) independent adjustments of lens with respect to film allow use of the Scheimpflug Principle. The Principle allows accurate focusing of any subject plane—even a tilted plane near to far— onto the film plane by correctly adjusting the lens orientation. Thus the camera focusing is made more general and precise than with ordinary cameras. Yes, there are tilting lenses in small camera photography, but people seldom purchase them.

After graduation we three moved to Superior, Wisconsin, near my home town of Cloquet, Minnesota with my expectation that I would be a physics professor at University of Wisconsin-Superior for the rest of my life. During my first year there, 1969, the university suffered declining enrollment, contrary to my goal of a permanent professorship. As time passed, our family increased by middle daughter Karen and youngest daughter Ruth. After serving five appointments to the university, I founded a partnership with Don Dettmann, A2D2 Electronics LLP, and worked my remaining years making instrumentation to sell to industry.

With excitement in 1969, I purchased my first ten sheets of 5×7 Kodak Ektachrome film to take scenic photographs of the local area. The great expense of color film constrained me to seek each picture carefully and compose it carefully. My criterion was that if the picture didn't look good upside down on the ground glass, it would not be a good picture. Each time I bungled the picture exposure I felt monetary pain. I wanted to photograph the scenes I knew from my childhood, chiefly the St. Louis River as it meandered through Cloquet and through Jay Cooke State Park, at 8800 acres the eighth largest state park in Minnesota. The common photographic big draw here has been Lake Superior, and more neglected has been the St. Louis River, yet I feel the River is my niche. My grandfather Herman Anway was a natural woodsman, and I feel I am keeping his tradition alive by pursuing this kind of photography.

My advice to others about photographic composition is the most simple possible: (a) fill the frame with important information for all pictures, (b) be close to the subject for portraits, (c) choose something near and something far, for scenery. However, good composition is too complex to rely on elaborate rules applied simply. Each kind of camera has its own type of viewfinder, which may help or hinder good composition. The stationary tripod-mounted view camera with its upside down image of the ground glass leads to a more contemplative consideration of the photograph. One sometimes 'walks' the camera around to achieve subtle improvements in the final picture-composition.

Dorothy and I converted an old backpack for me to carry the view camera and lenses into the field. She sewed a new cloth backing (multiple times for lens additions) and I machined the mechanical fittings. That way I could carry all my lenses and extra film holders long distances, at least when I was younger. Now at older age I carry lightweight lenses and fewer of them.

I quickly made friends of the Jay Cooke Park Rangers: now-retired director Eunice Luedtke, naturalists Kristine Hiller and Carly Hawkinson, and present director Gary Hoeft. Assistant director Mark Luschen would urge me to check back after my winter trips, and I appreciate his concern. All of the rangers have given me wise advice over the years, and I have enjoyed sharing with them my unusual discoveries in the park. As I explored the park more and more I got lost more and more and learned how to find myself again. How do you know you are lost? You come to a river and it is flowing the wrong way. Then you are lost.

Picture taking has become a family event rather than just my very own indulgence. Dorothy accompanied me many times into the forest, and we would seek pictures together. I started photography with the idea that I could 'store' a picture in my mind and come back the next day to the same site and take it. Instead I have found the hard way that it can't be done. The scene changes, the lighting changes, I can't find the location, and that which moved me no longer moves me. So my rule is, take the picture now, because I won't be able to take it later.

Jay Cooke Park has changed through the years. Its iconic structure is the "Swinging Bridge" crossing the St. Louis River, first erected after World War I. In my lifetime in 1950 the flooded river destroyed the 3rd bridge. In 2012 the flooded river destroyed the 4th (higher) bridge again. After this flood I called up Naturalist Kristine, and invited myself into the park, and invited her to be my guide. She took it well, giving Dorothy and me a formal tour and I was able to document the flood destruction with my 5×7 camera. Geology had changed before our eyes in a matter of hours, including new beaches and new slumped hills baring their clay insides, severing Highway 210 inside the park. Minnesota has agreed to restore the highway in two years from this writing. Dorothy and I were pleased to urge this rebuilding at public hearings.

Gradually I found other view camera enthusiasts in our local region: David Porter, Ron Yardley, and Henry Roberts. David and Ron have accompanied me on various photographic expeditions. In 2006 at a Rotary meeting, Henry told me, "Stick around." So I did and afterwards he took me to his car to show me a 5×7 Gowland monorail camera without lens, which he offered to give me. So I accepted it, later sending an e-mail to my three grown daughters to see if anyone would want this. Deafening silence. Then a letter from Carol wondering if I could provide a lens. I bought one from Jeff Frey of Custom Photo Lab, and my son-in-law Keith was on his way to entering a new hobby. He now has two 4×5 cameras, one 5×7, and an 8×10 Toyo heavily modified in his own machine shop. Keith, Carol, and daughter Lily as a family now explore and photograph scenic areas the world over.

As Keith and I bring our cameras along to take pictures, we stir up a minor flurry of interest among spectators. The fastest we can take one picture is 15 minutes to set up and put away. We are always happy to give spectators a peek at the ground glass image, shielded from the sun by a dark cloth ("so that's what the black cloth is for!"). We enjoy interacting, even though the questions are the same: "Is this an old camera?" *"No, it is a new camera."* "Do you take pictures of wildlife?" *"I can take pictures of dead wildlife. Although, once I took a picture of a turtle, which left afterwards."*

Another source of pleasure for me has been walking off trail through Jay Cooke Park with a non-photographic friend, typically Jim Taylor. One winter I walked up an unnamed snowy river to an unnamed 44 foot cascade waterfall, a favorite destination, to take a picture. On the way back with all my climbing over and under fallen trees, I lost my 210 mm lens, a gift from Keith. It fell off the front of my camera. Only when I got back home did I painfully realize its loss. Two days later I retraced my steps, trying to find a 4x4 inch black lens board against a 2 inch layer of white snow on ice. Certain that I left it at the waterfall, I returned to the exact spots I had taken pictures, but found no lens. Downhearted, I returned to my parked car. 100 yards from highway 210, I looked back, and there it was, lying in the snow beside my trail. All was intact with no damage, but the front lens cap was missing. A few days later I reconstructed the same trip, but with Jim Taylor, humorously telling him to be on the look-out for the missing lens cap. As we approached the waterfall, Jim plucked the black plastic from the snow (far from the prior lens discovery) and showed it to me. An animal had chomped on it and spit it out, indenting it with dual tooth marks. I use the lens and marked cap constantly to this day, and Jim and I still chuckle over the story. Now I keep all lenses inside my pack and not on the camera. As I write this today, Jim and I just found pilings 50 to 100 years old placed into Silver Creek in the park, showing our photos to naturalist Kristine.

In 1999, the wearing out and looseness of the 1940s vintage Chicago-made 5×7 Grover camera began to grate upon my nerves, so I upgraded to the Wyoming-made 5×7 wooden K B Canham camera, a considerable improvement. But I was so used to the Grover, just loosening, grabbing anything, and then securing, that it took me years to become proficient with the Canham with its different but improved controls.

5×7 cut film size is an oddball size compared with the most popular 4×5 and next most popular 8×10 size. 5×7 cameras are sometimes considered to be portable versions of 8×10 cameras which are too heavy to be carried easily. 5×7 film is rare, so much so, that I now purchase 8×10 film and cut it accurately in the dark with a wheel cutter and special jigs for positioning. One must not cut the nominal 10 inches in half to make the 5 inch nominal dimension. All cut film holders require accurate film size to fit properly into their slots.

Mostly I have not exploited these pictures, but there are a few exceptions. Service Printers, Duluth, Minnesota, has published some calendars of my photographs.

I donated the use of my pictures to Miller-Dwan Hospital, and the hospital paid reproduction and framing costs. Their purpose was to bring peacefulness and serenity to the staff and patients, and I still get commendations from the 5th floor day surgery nurses. Black Bear Casino, Carlton, Minnesota, purchased my pictures for one of their restaurants. Interviewing the purchasers, I found that each person has a different concept of beauty that appeals, and I learned to accept the validity of their choice. My most recent picture is serial number 2368, and my personal favorite is serial number 67.

David Windsor died recently, survived by his widow Lynn, who herself is accomplished in graphic arts. I tell this tale in love of him: Various friends would have difficult photographic questions. I referred them to David, being sure to tell them in advance so they would not become angry, "You get the first sentence, but David gets all the other sentences."

Ruth Anway selected the photographs presented here, mostly from Jay Cooke Park, but not all of them. Ruth selected the cover picture to be compatible with the required printing. The cover picture is the showy lady slipper orchid, the Minnesota state flower, photographed in Jay Cooke State Park. Ruth also scanned and Photoshopped her selected 5×7 positive transparencies for dust removal, but did not change the color saturation of the original. Ruth Photoshopped picture serial number 67 to repair fading from excessive light damage and picture serial number 106 to repair a break in the emulsion.

Susan Rubendall, retired from her editorship at Pfeifer-Hamilton Publisher, donated her time to setting up this book from the parts created by Ruth and me. We appreciate her expertise, advice, and hard work for us in all aspects of publishing this book. I received additional book-publishing advice from Anita Zager and Richard Carlson.

In my youth I read *Modern Photography* magazine, which often expressed that with a little pluck and zeal, any hobbyist could take better pictures than any professional. Now I am older and realize that in some of my familiar fields—physics, photography, electronics, and machining—the professional normally is ten times more proficient than the hobbyist. Despite this, I hope that you, the reader, will indulge my hobby pictures.

—Allen and Ruth, October, 2014.

W I N T E R 1–20

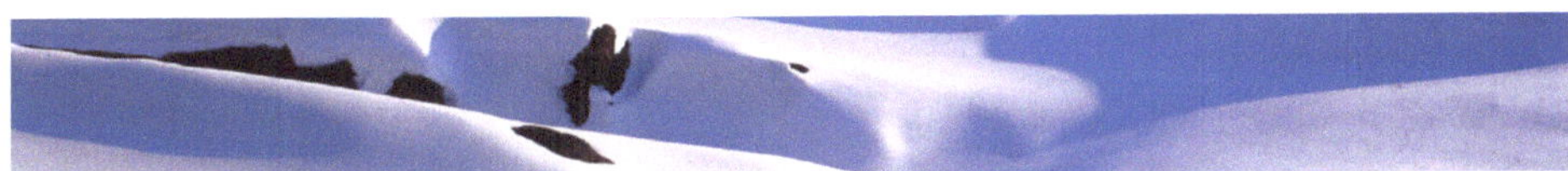

Old shutter lenses with crude oils function poorly in this harsh environment. New shutter lenses with their silicone oils work well, but the photographer is still cold. In 1970s I worked for Plaunt and Anderson Co. on an invention (Patent 4 083 229), sometimes for days outside in the winter. Plaunt explained to me that no matter how much a person bundled up against the cold, the person would only be able to work half as fast as in the summertime.

This holds true for winter view camera photography. My 15 minutes fastest speed becomes 30 minutes for camera setup. Some of the camera adjustments need bare fingers. My breath fogs the ground glass viewing screen. My light meter and GPS require lithium batteries to work in the cold. Deep snow and short days force shorter journeys. So I have fewer winter pictures. However, the low winter sun even at noon makes beautiful long shadows on the pristine snow, so I look for these pictures. But, at least there are no bugs to torment one.

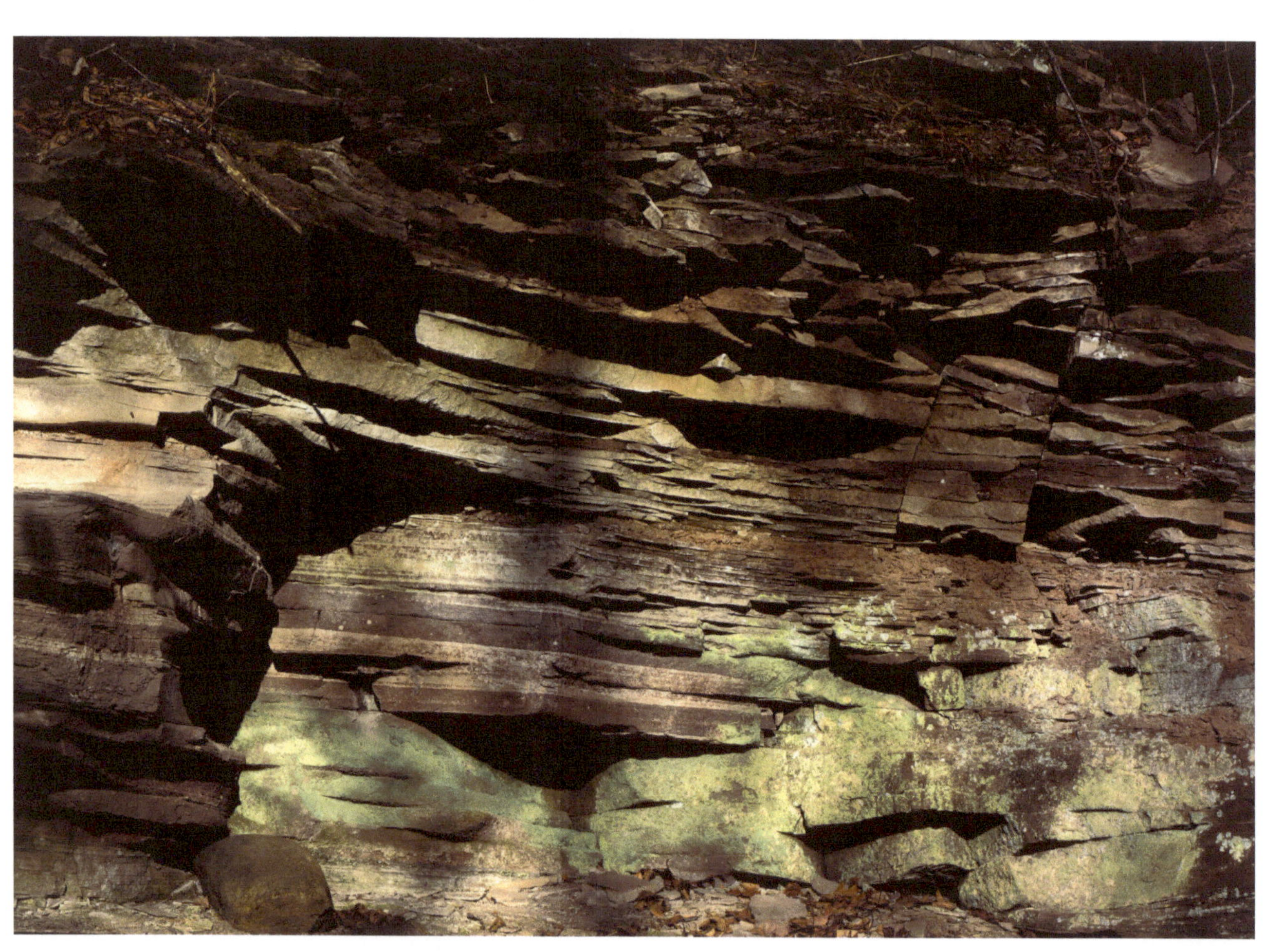

       Fond du Lac, Duluth, Minnesota

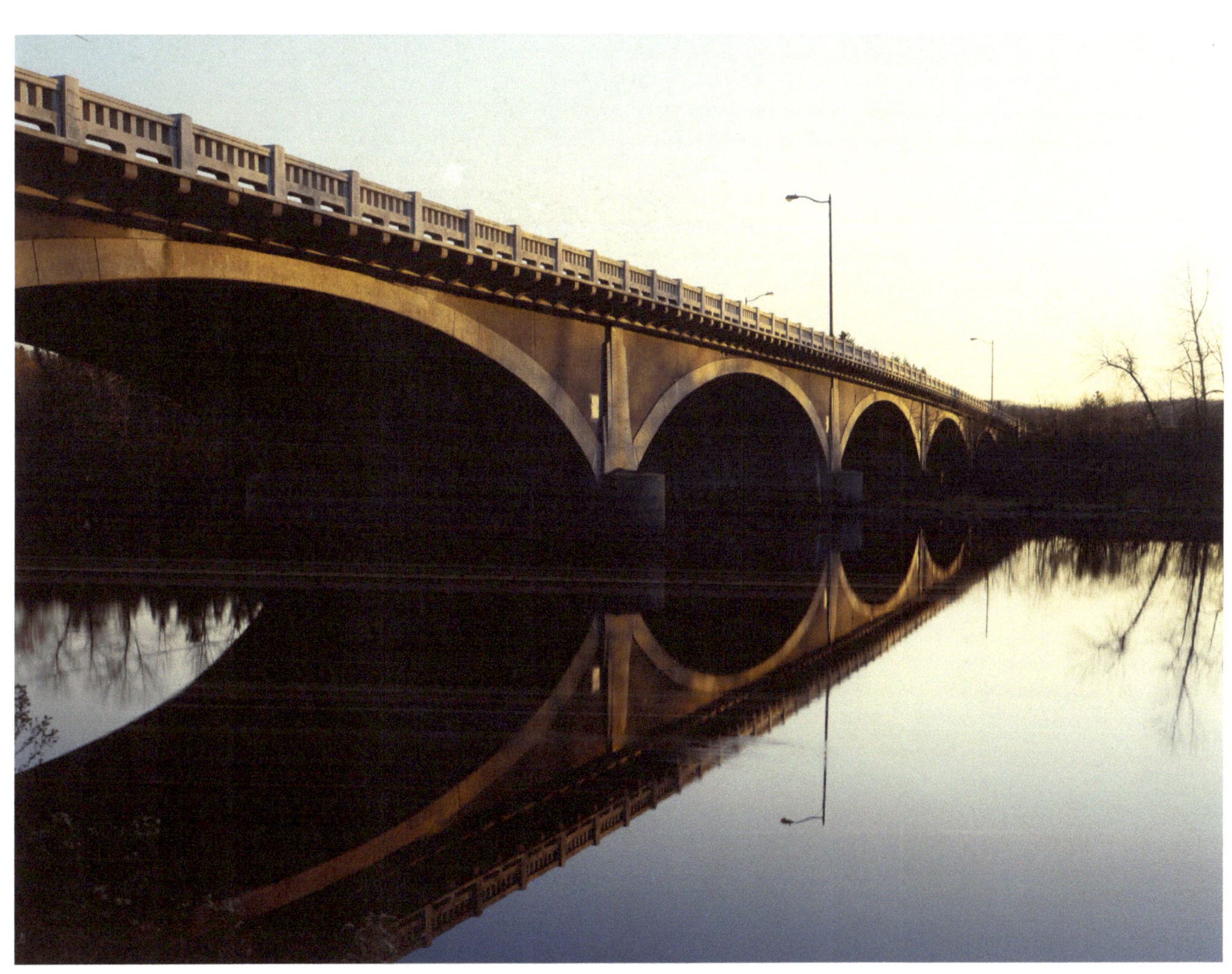

2   324   Fond du Lac, Duluth, Minnesota

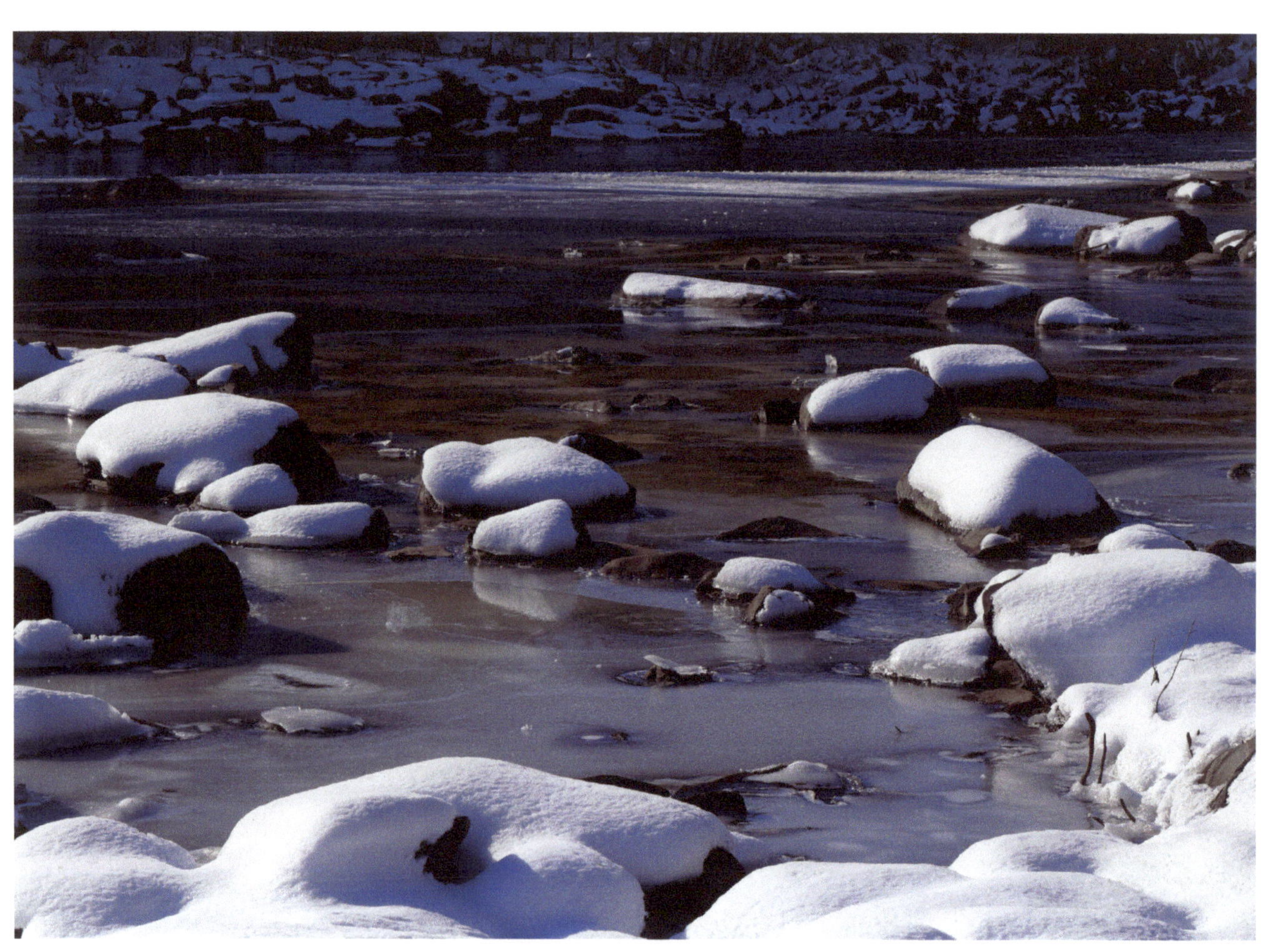

3   1443   Jay Cooke State Park, Minnesota

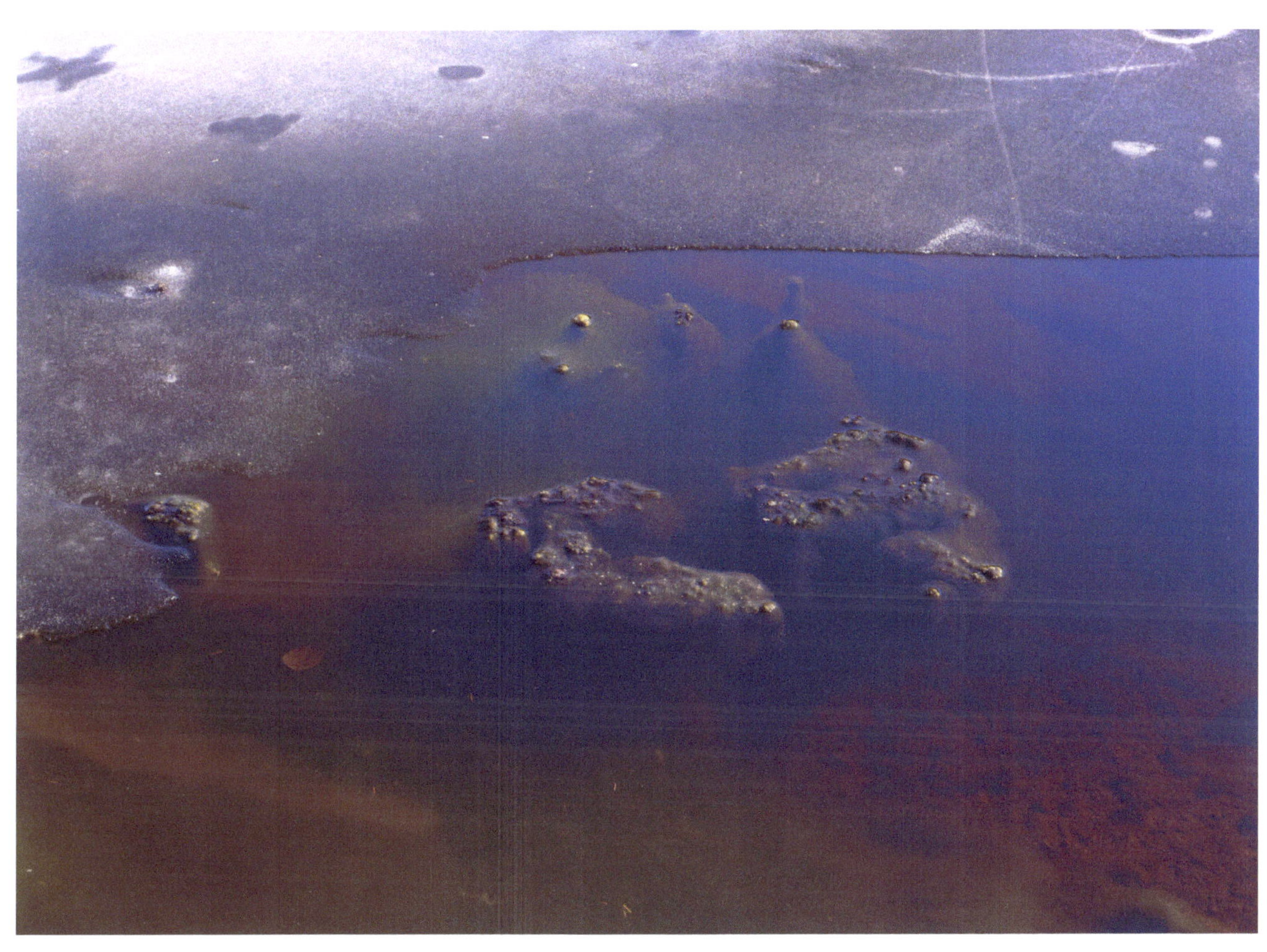

4   1448   Jay Cooke State Park, Minnesota

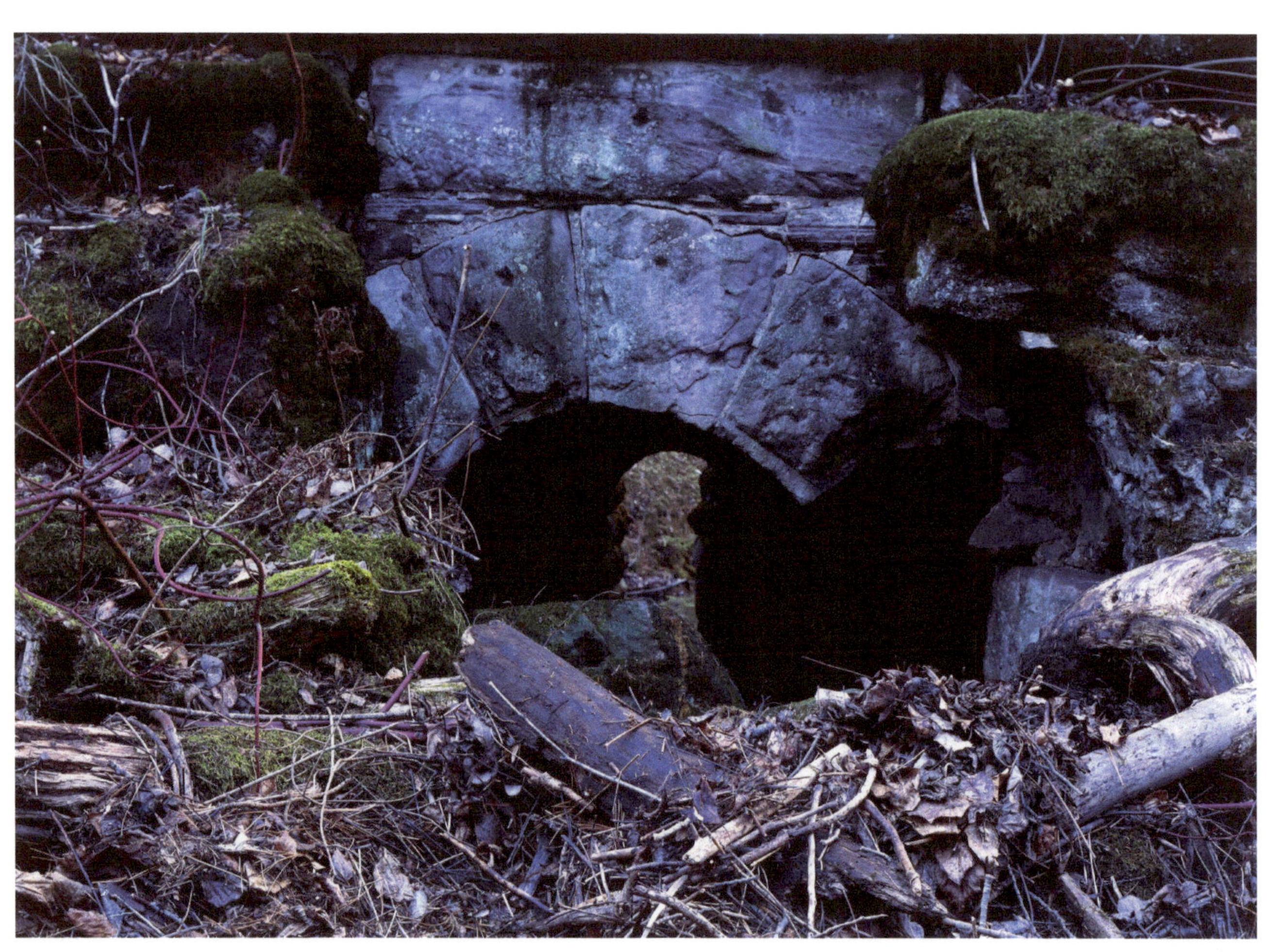

    Jay Cooke State Park, Minnesota

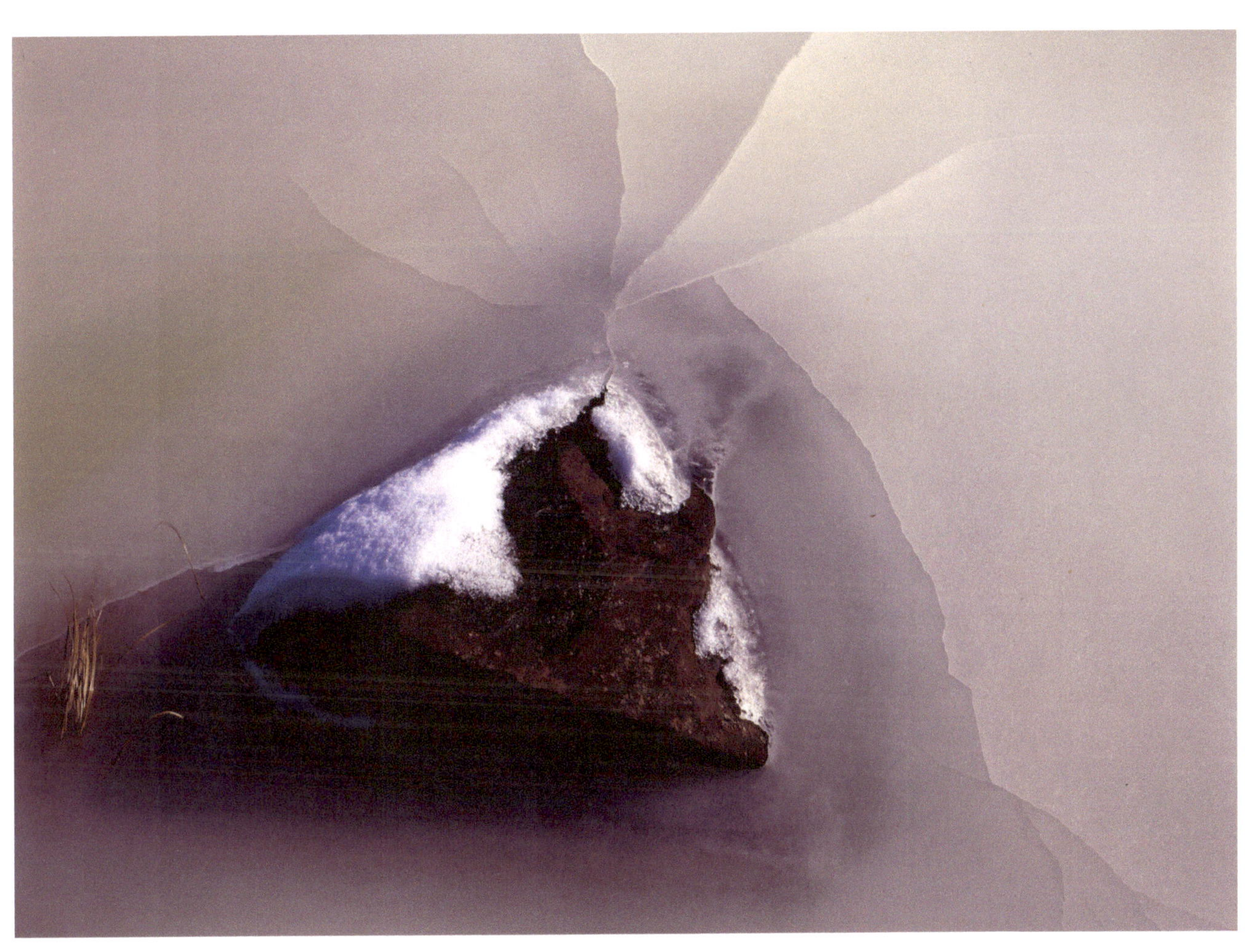

6   1696   Jay Cooke State Park, Minnesota

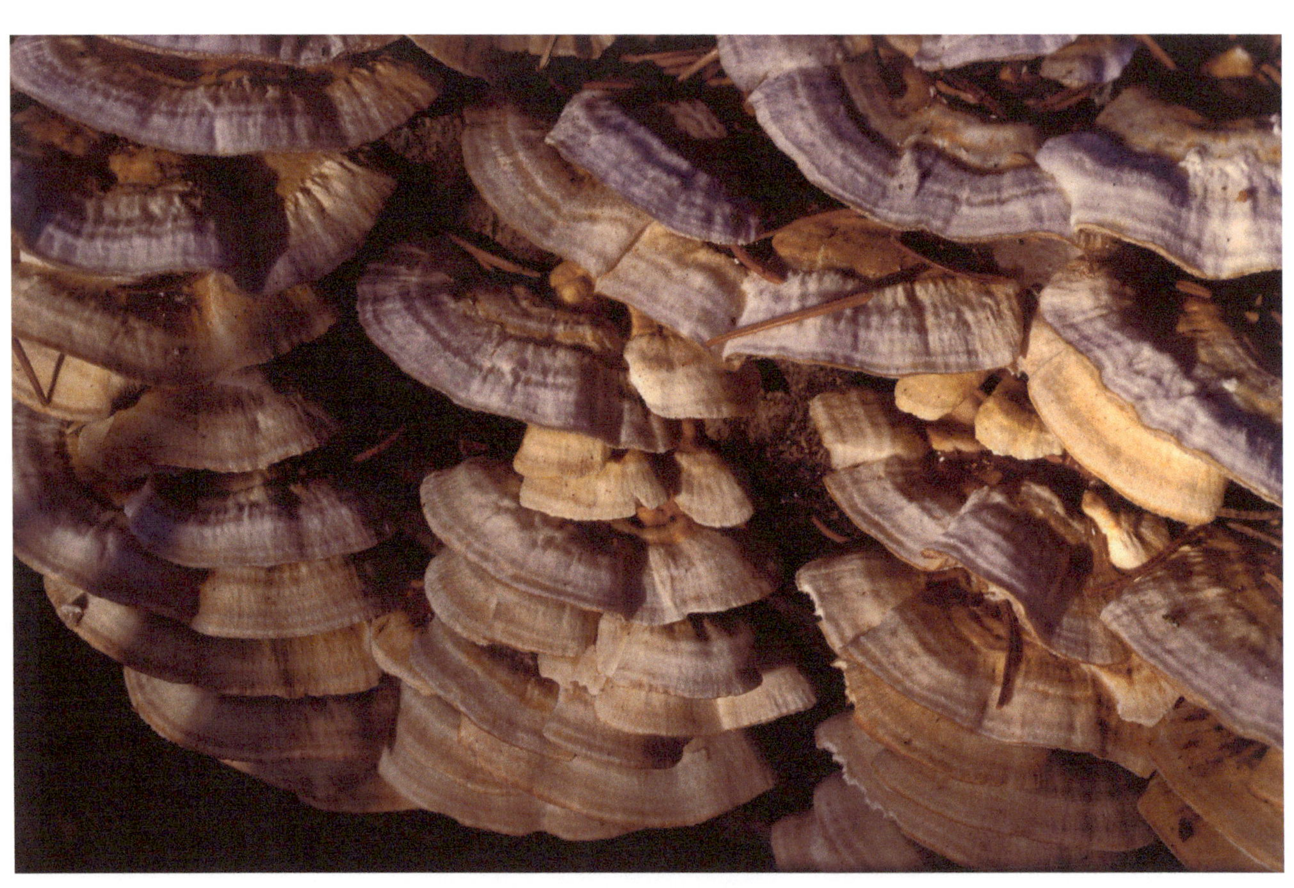

7   I 700   Jay Cooke State Park, Minnesota

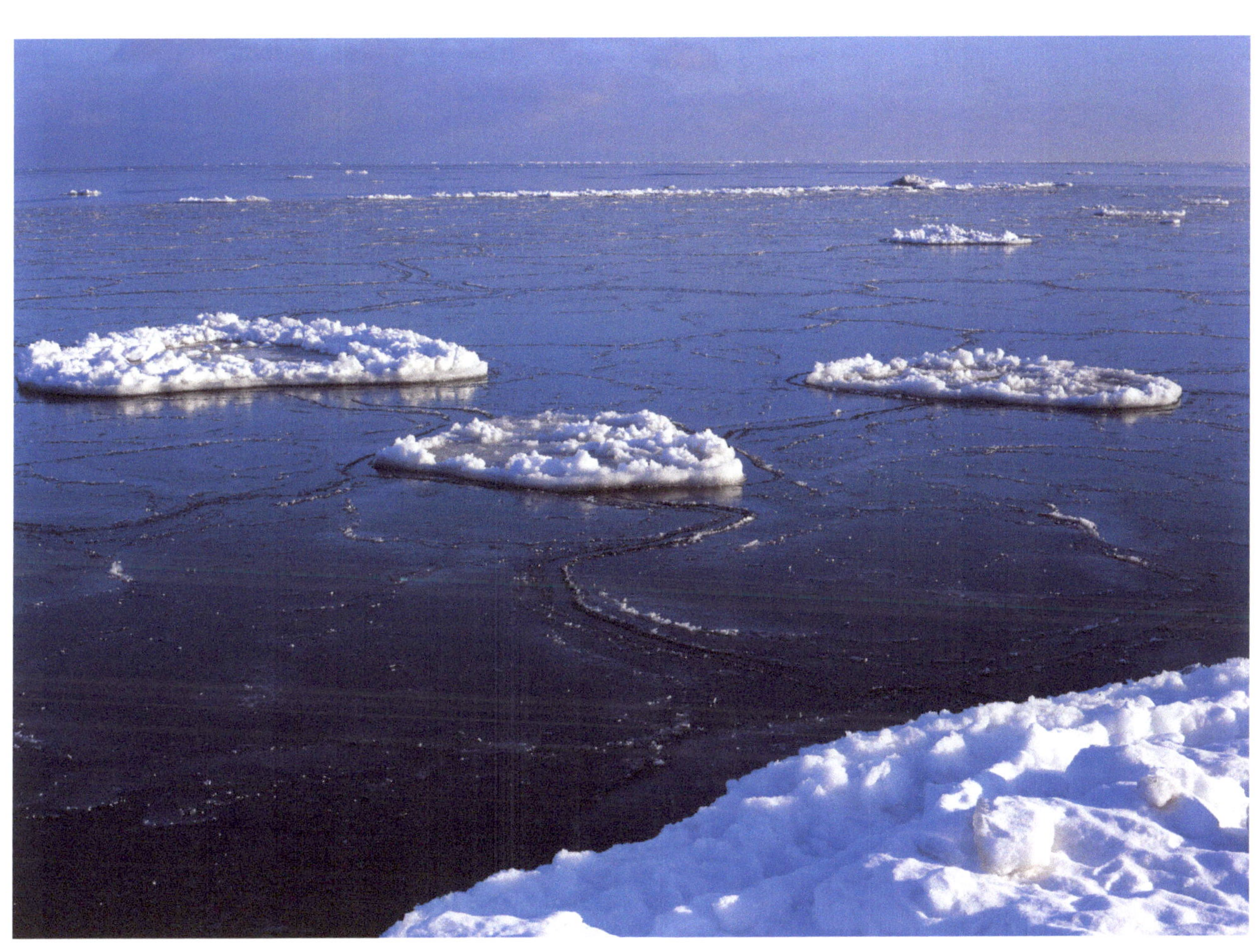

8   2068   Dutchman Creek, Superior, Wisconsin

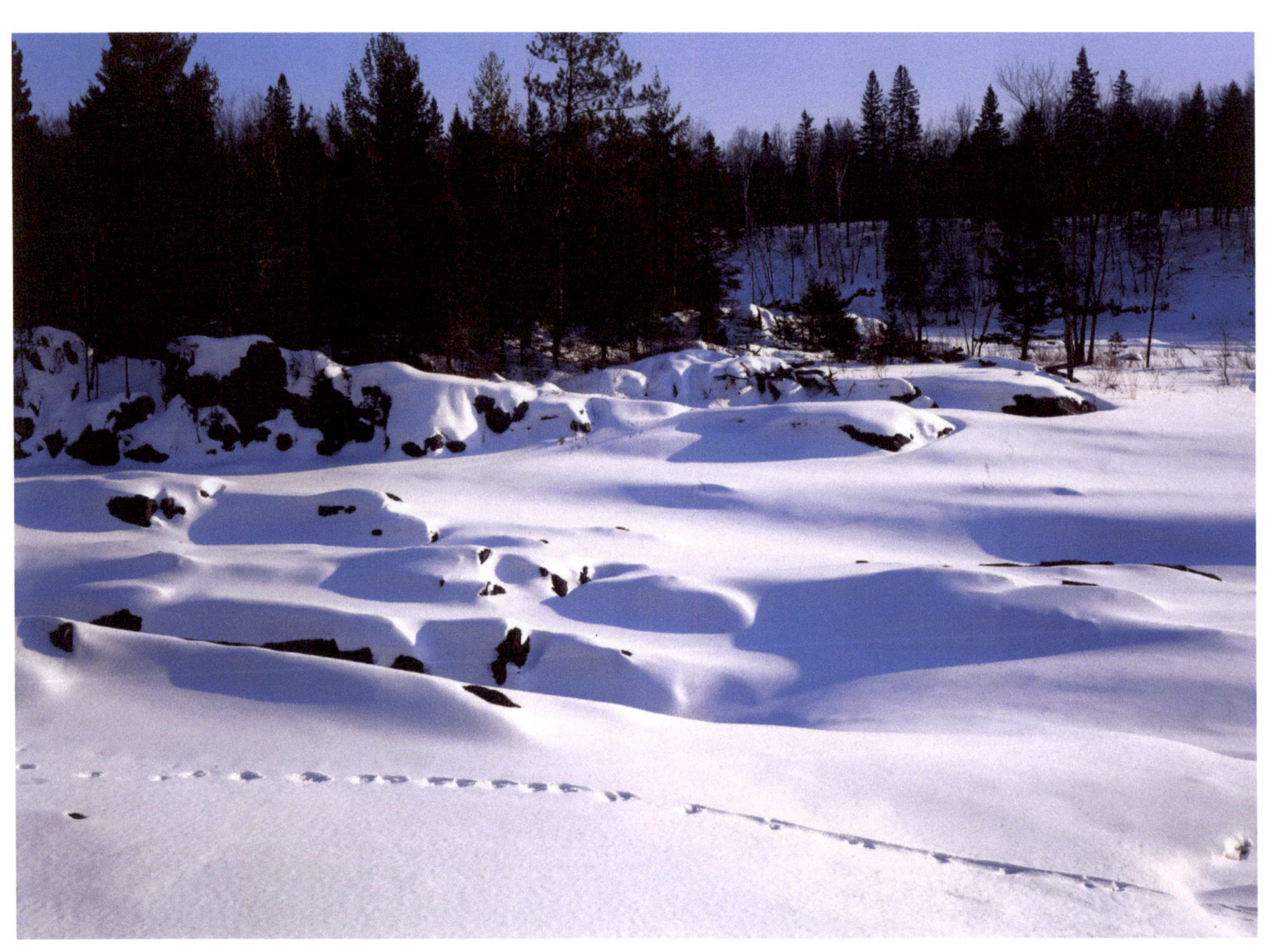

     Jay Cooke State Park, Minnesota

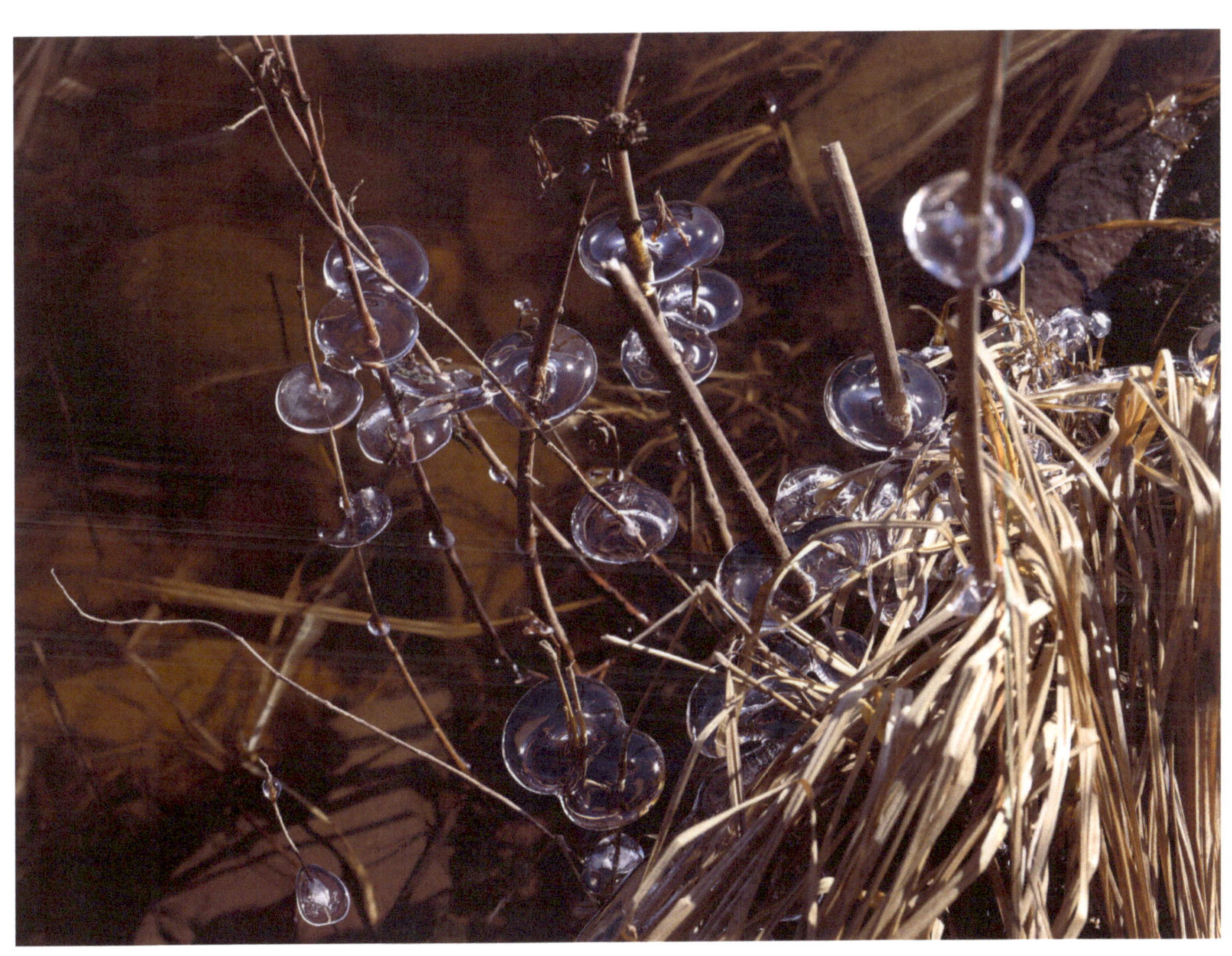

    Jay Cooke State Park, Minnesota

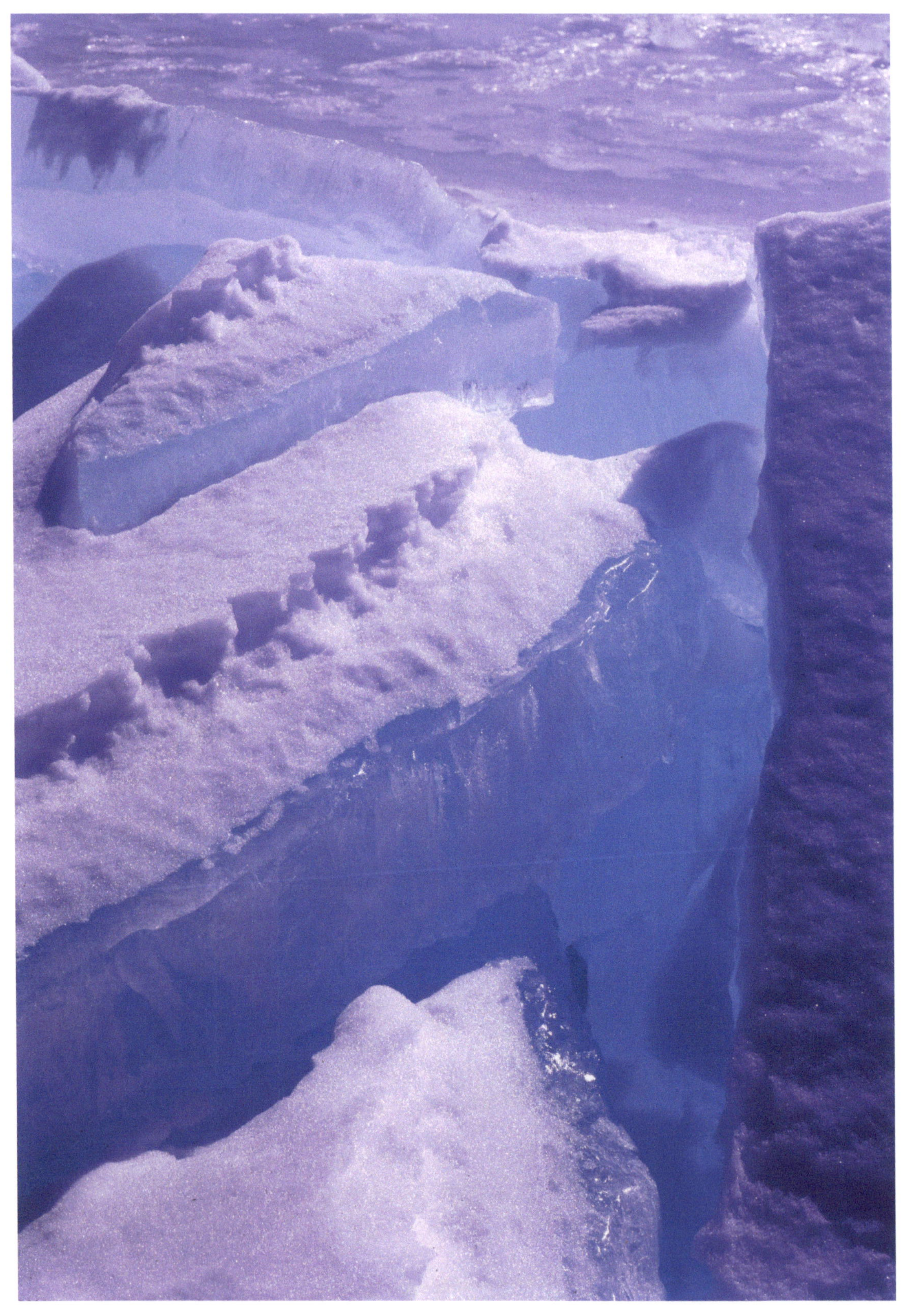

11   1884   Lester River, Duluth, Minnesota

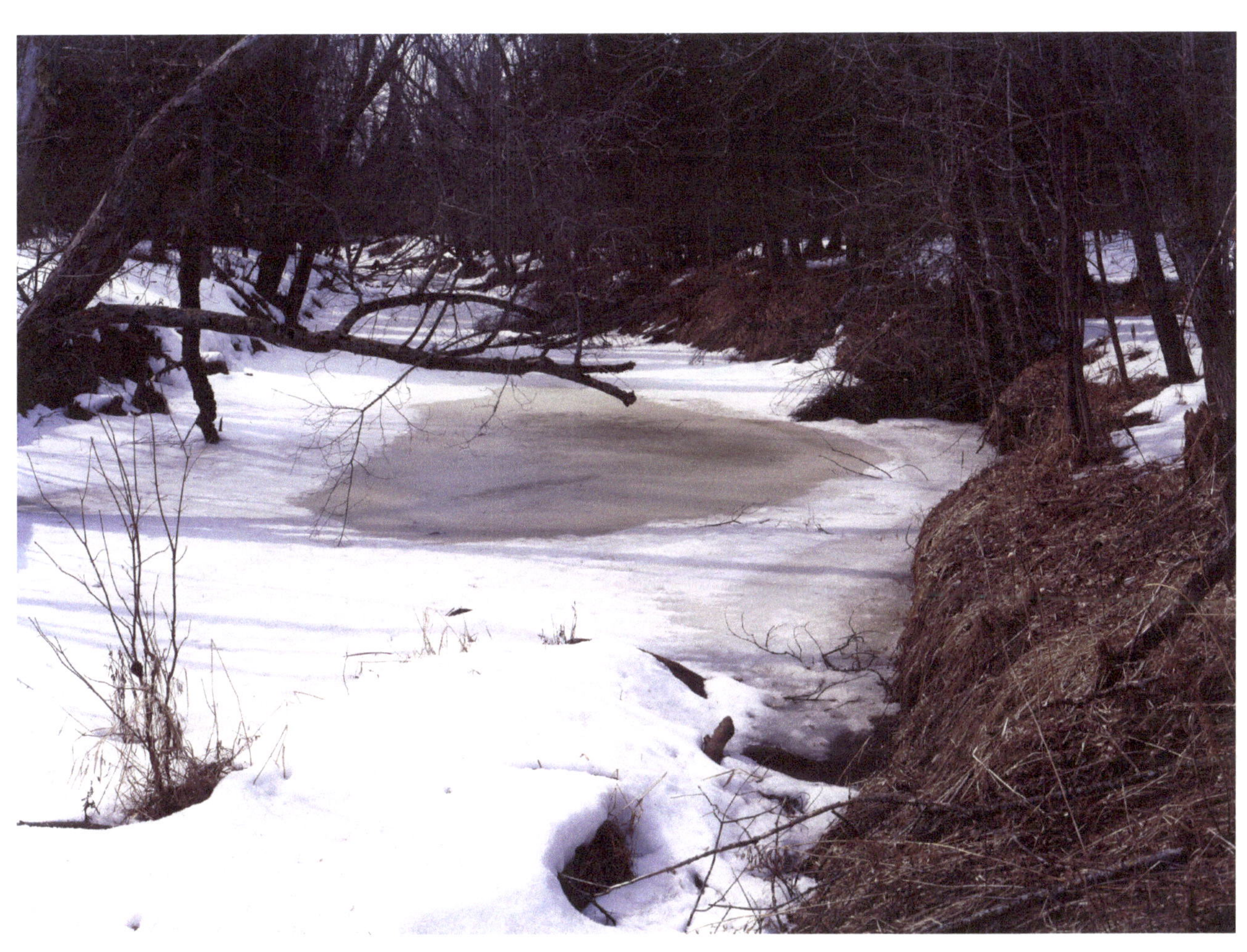

12   2074   Scanlon - Carlton, Minnesota

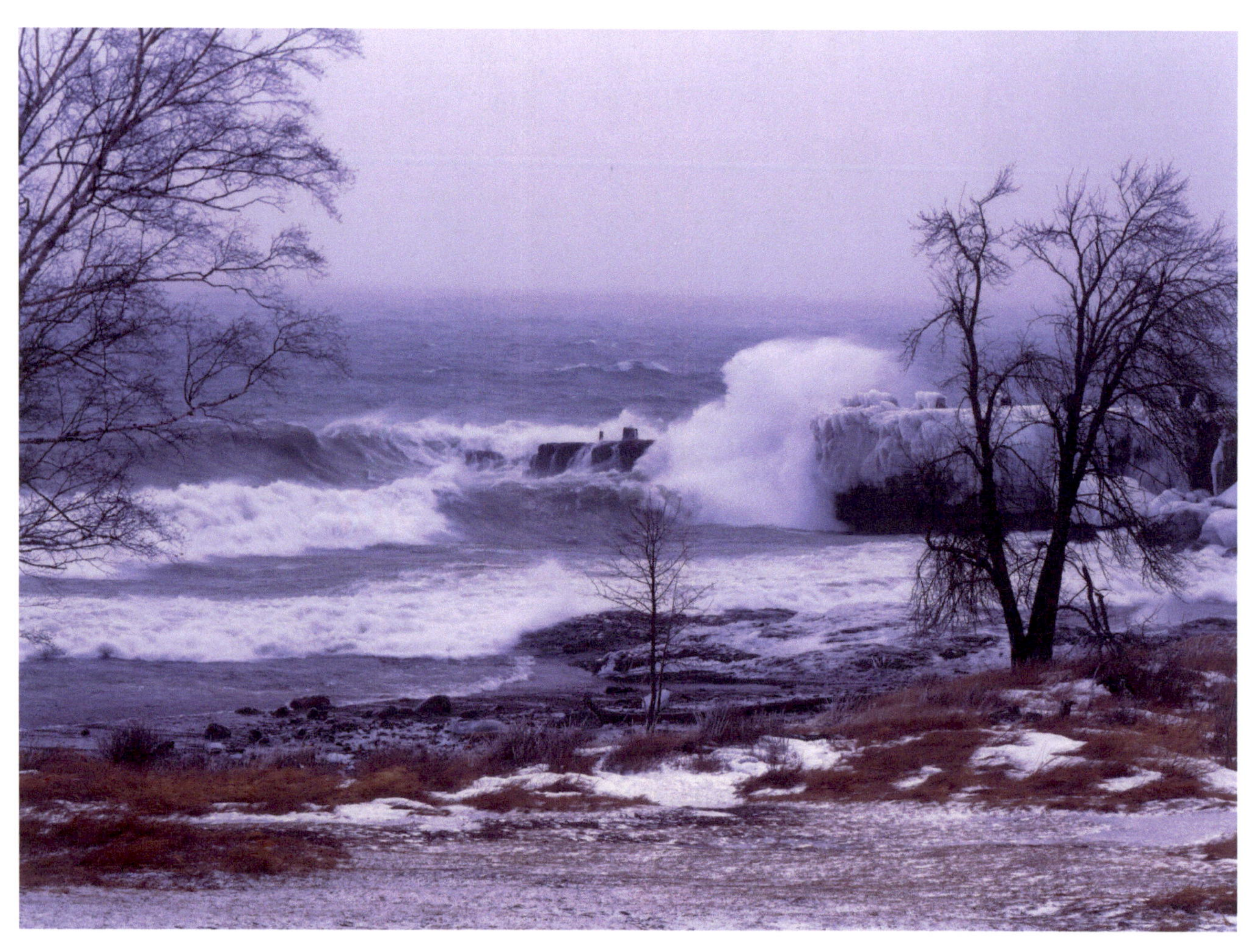

13   2075   Gooseberry Falls State Park, Minnesota

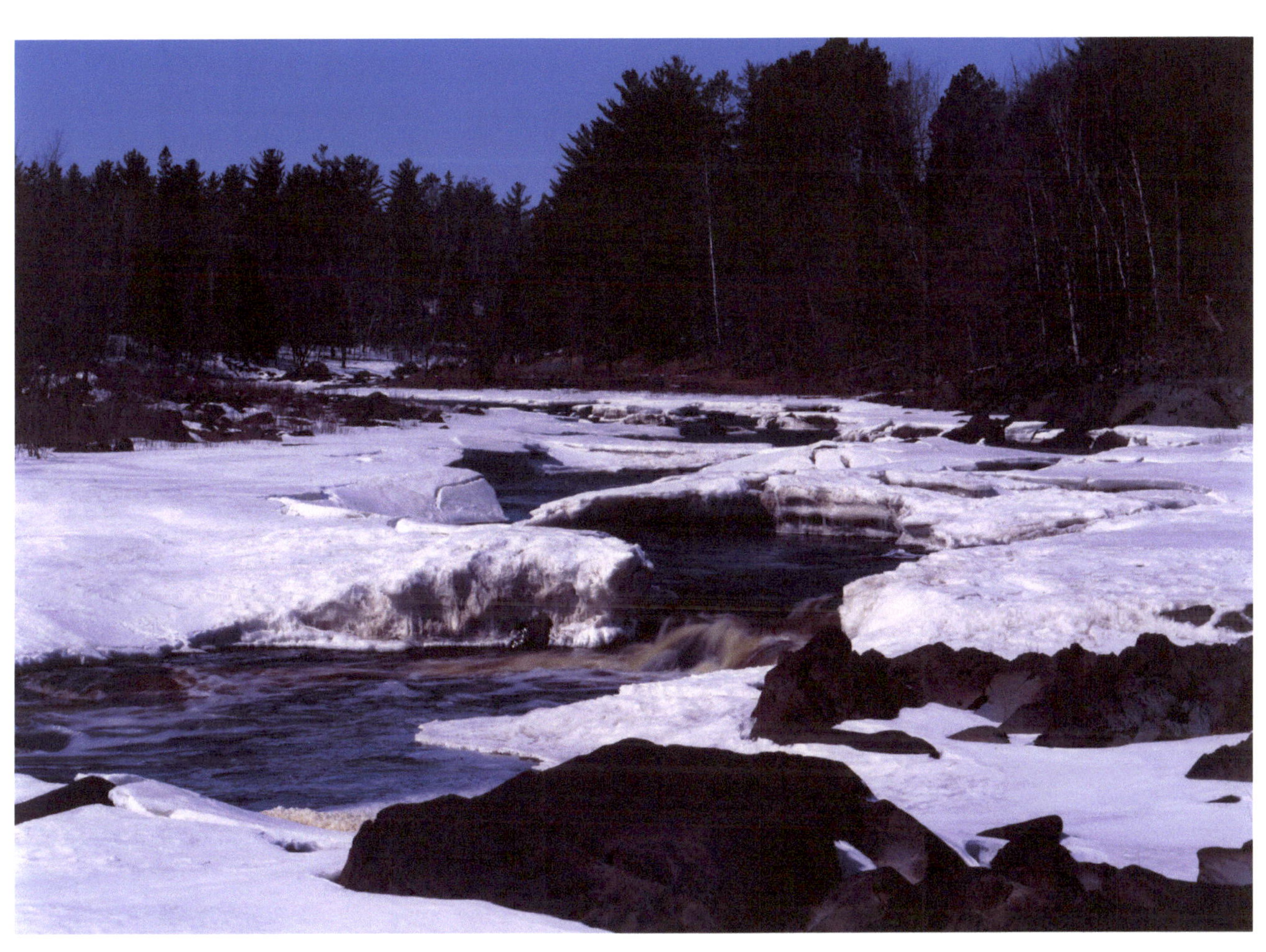

14   2076   Jay Cooke State Park, Minnesota

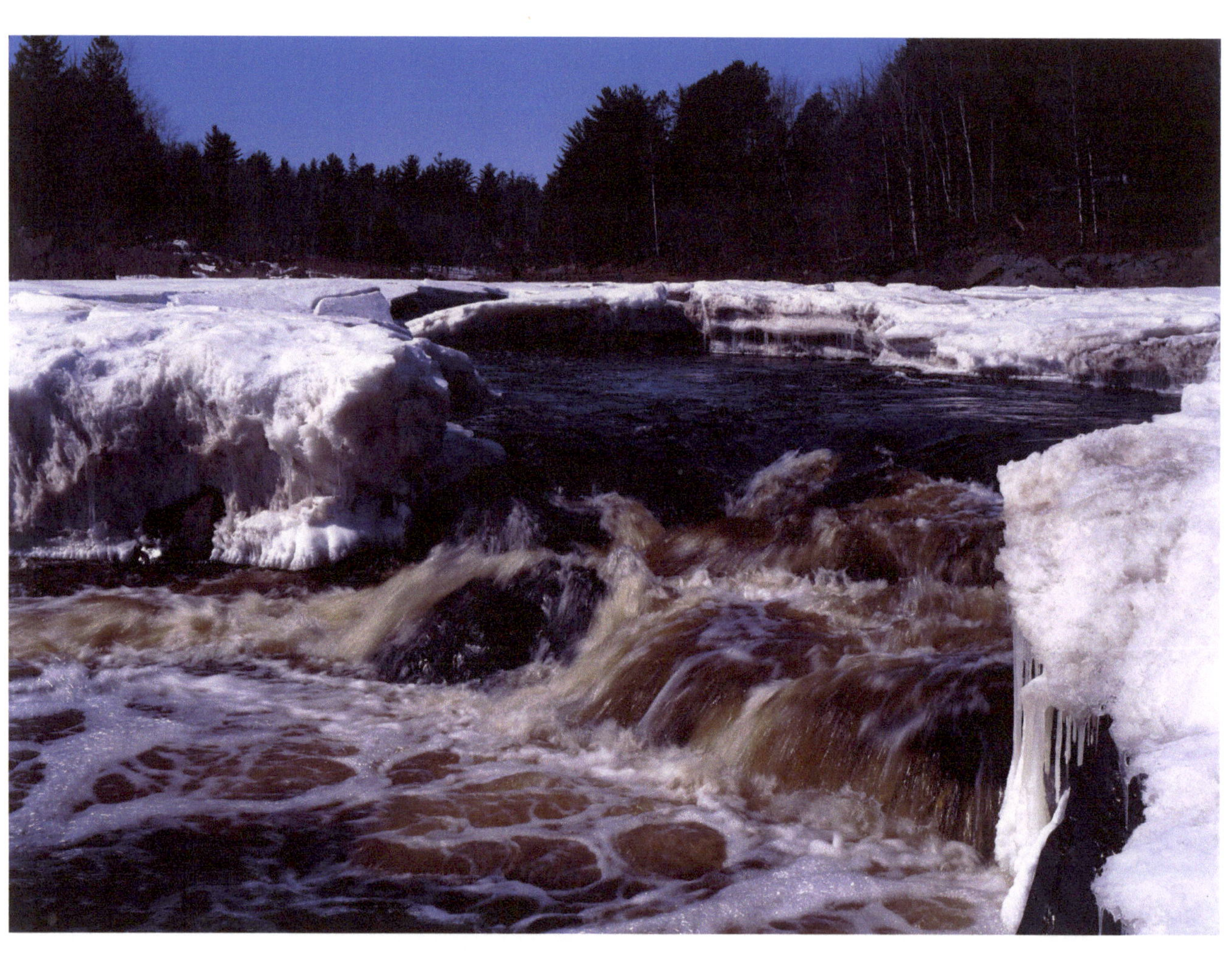

15   2077   Jay Cooke State Park, Minnesota

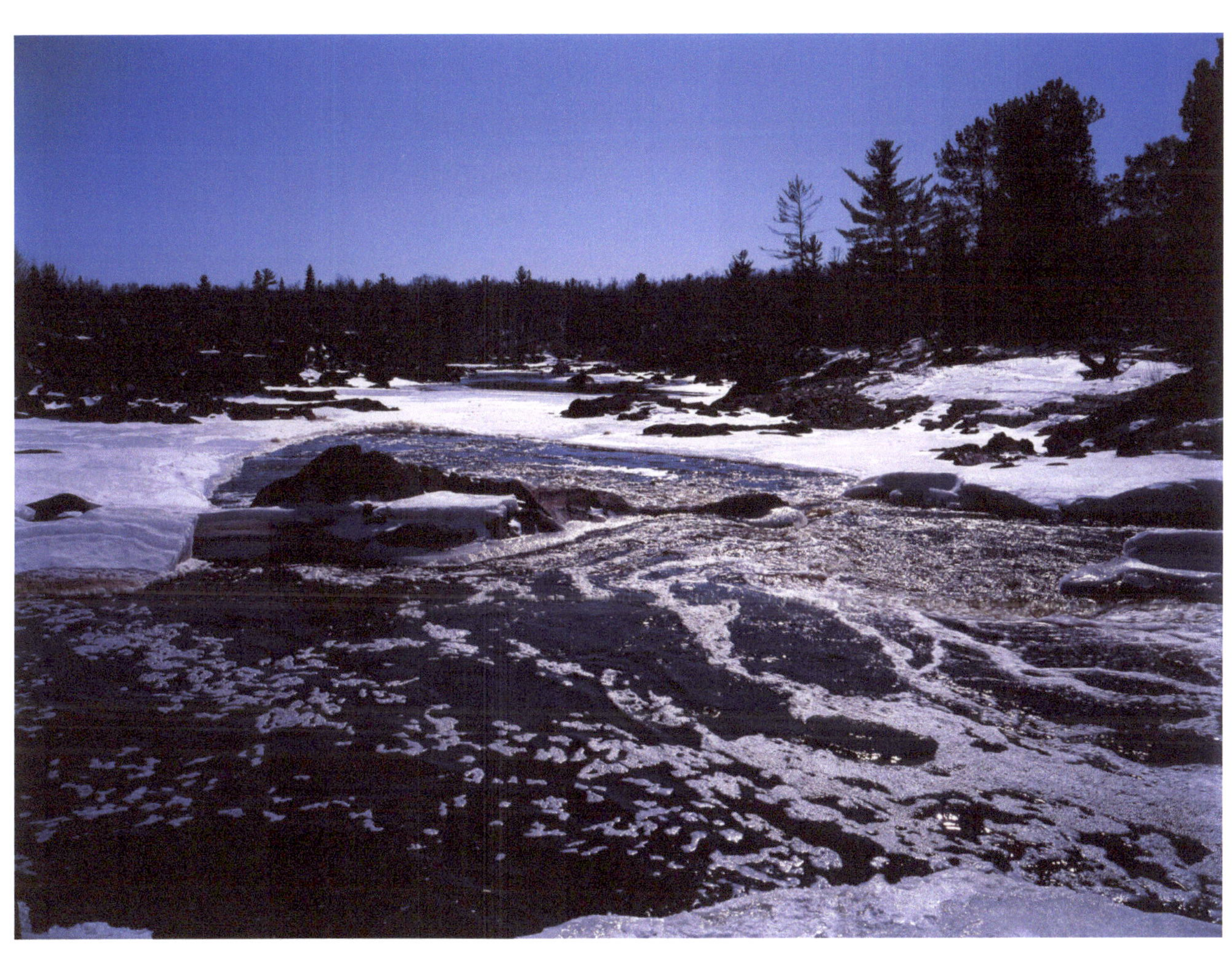

16   2078   Jay Cooke State Park, Minnesota

17   2153   Cascade River State Park, Minnesota

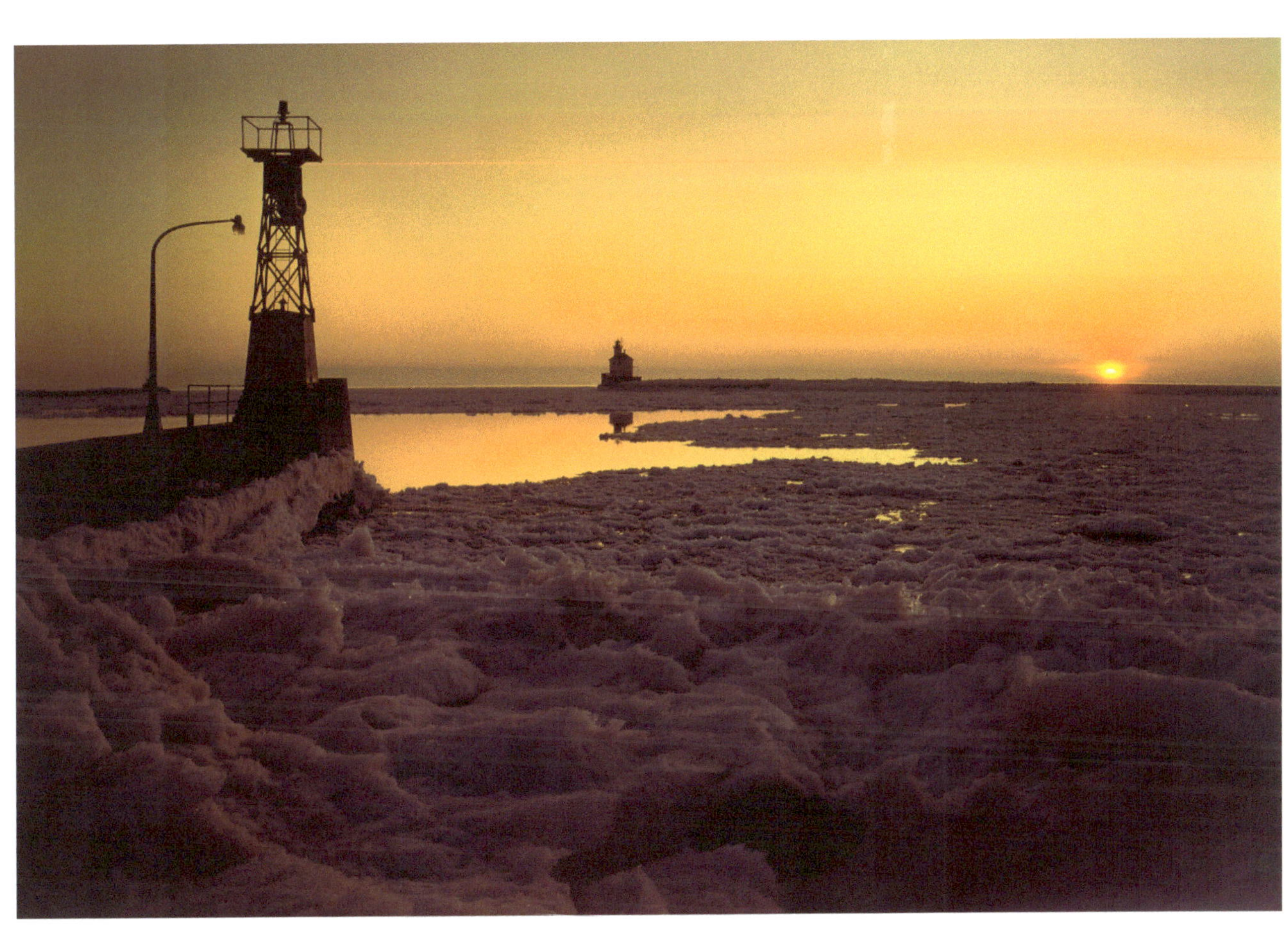

     Superior Entry, Superior, Wisconsin

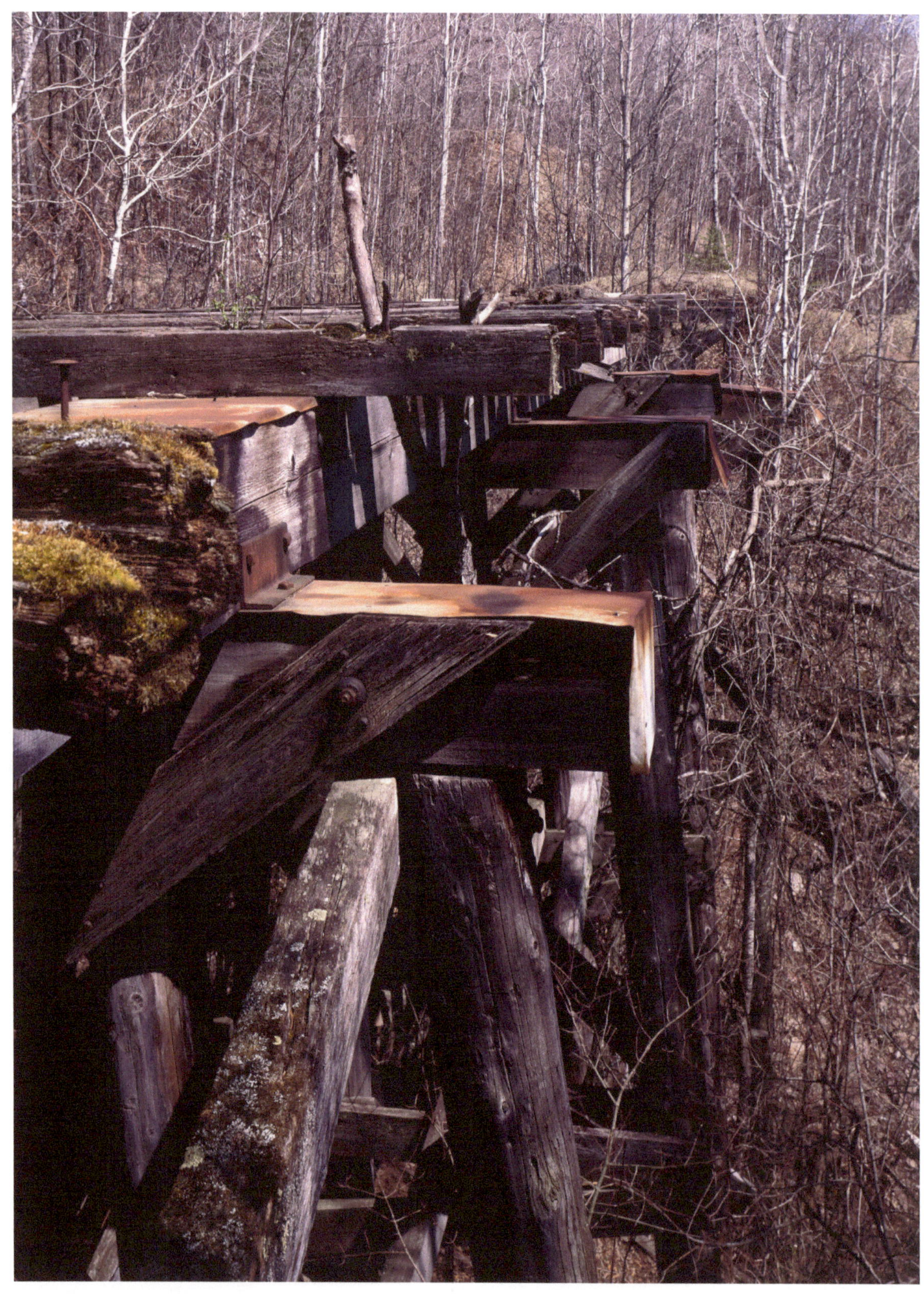

19   914   Fond du Lac, Duluth, Minnesota

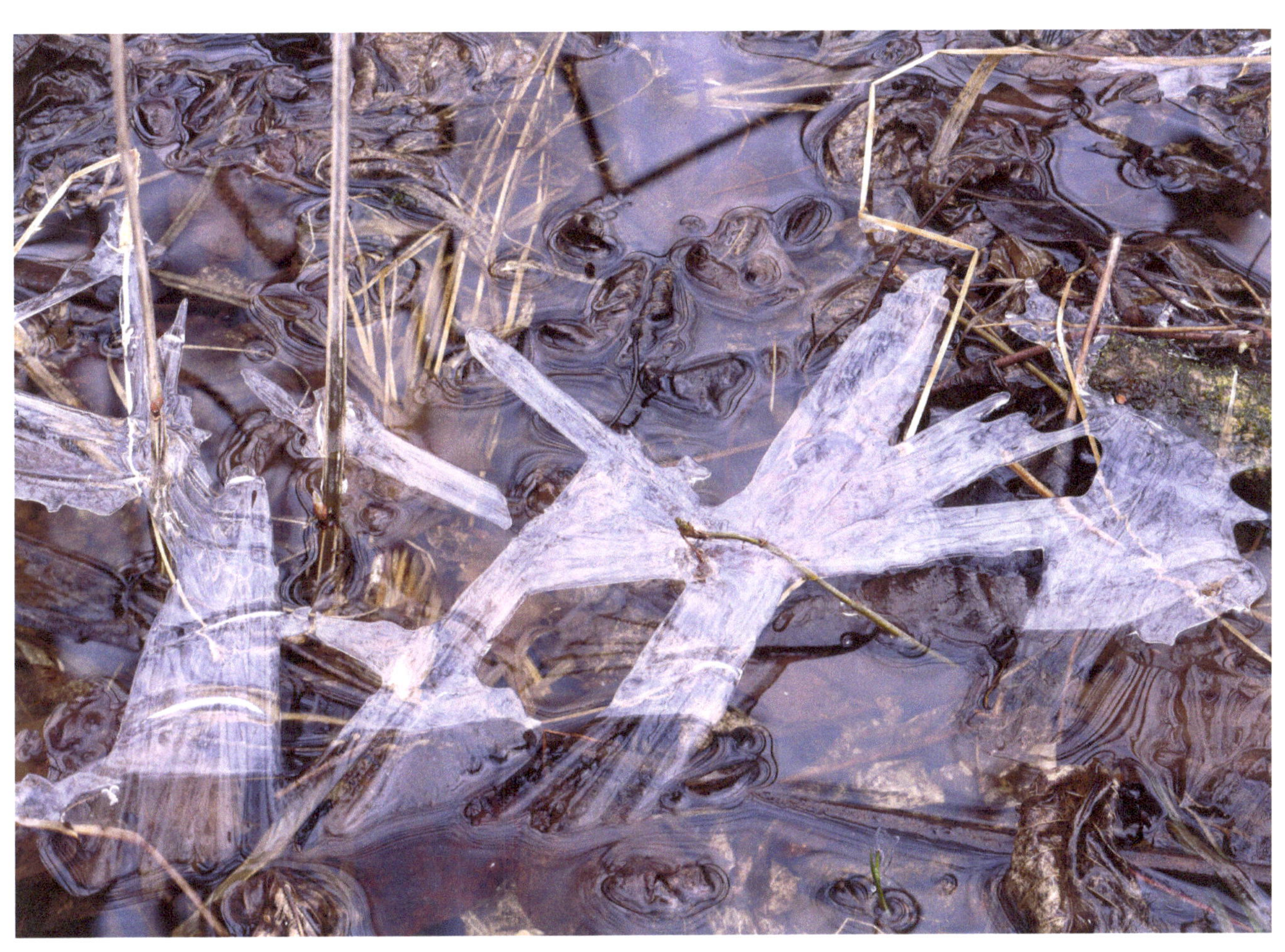

     Jay Cooke State Park, Minnesota

SPRING 21–52

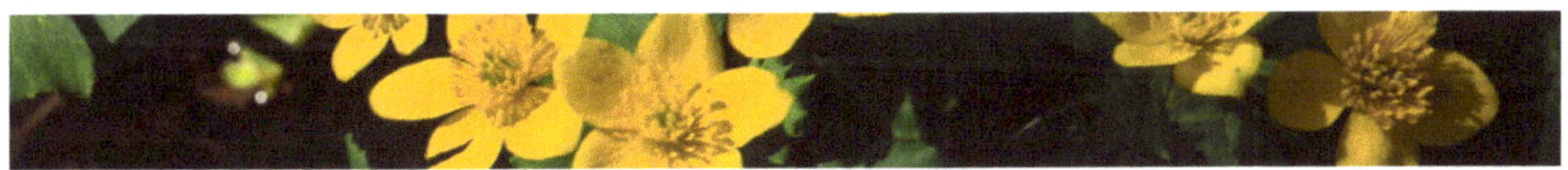

Spring is the time of heavy river runoff from melting snow, opportunity for dramatic photographs of the surging water or ice flows. Sometimes rivers have changed in front of me as I have paused to watch. Ice flows may only last for hours. When I was 9 years old, 1950, my mother took us children to see the flood destroying the 3rd Swinging Bridge in Jay Cooke. It was as if the snow had melted in one day. That day, I saw the water was much higher than I have seen in the published park pictures. It is essential to be there at the dramatic moment.

Near Leech Lake, Minnesota, where my Anway ancestors settled, is the aptly named Wood Tick Trail. My family of 5 has been there and come back all infested. Wood ticks come out just after the snow has melted. At a former convenience store in Thomson, Minnesota, I met a man permanently afflicted by Lyme disease, spread by wood ticks. The disease slowed his movements to half speed, but he told me, ruefully, "I can go out into the woods now at any time and not get Lyme disease."

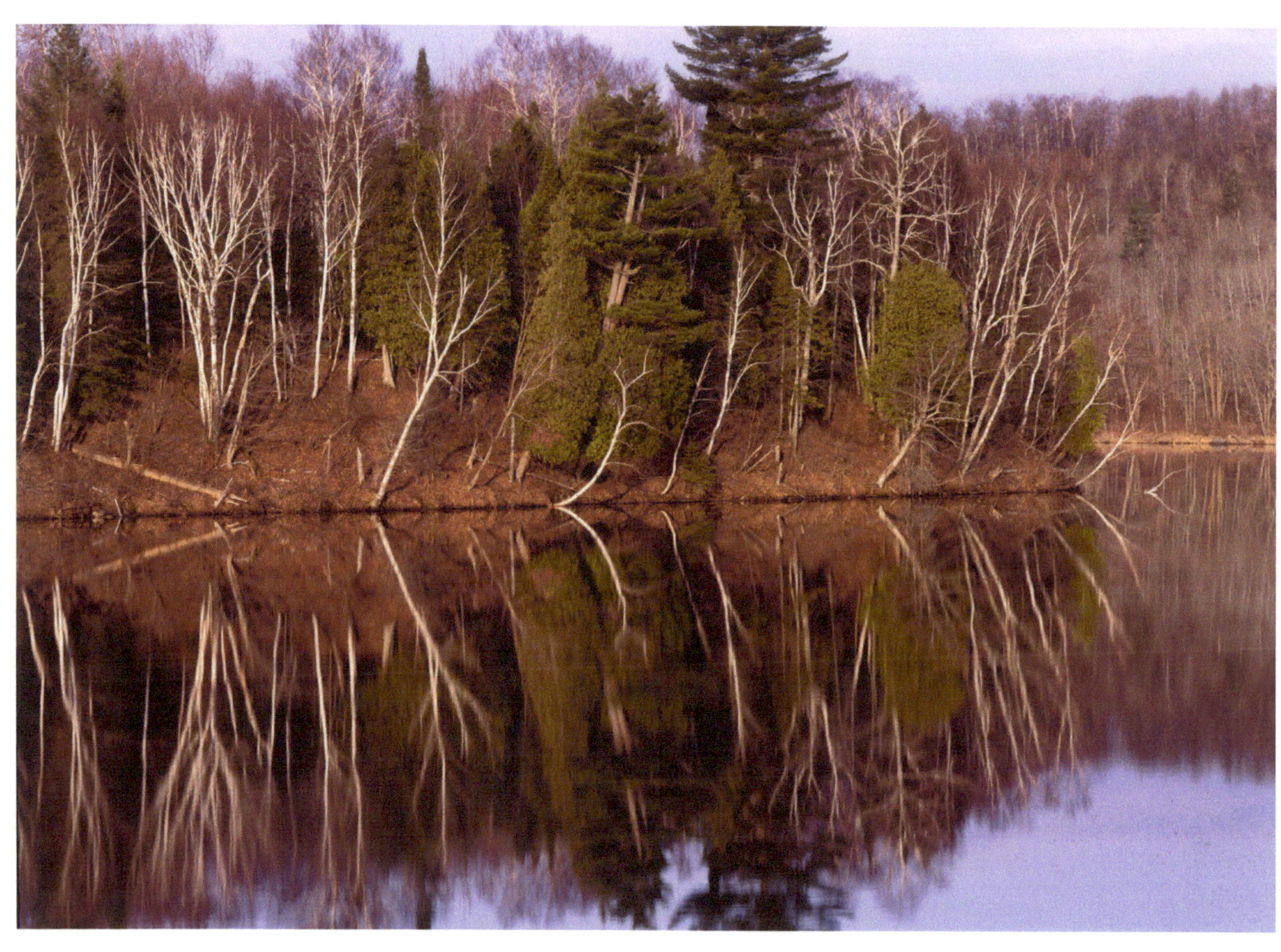

21   1471   Jay Cooke State Park, Minnesota

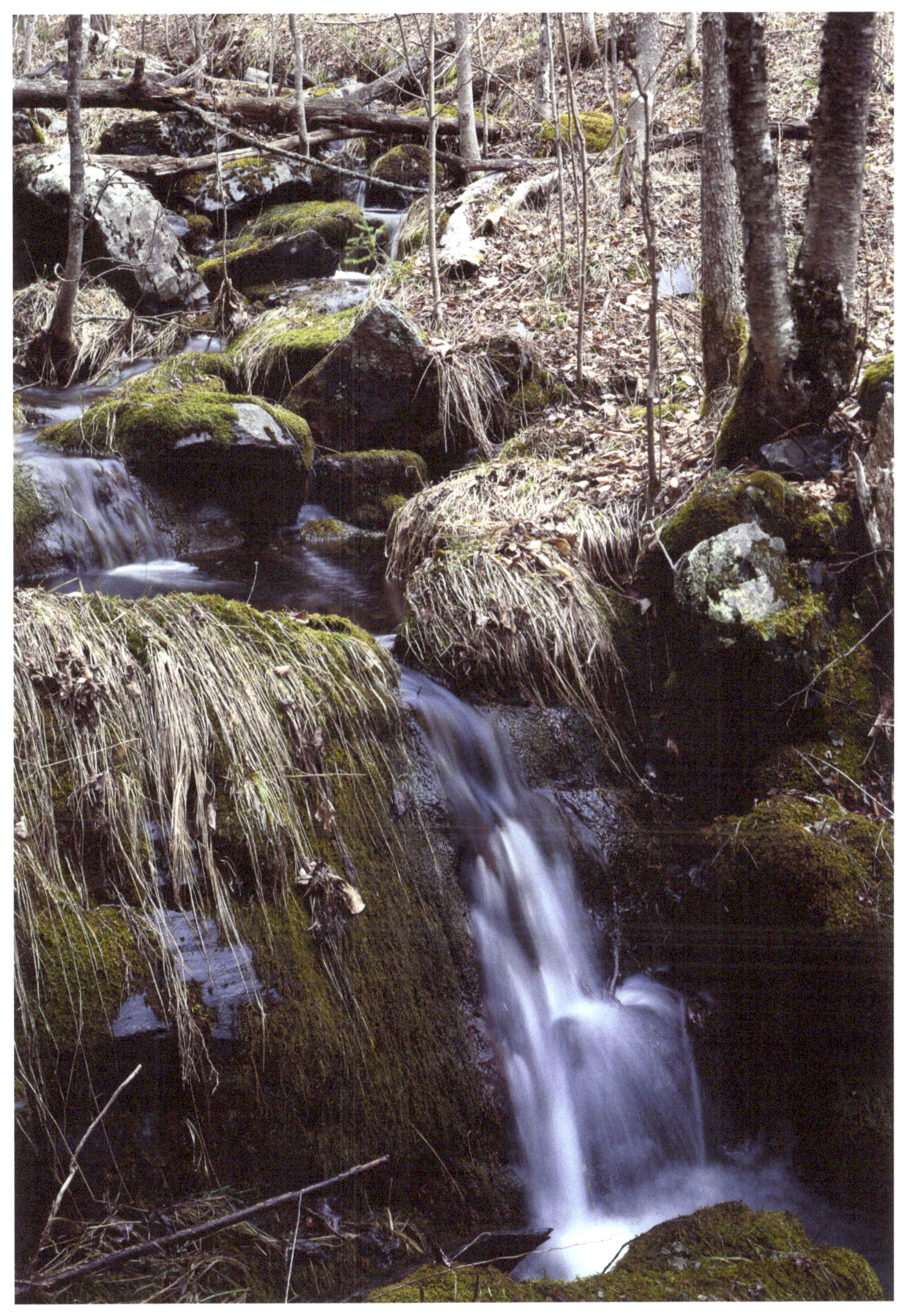

    Jay Cooke State Park, Minnesota

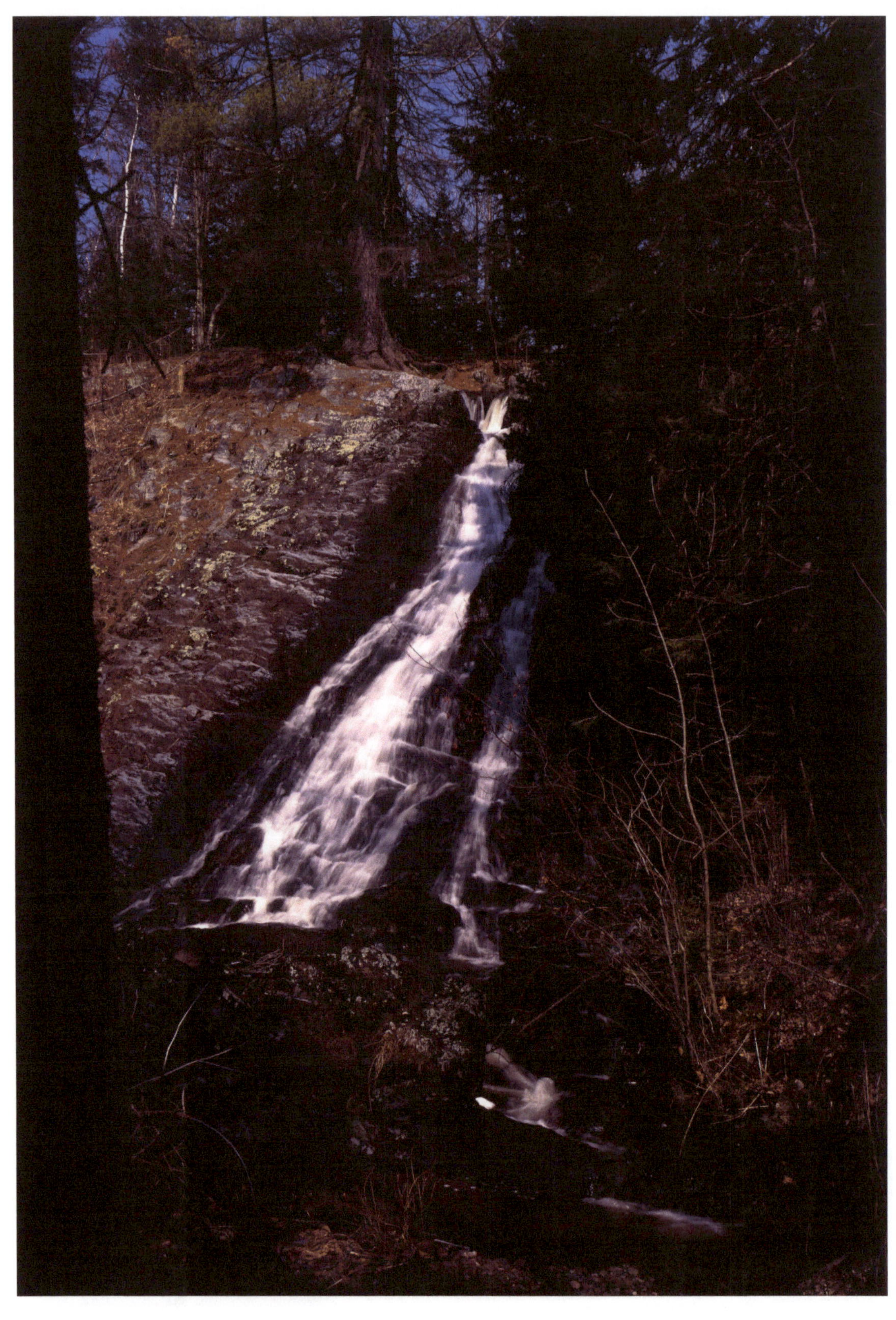

23   2082   Jay Cooke State Park, Minnesota

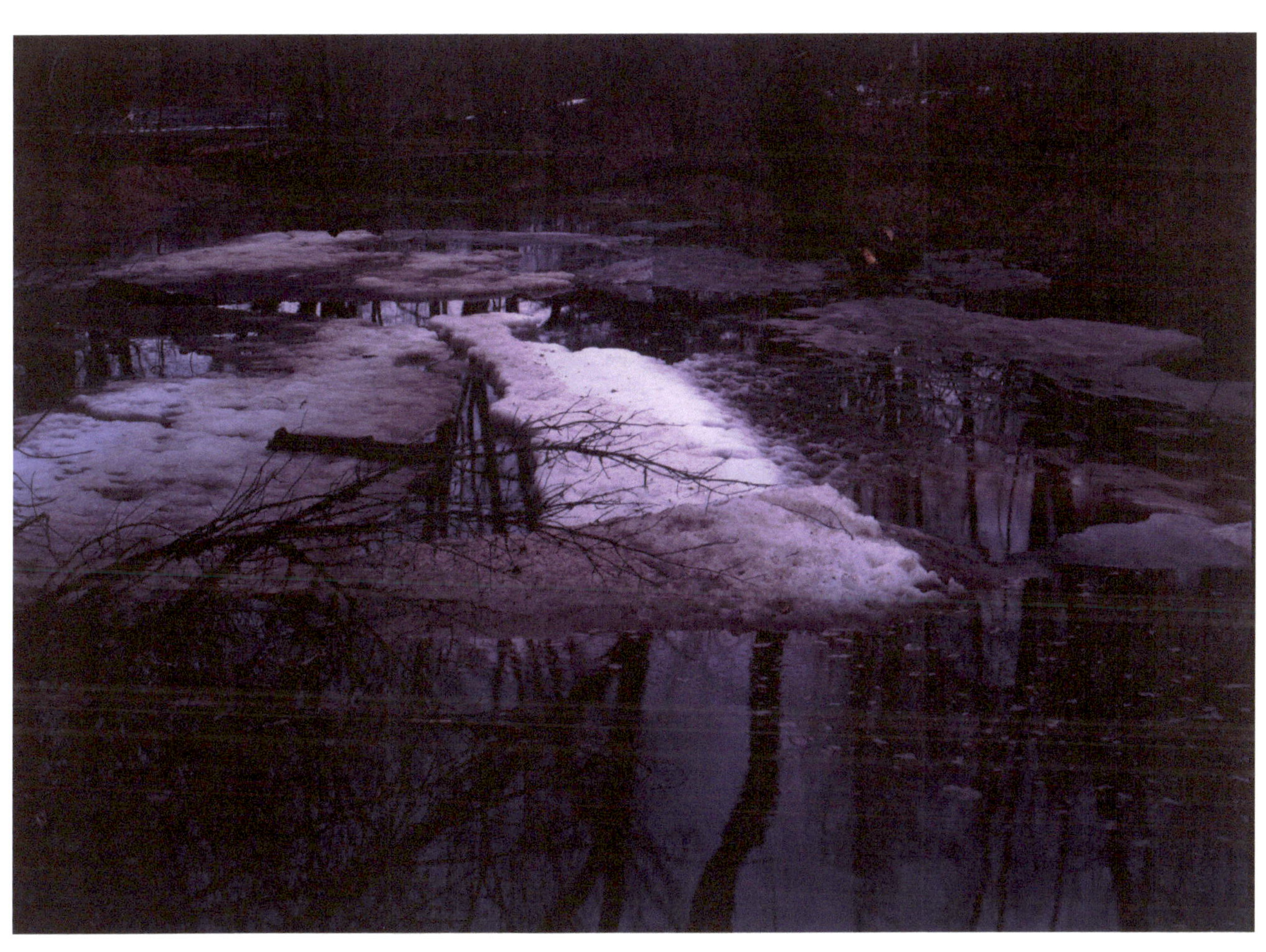

24   2083   Scanlon - Carlton, Minnesota

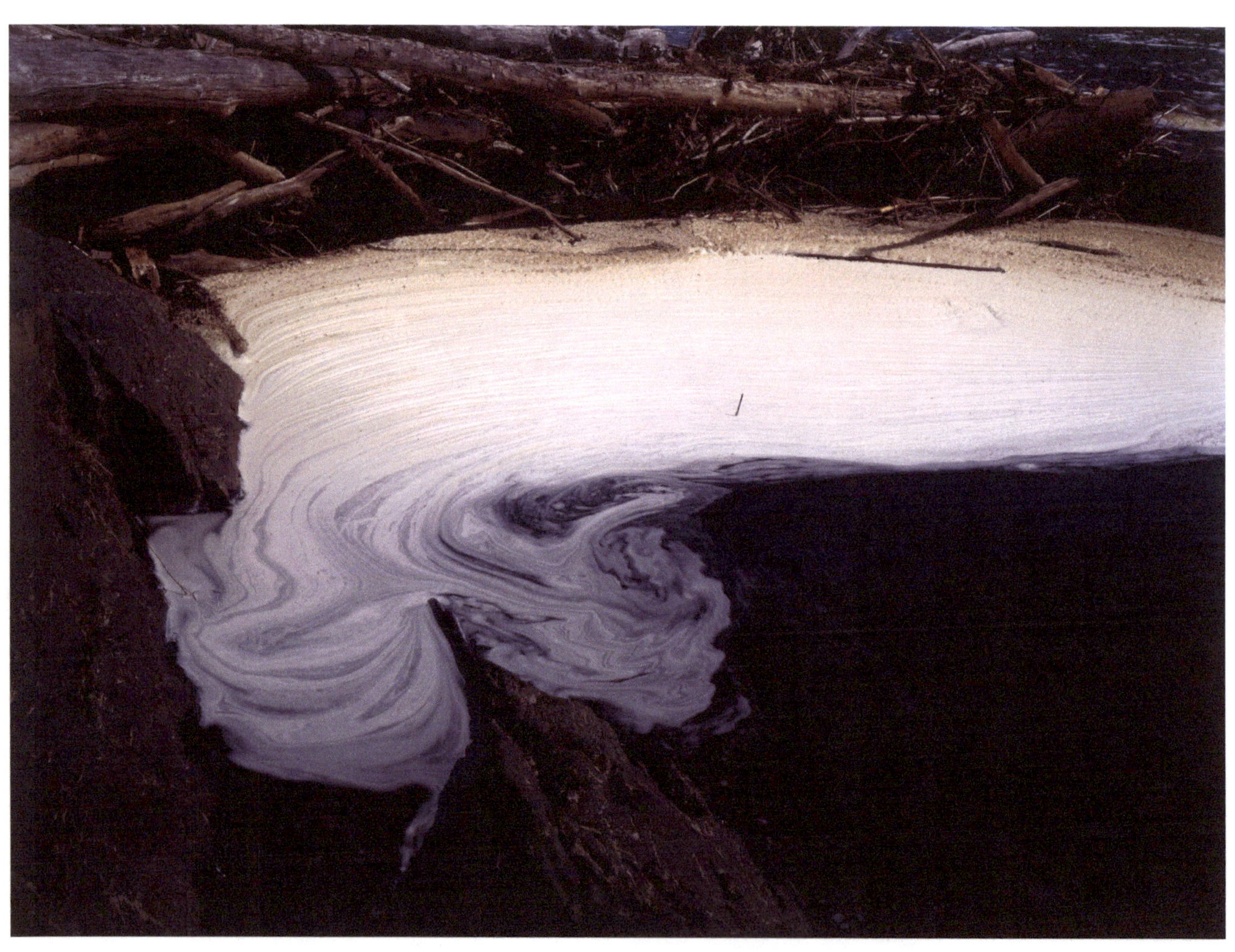

25   2085   Jay Cooke State Park, Minnesota

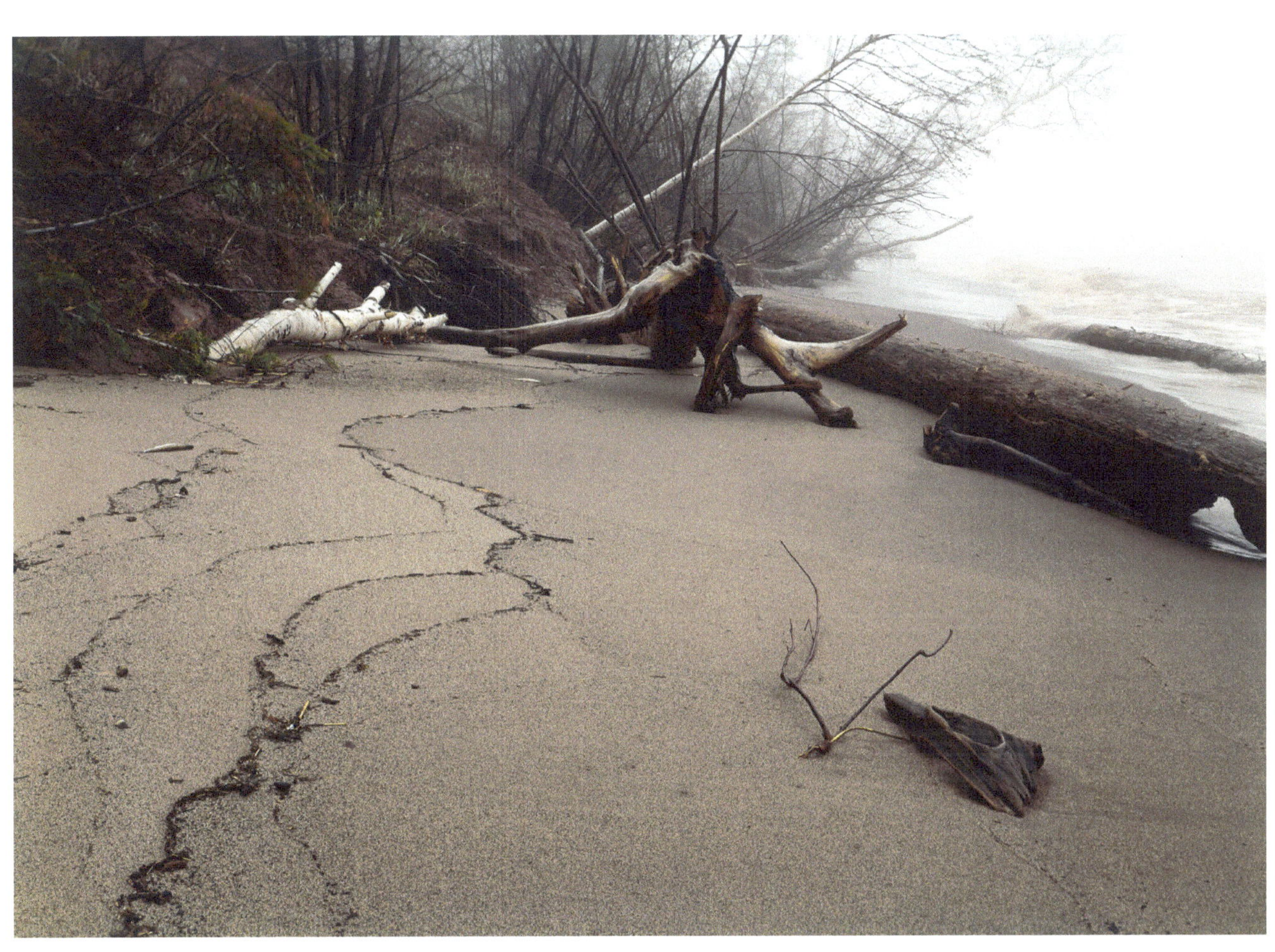

26   67   Dutchman Creek, Superior, Wisconsin

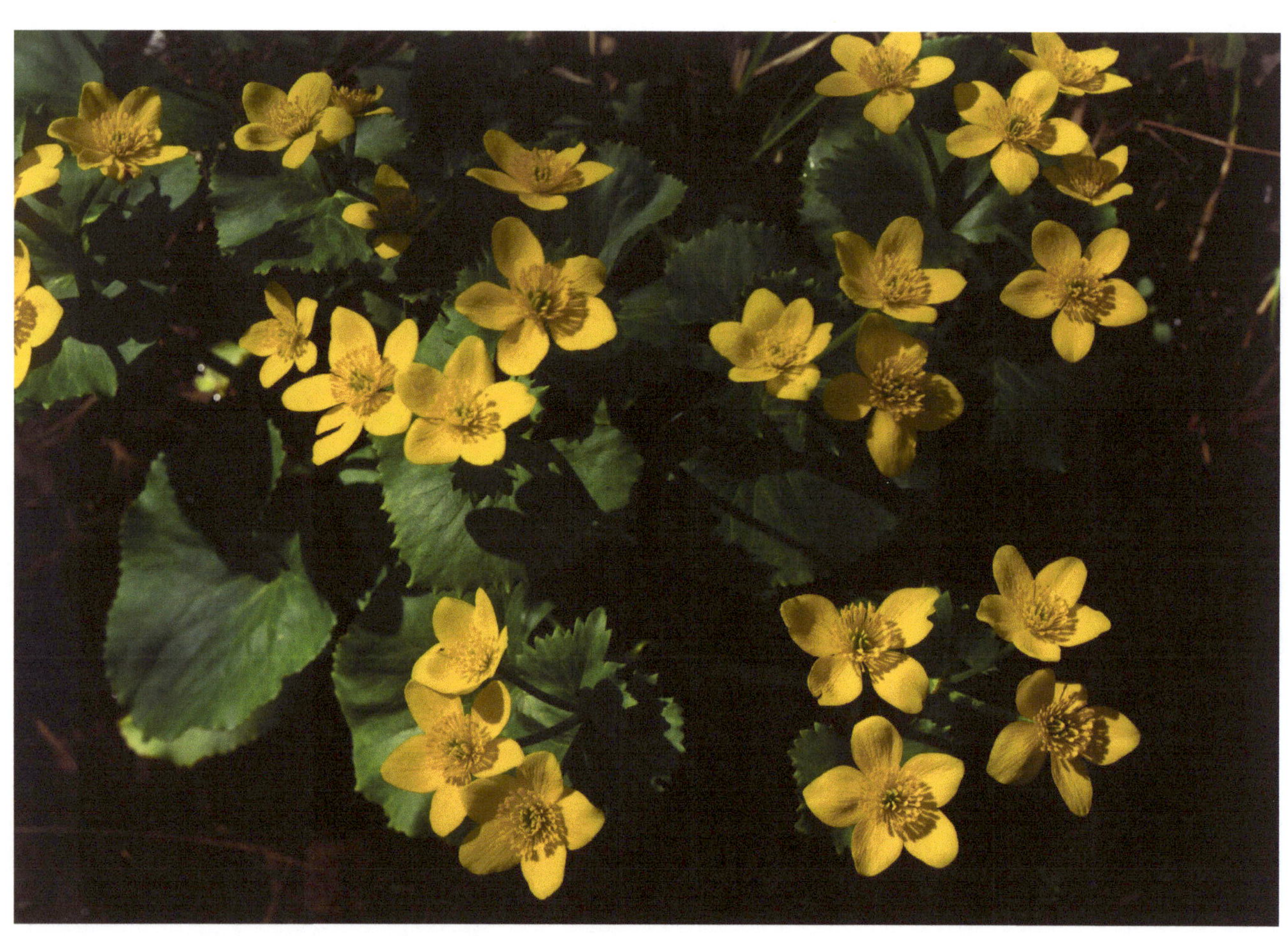

 Jay Cooke State Park, Minnesota

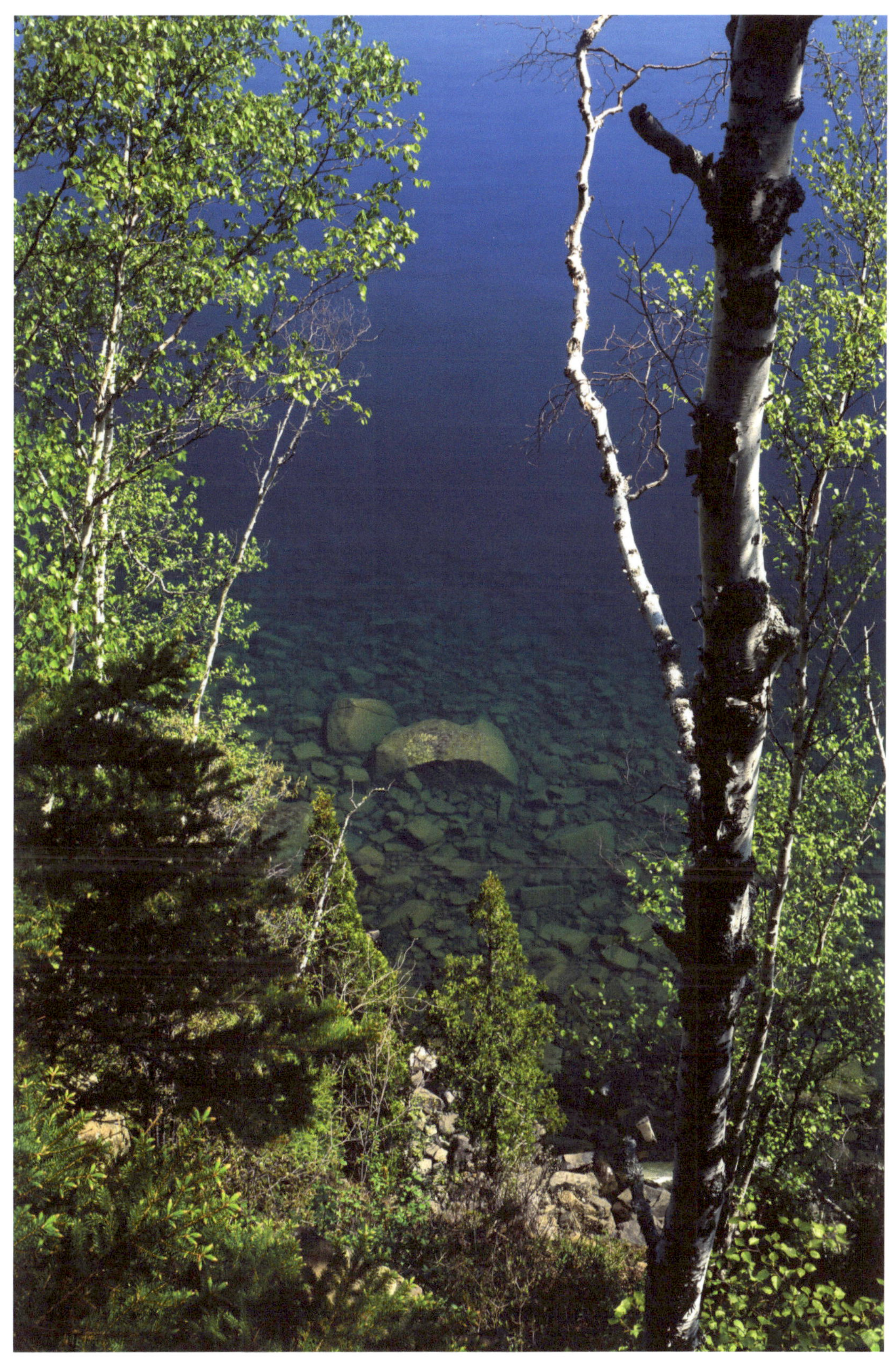

28   335   Split Rock Lighthouse State Park, Minnesota

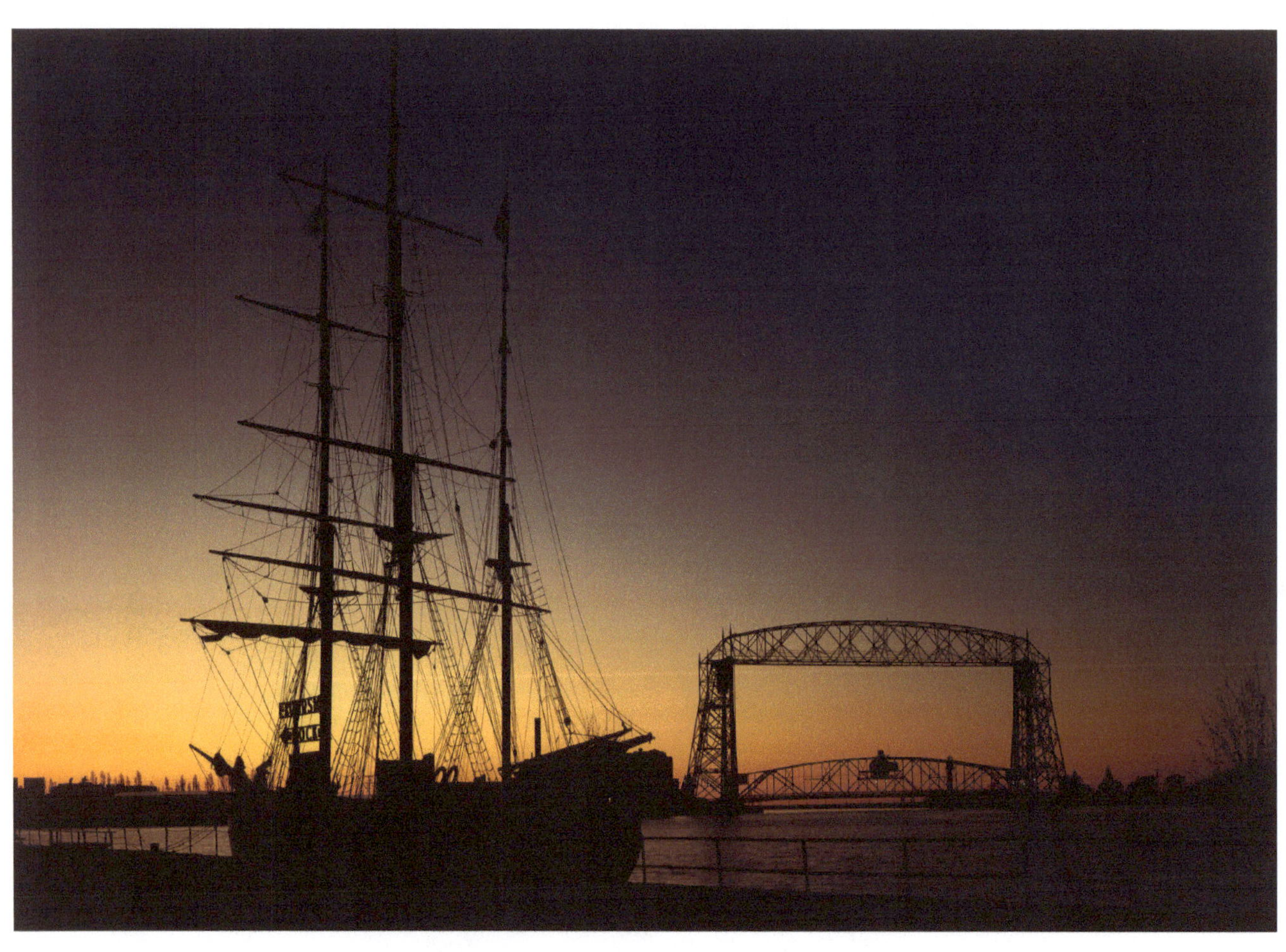

Duluth, Minnesota

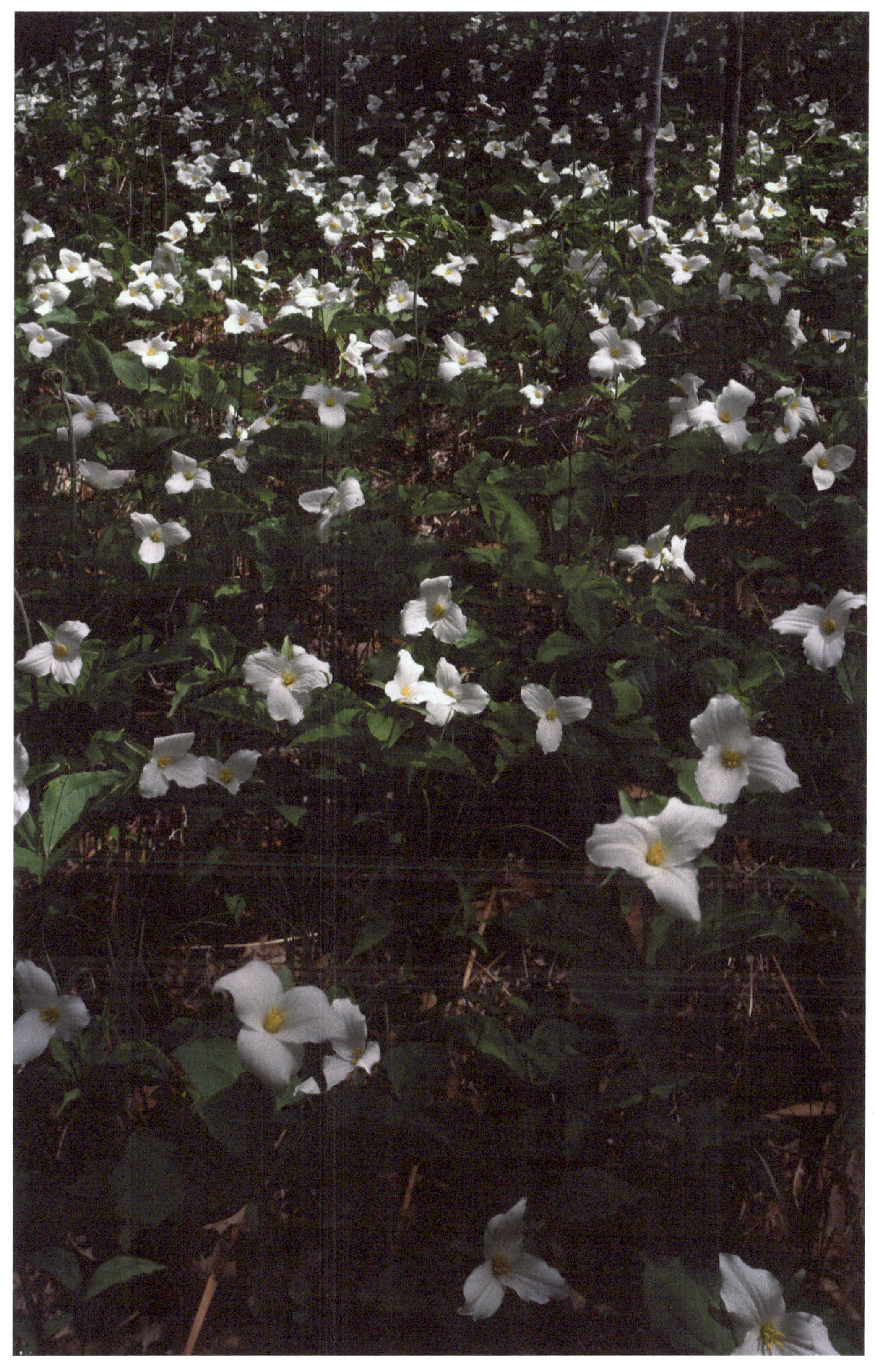

30   426   Jay Cooke State Park, Minnesota

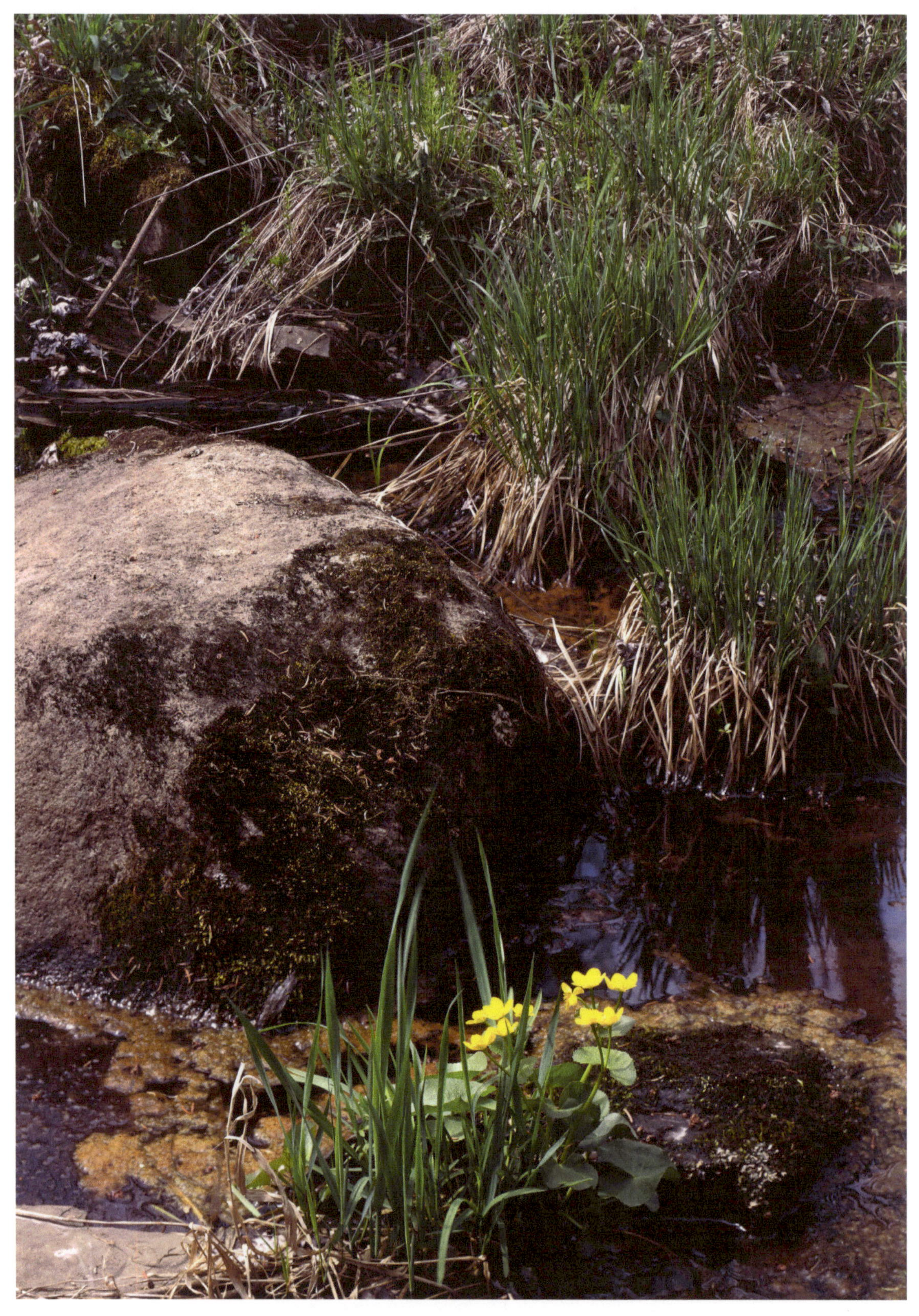

  Scanlon - Carlton, Minnesota

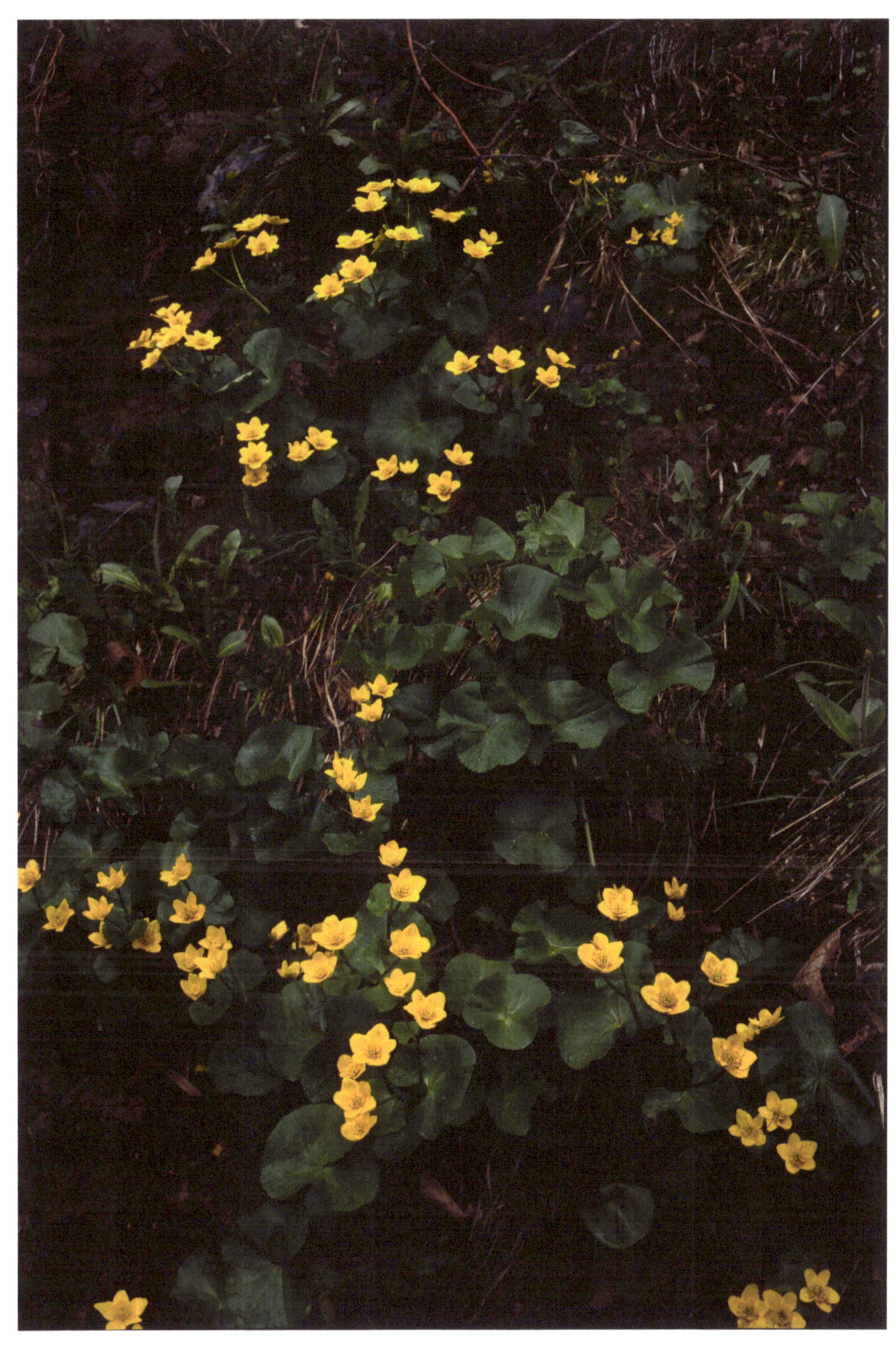

    Jay Cooke State Park, Minnesota

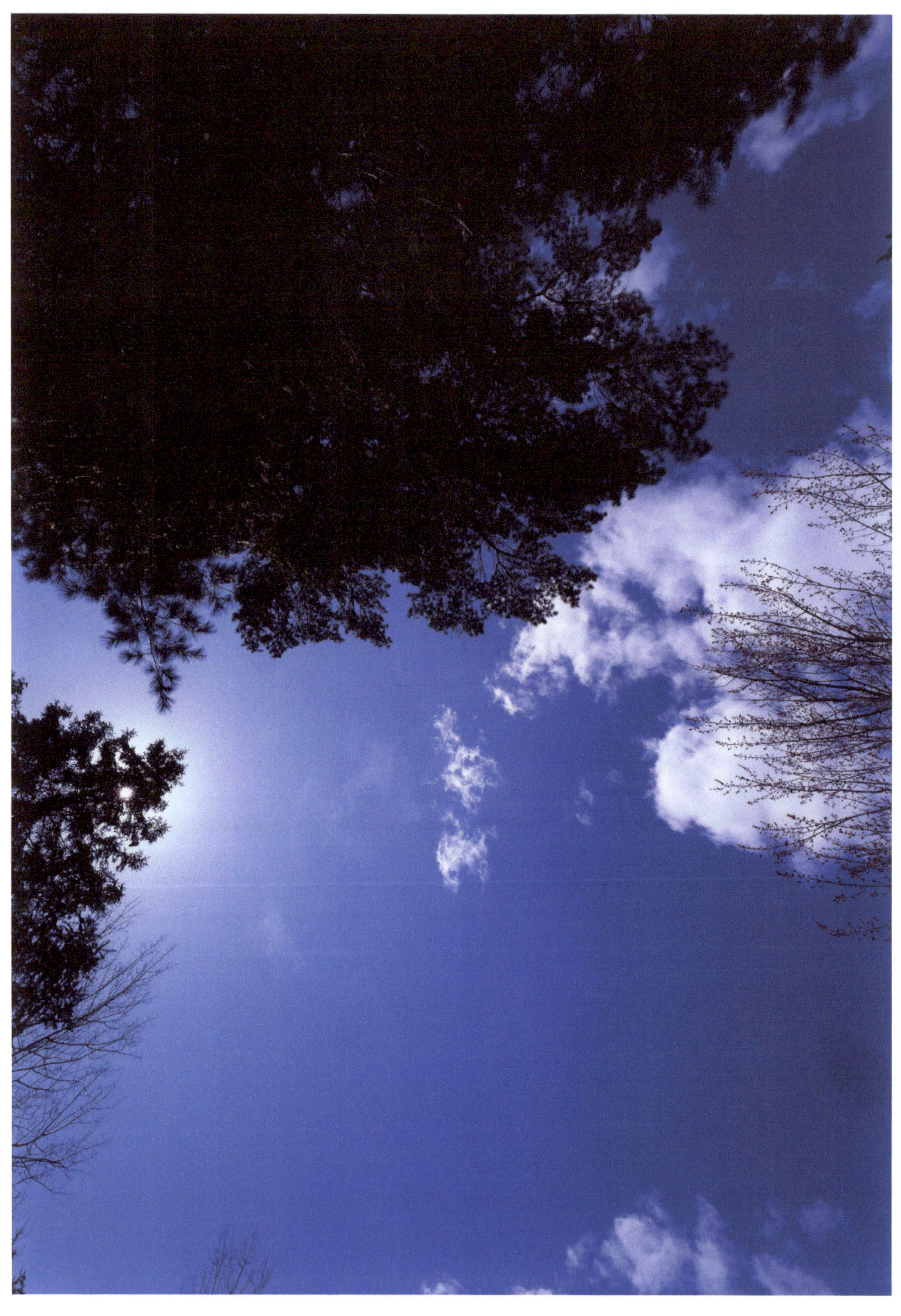

    1900   Jay Cooke State Park, Minnesota

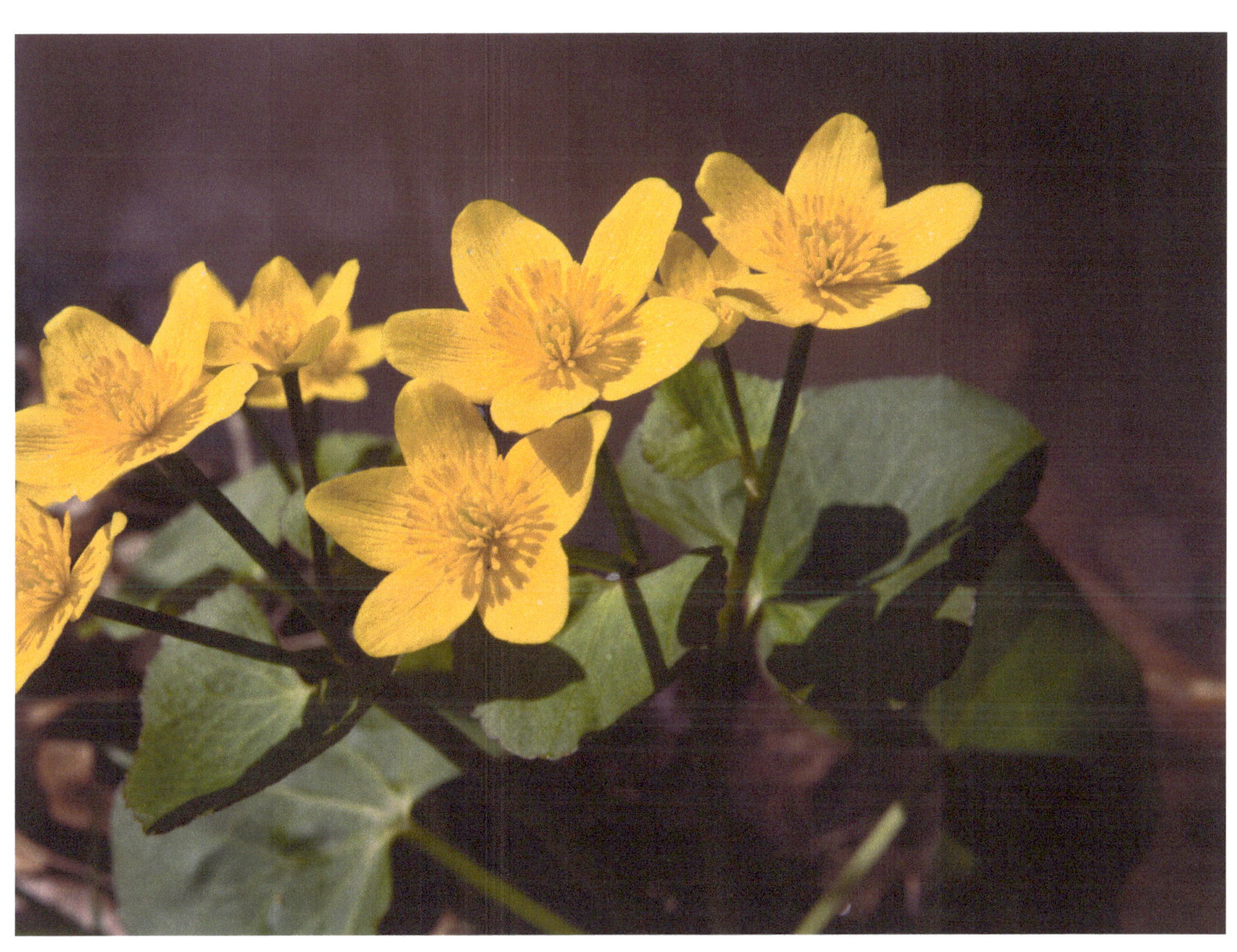

    Jay Cooke State Park, Minnesota

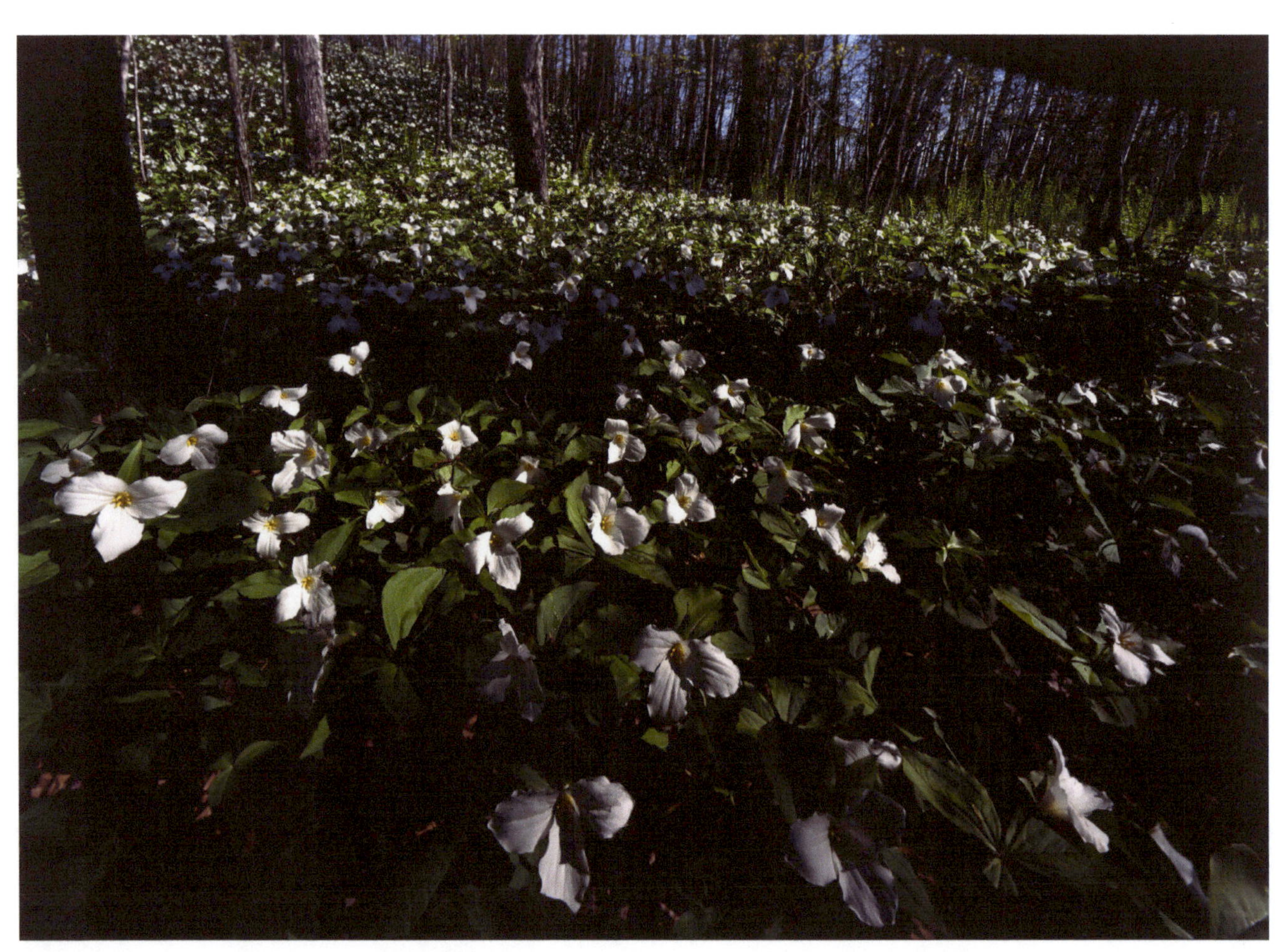

35   1988   Carlton County Road 4, Minnesota

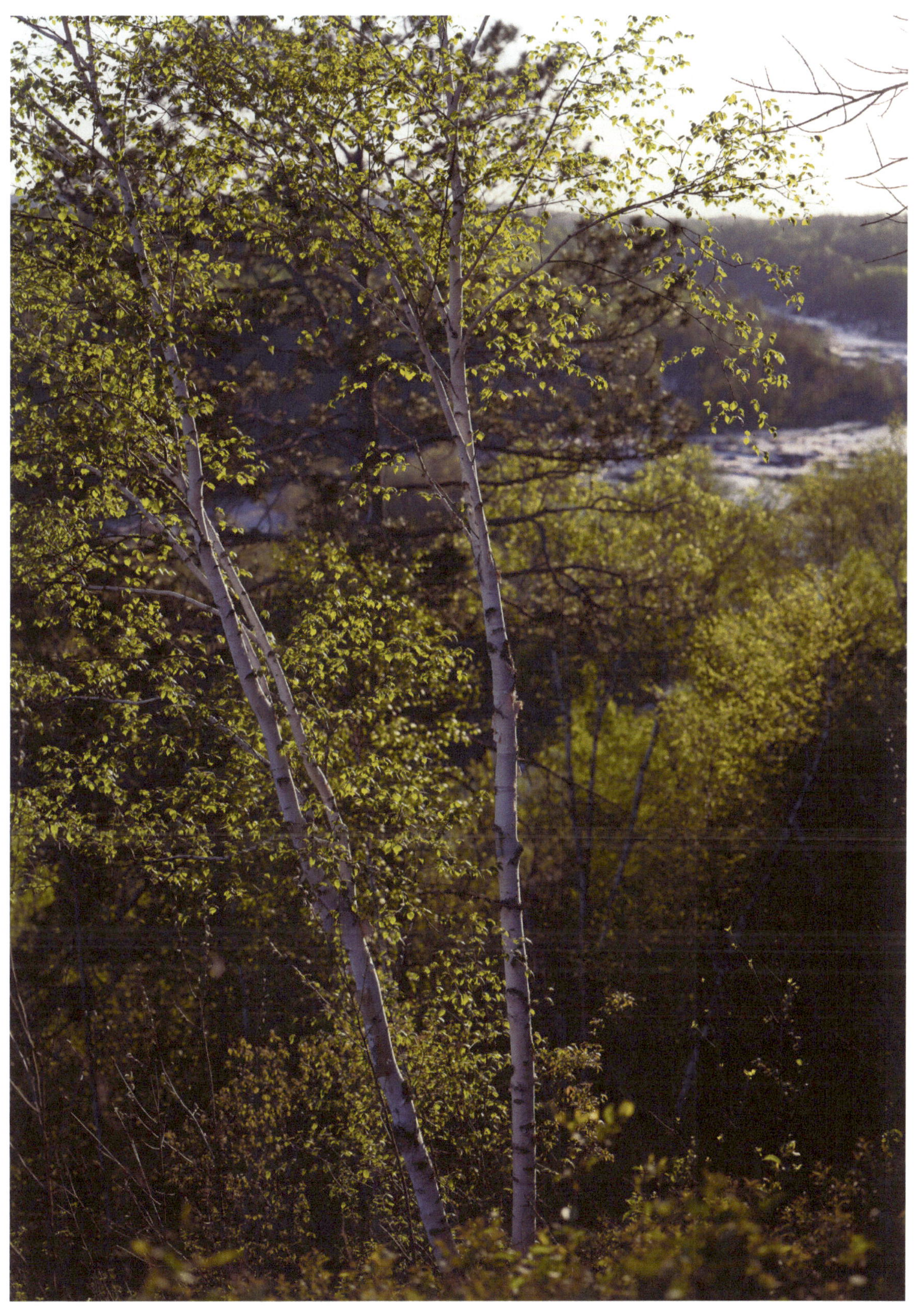

36   1994   Jay Cooke State Park, Minnesota

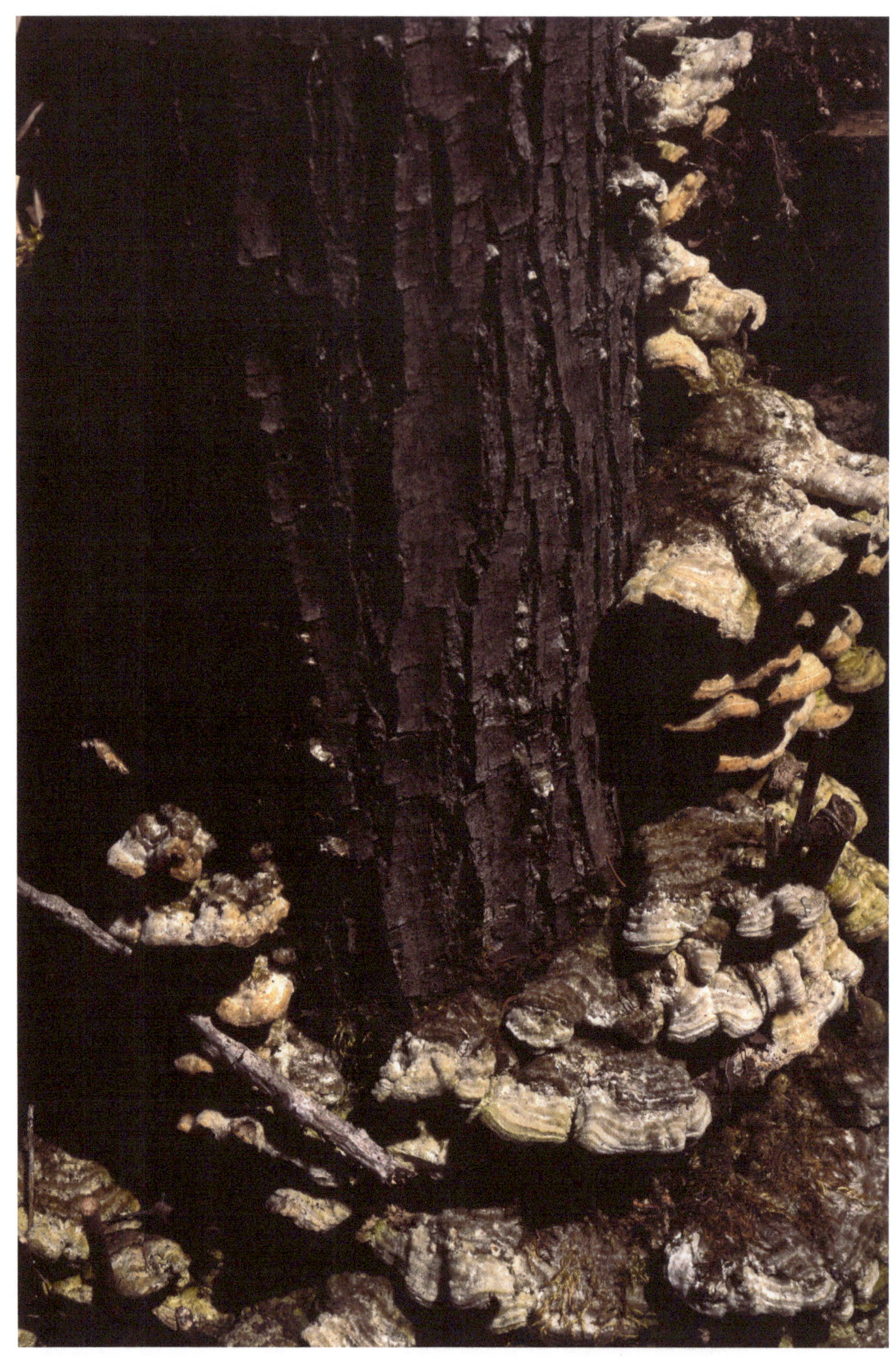

     Jay Cooke State Park, Minnesota

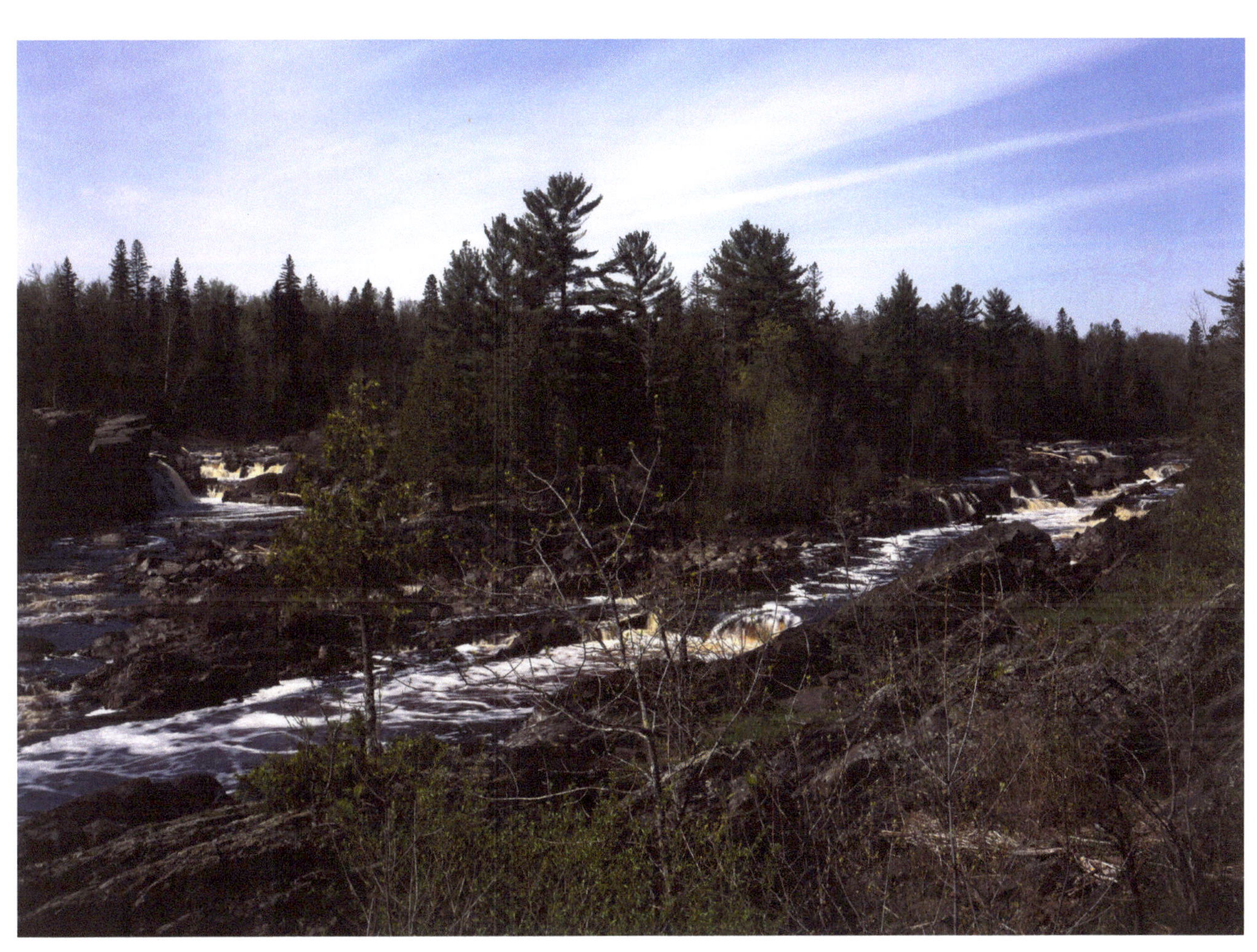

38   2095   Jay Cooke State Park, Minnesota

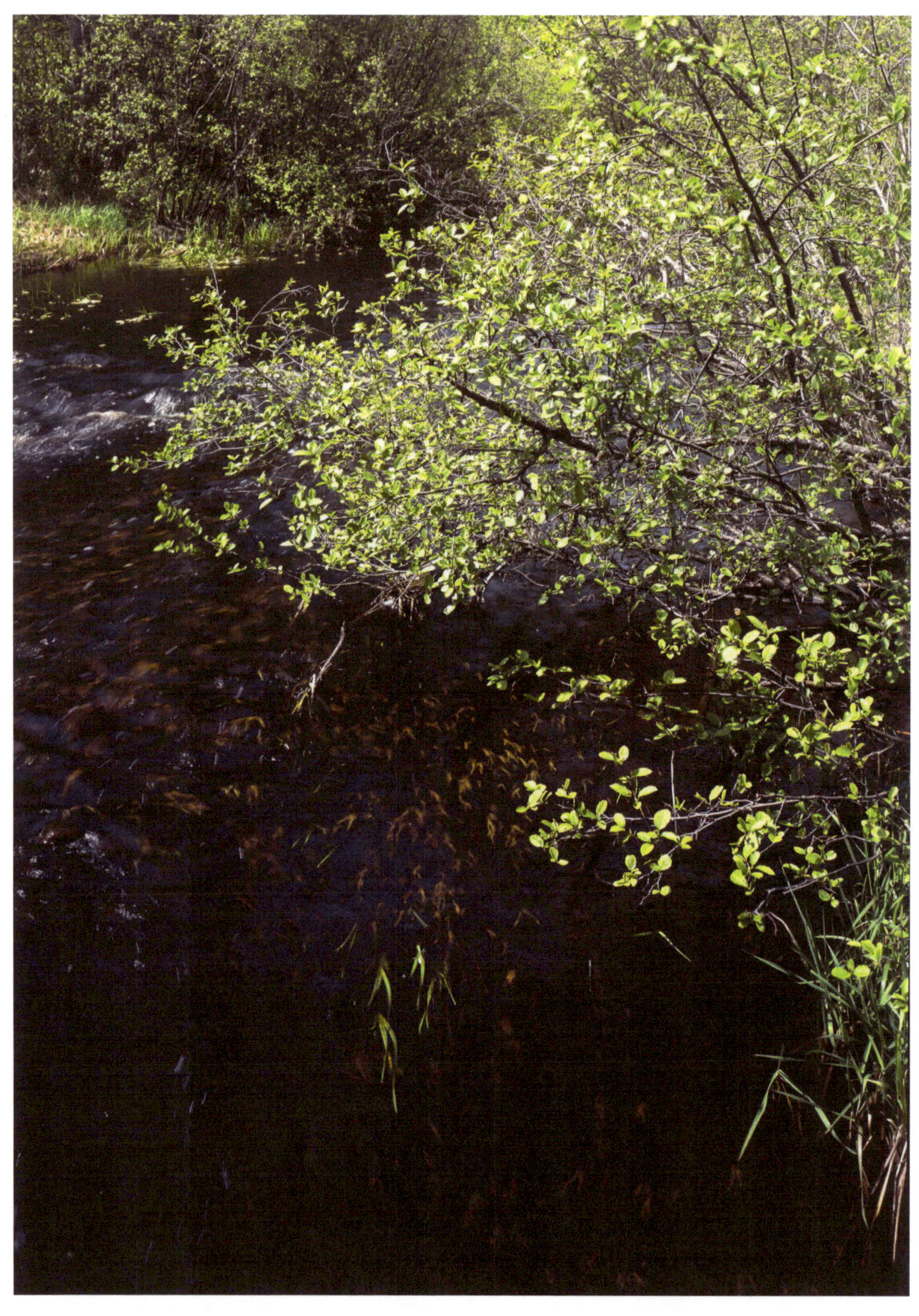

39   2096   St. Louis County Road 8, Minnesota

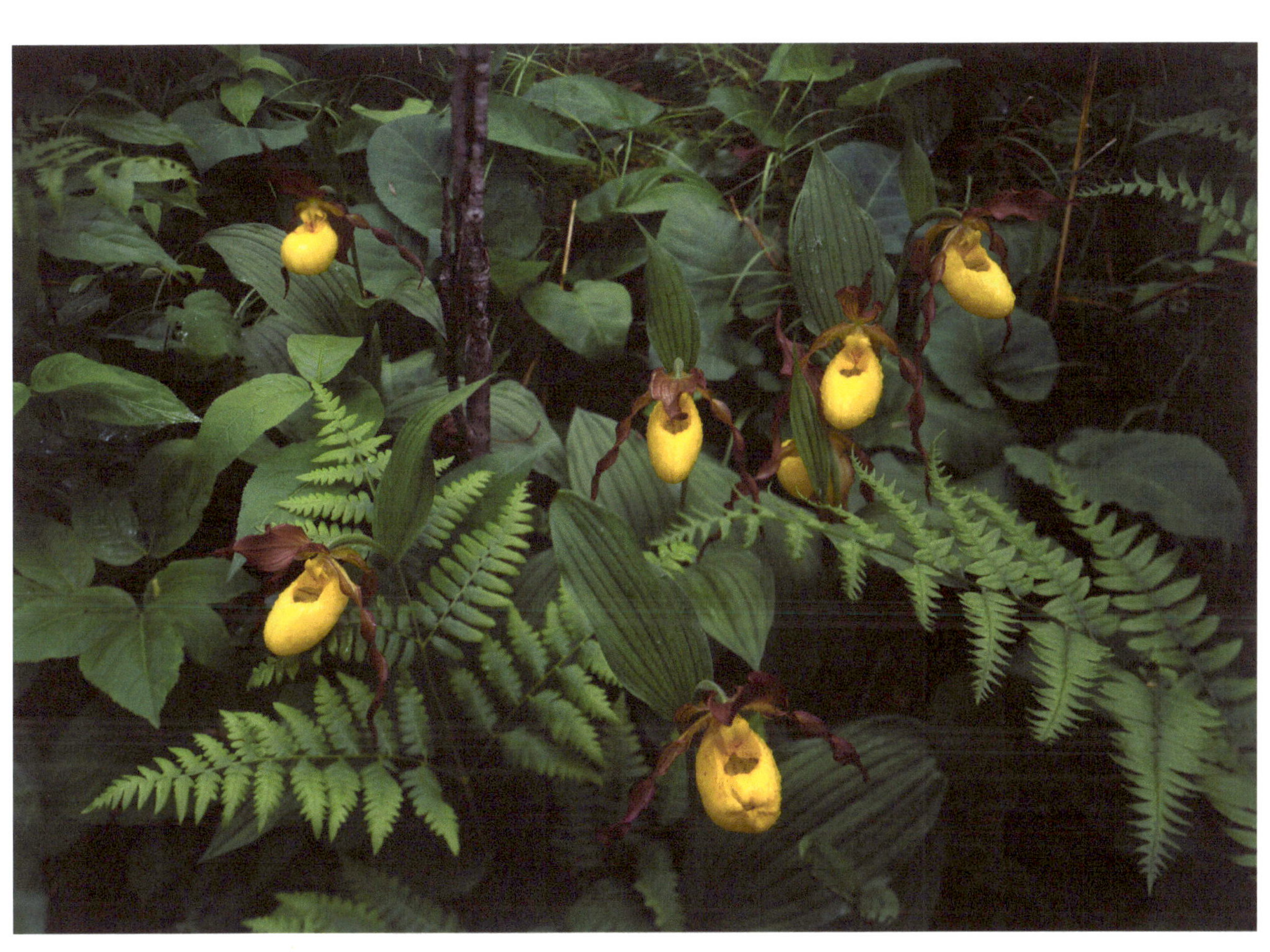

40   2160   Jay Cooke State Park, Minnesota

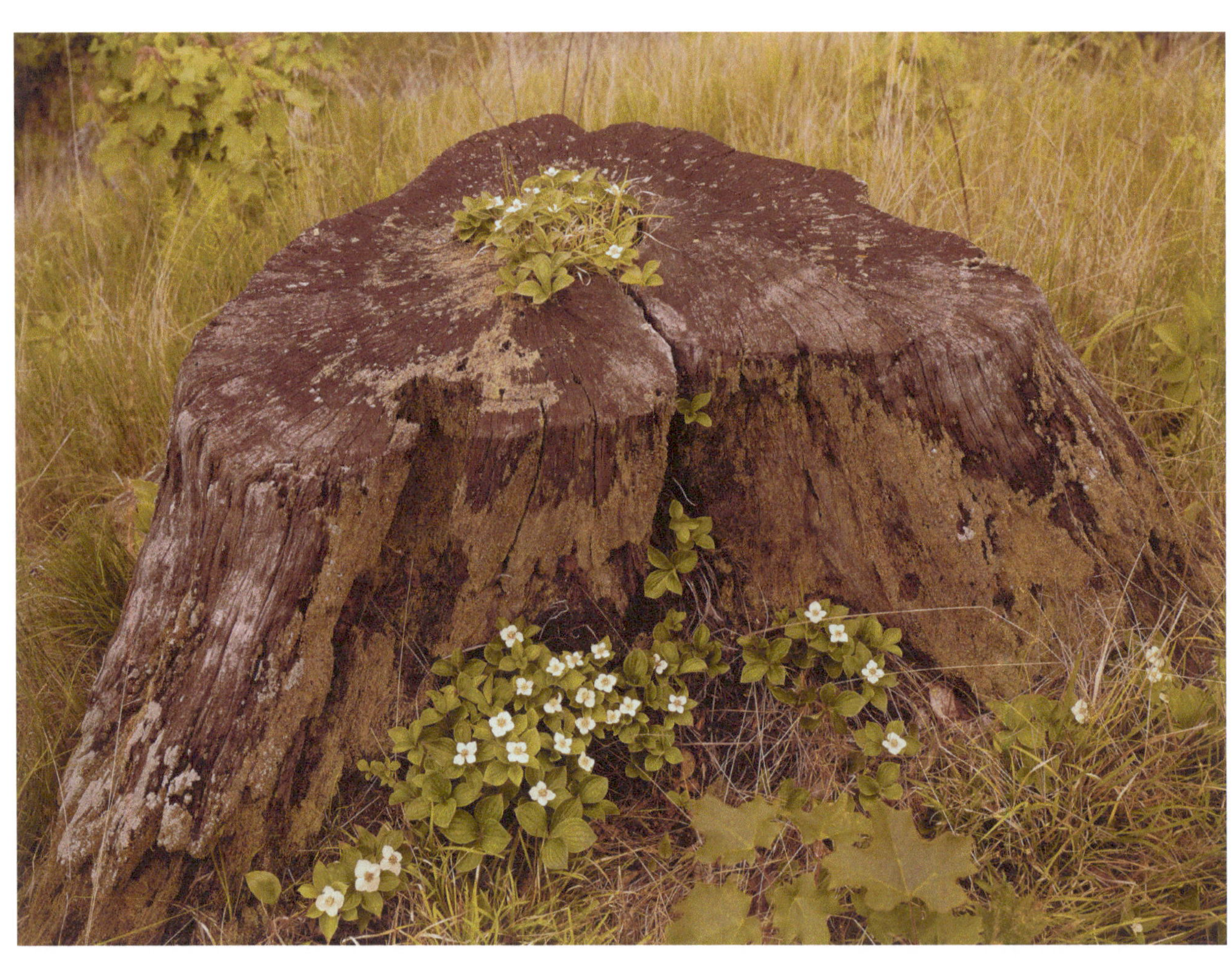

    Jay Cooke State Park, Minnesota

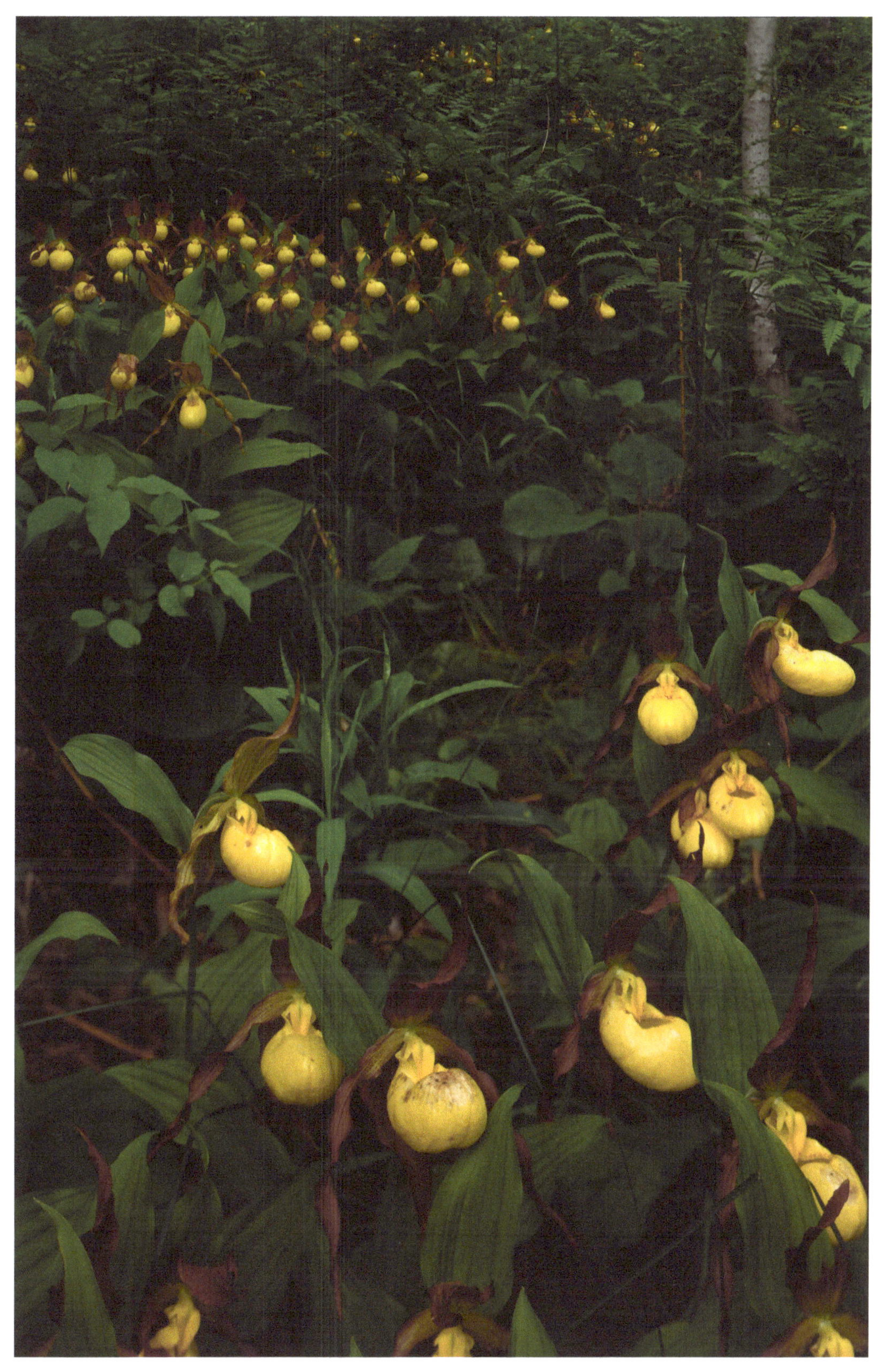

42   931   Jay Cooke State Park, Minnesota

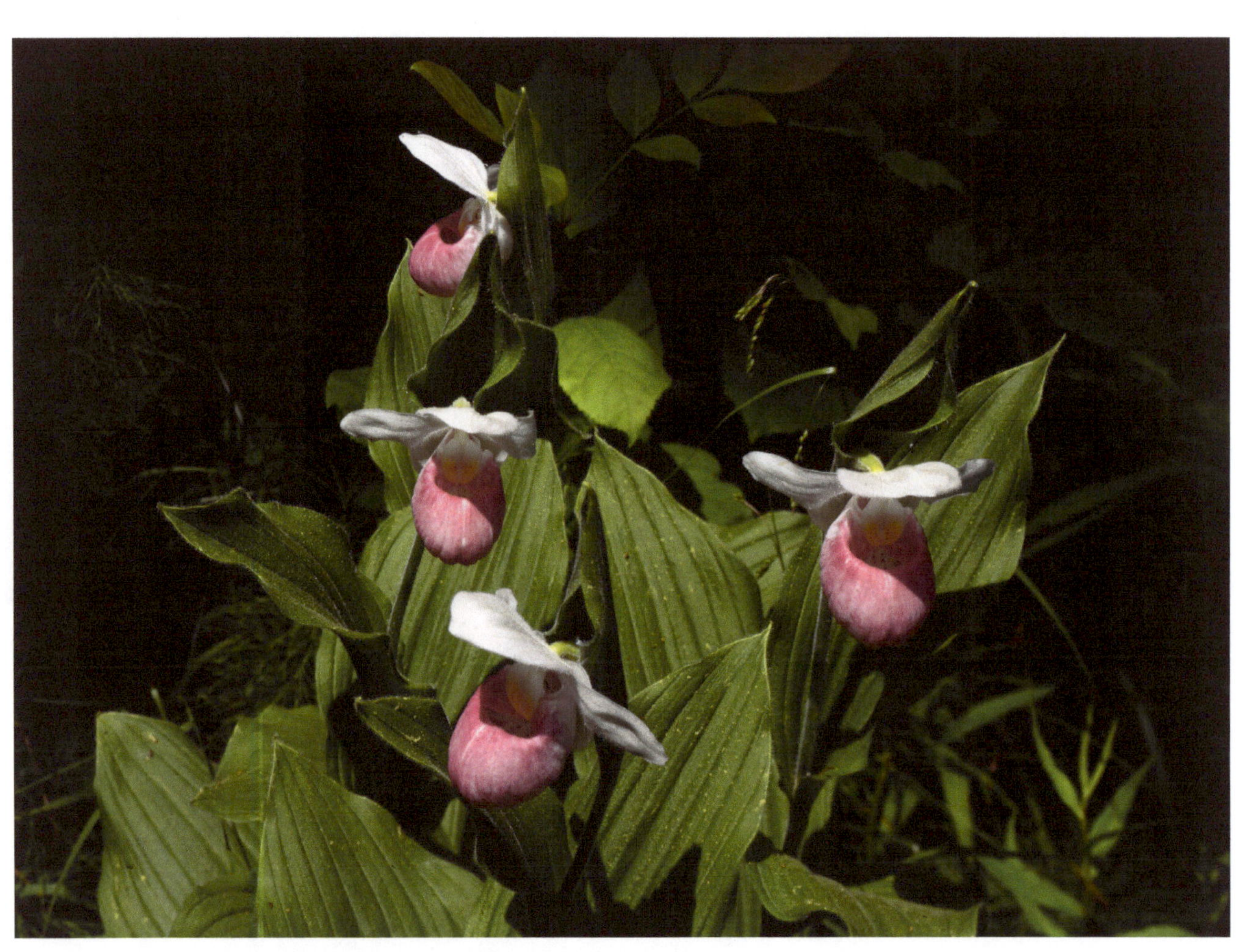

43   1073   Jay Cooke State Park, Minnesota

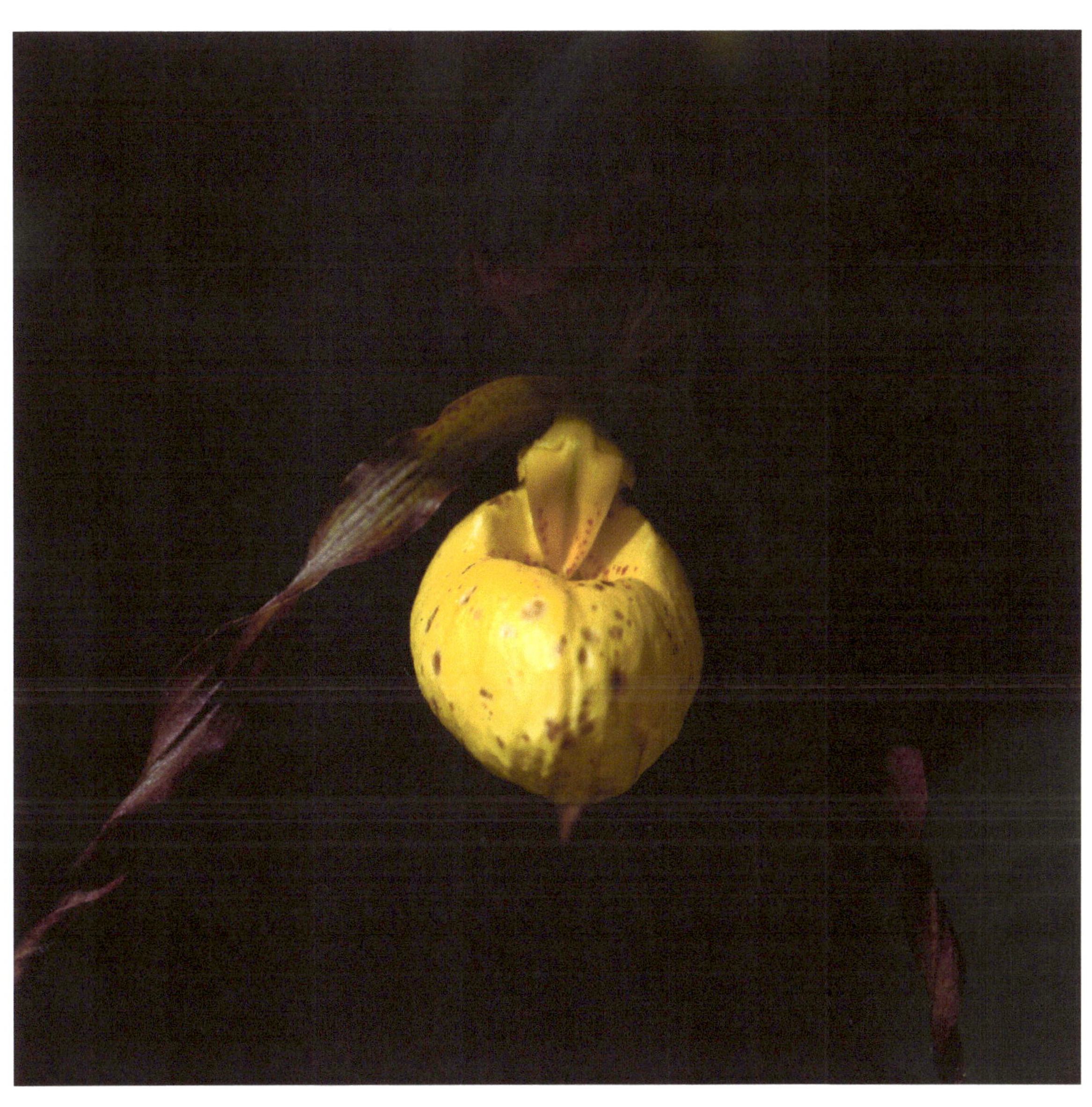

44   1744   Jay Cooke State Park, Minnesota

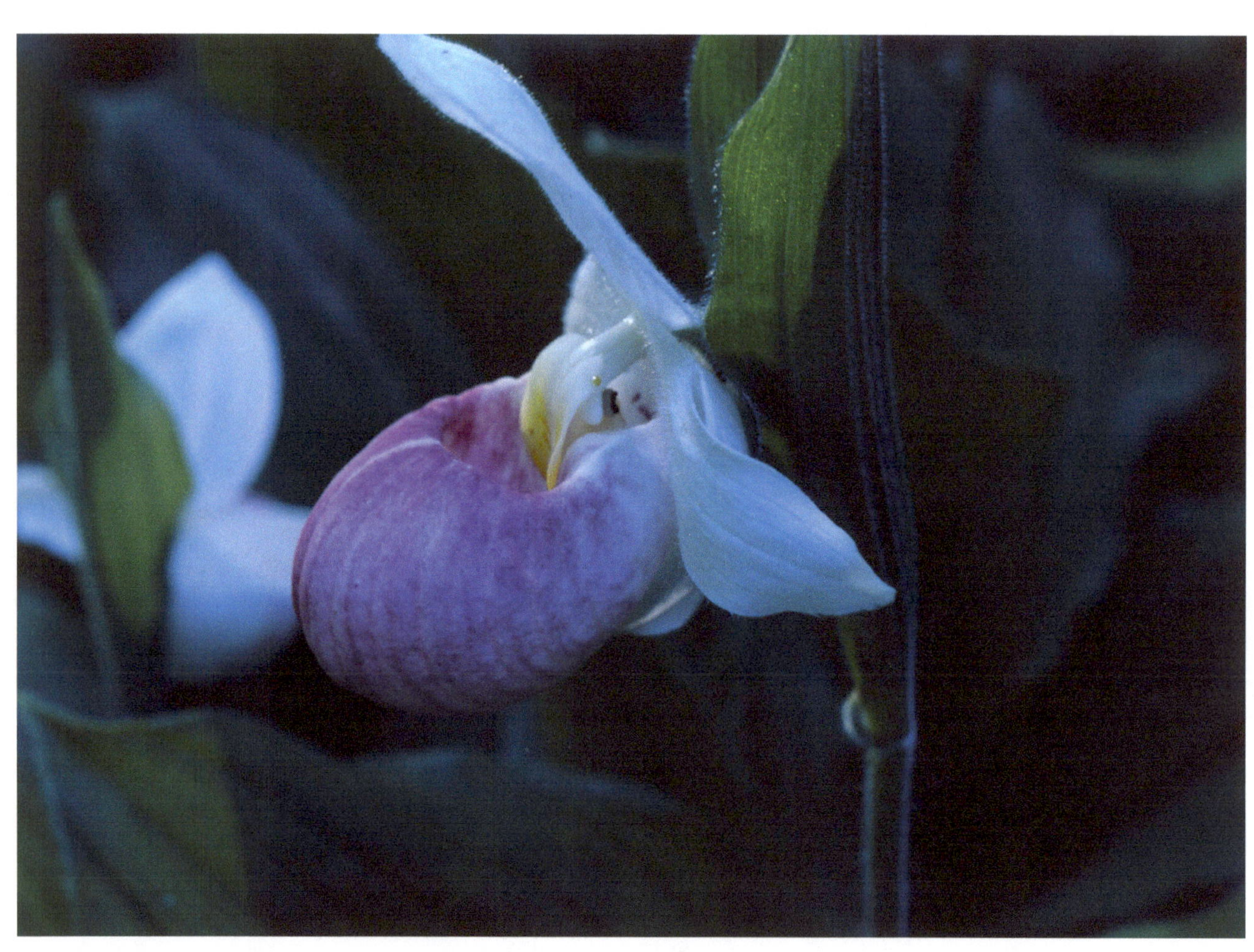

45   1751   Jay Cooke State Park, Minnesota

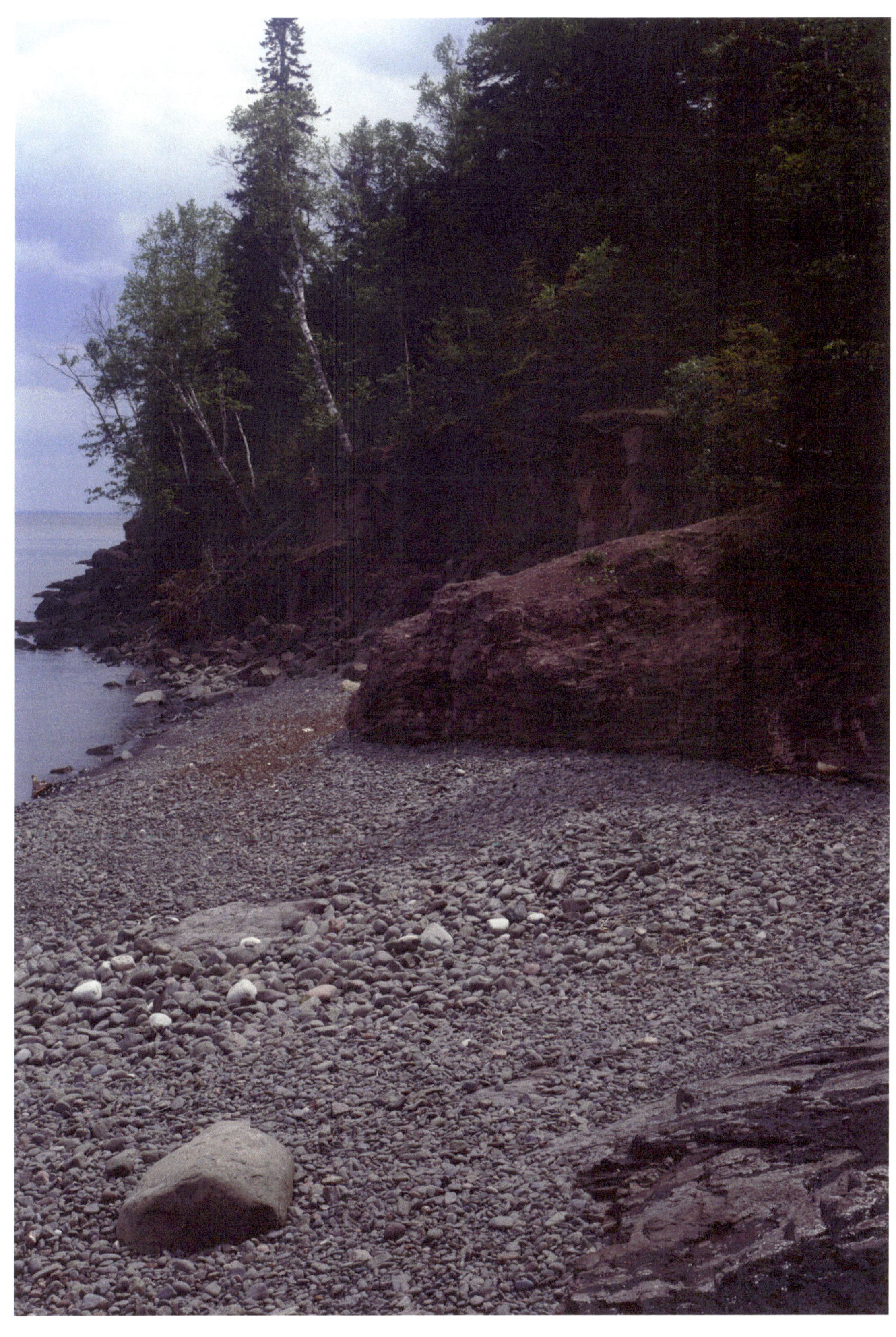

    Burlington Bay, Two Harbors, Minnesota

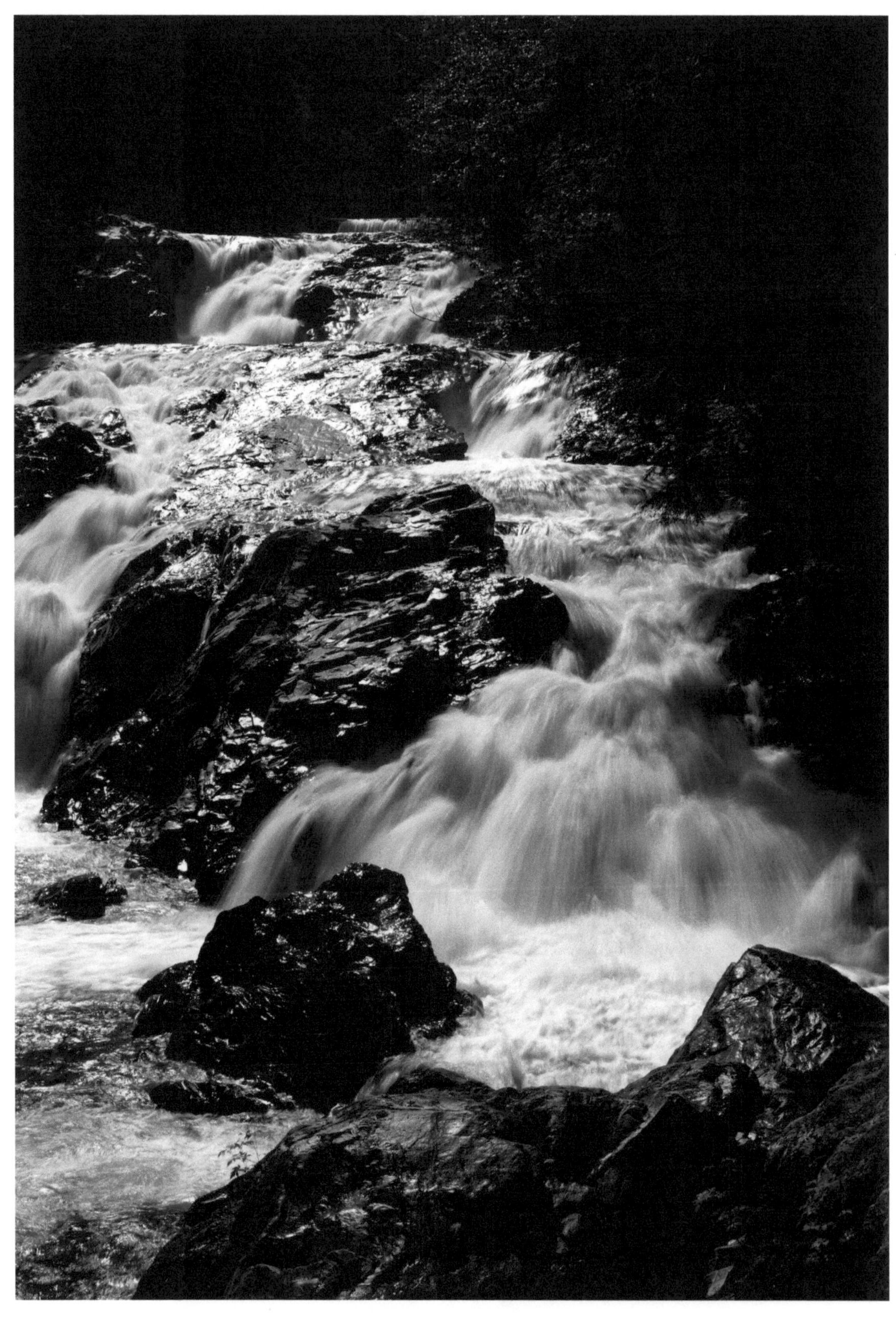

47   1907   Olallie State Park, Washington

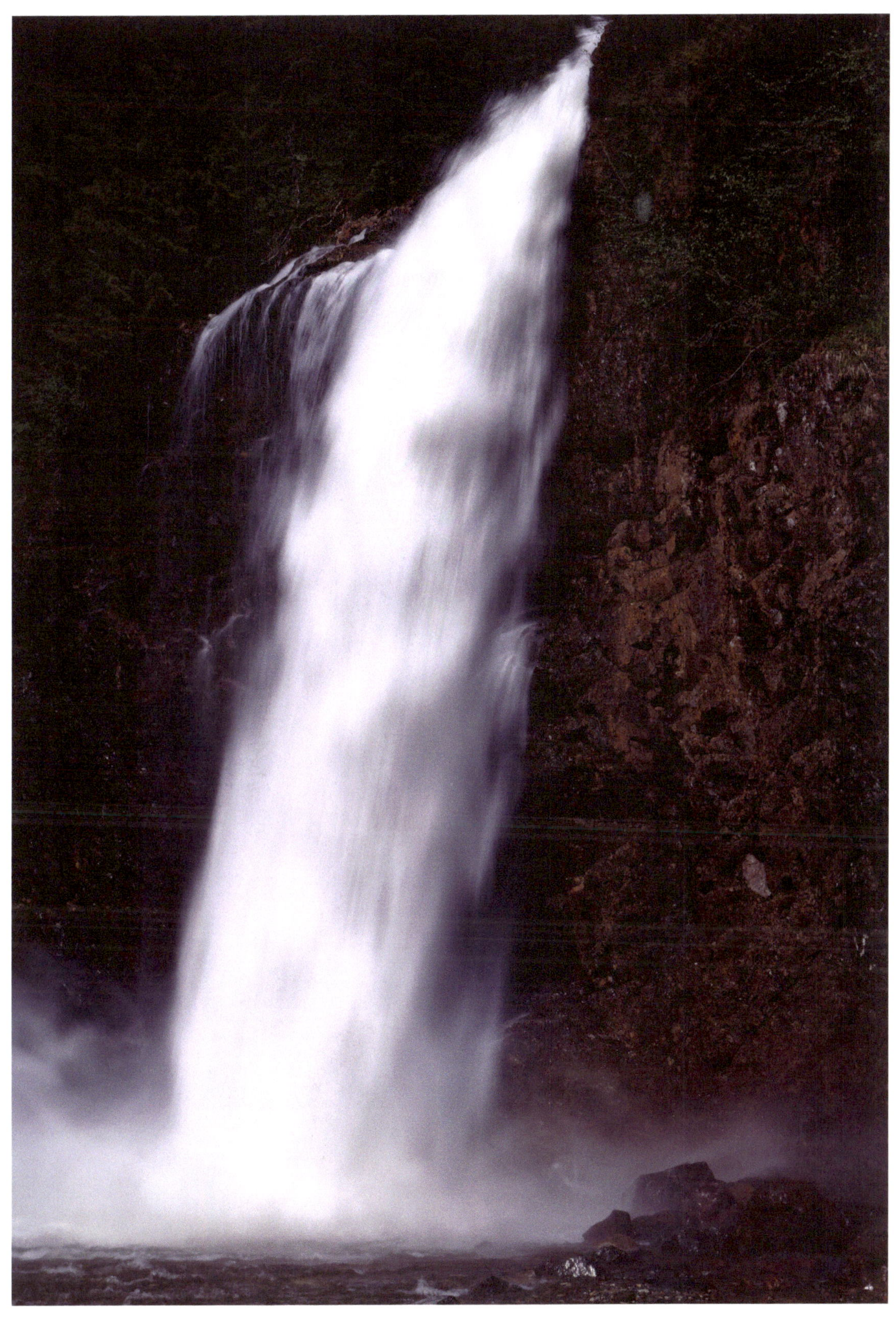

48   1913   Franklin Falls, Washington

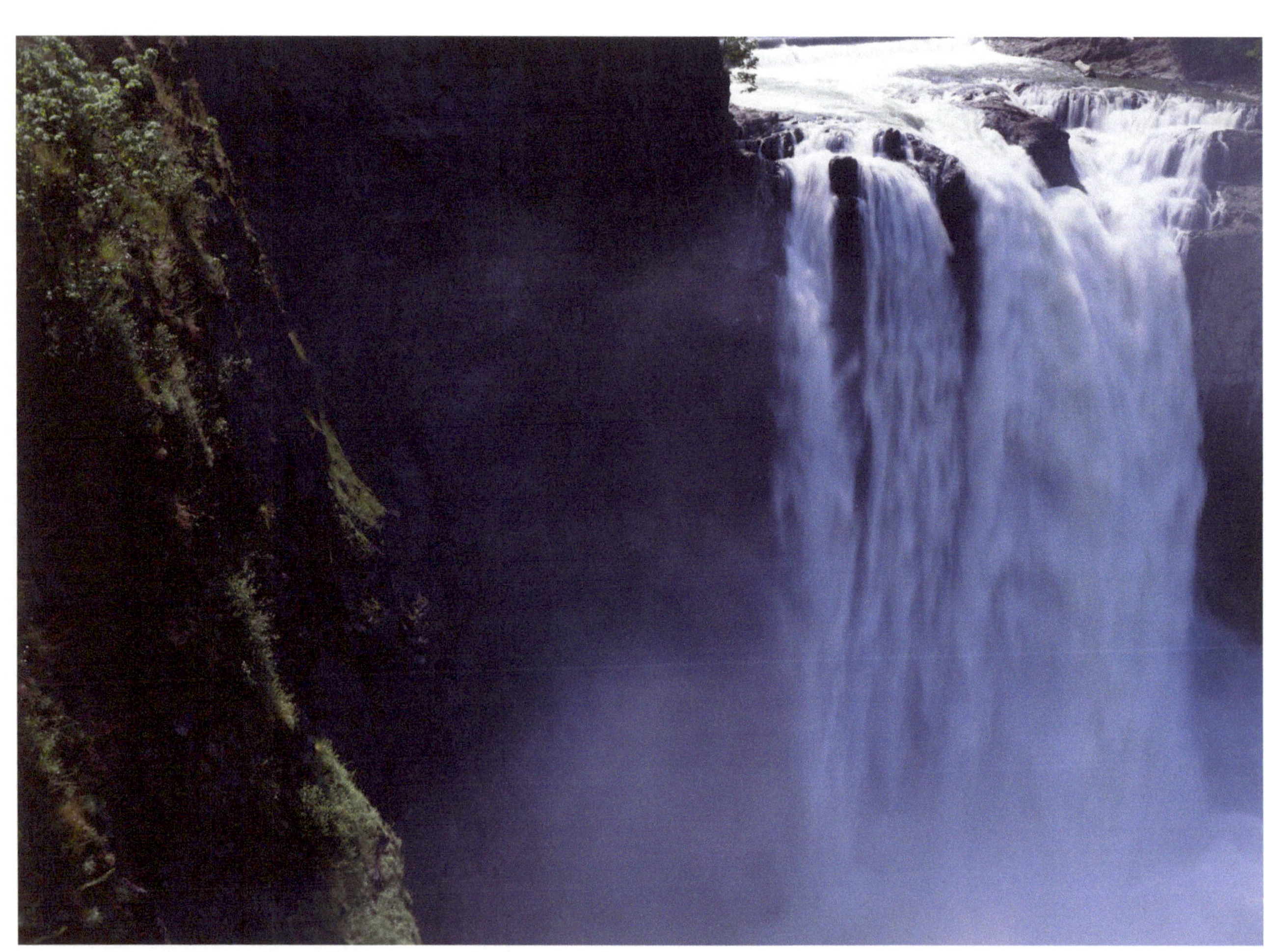

49   1918   Snoqualmie, Washington

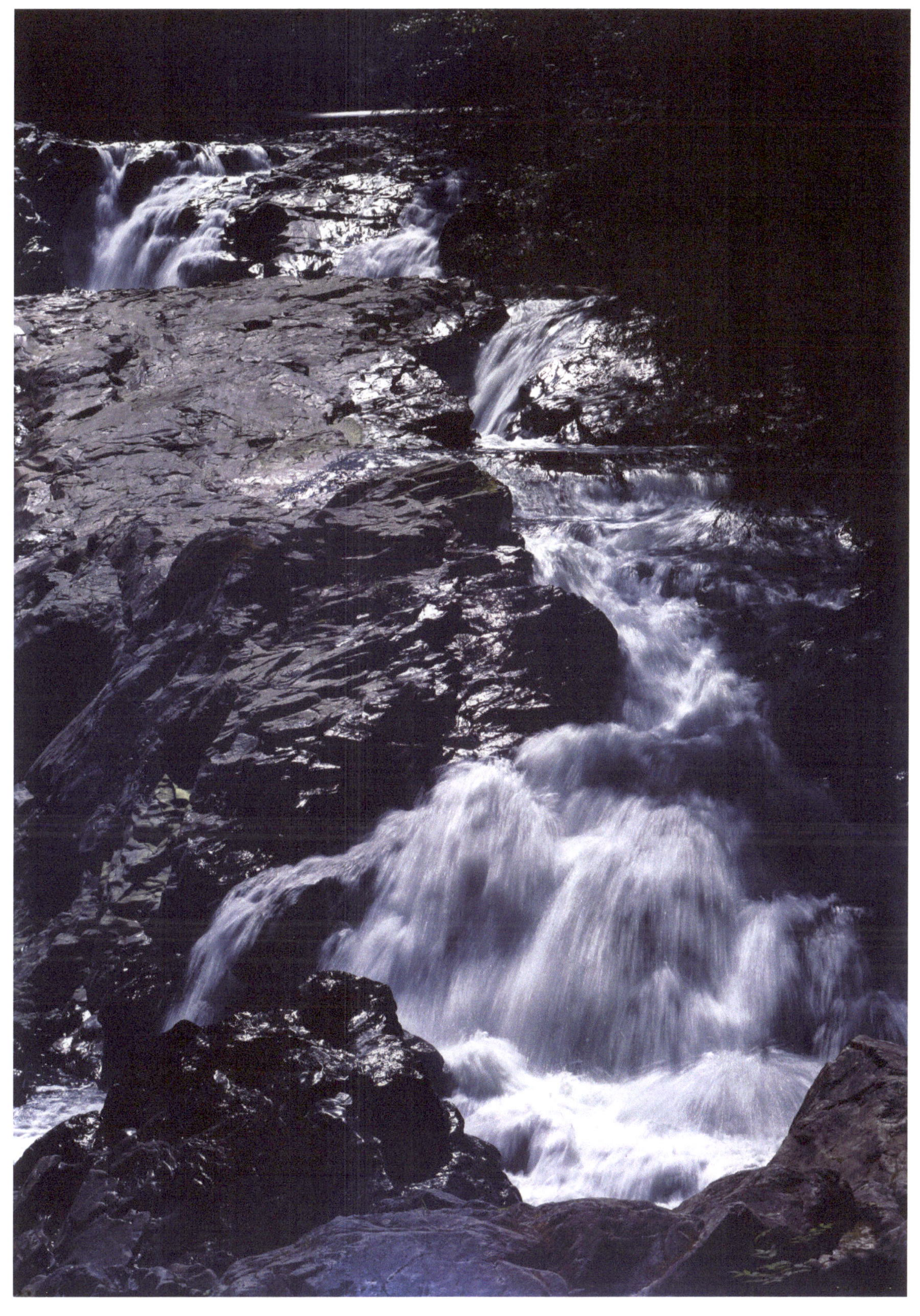

50   2001   Olallie State Park, Washington

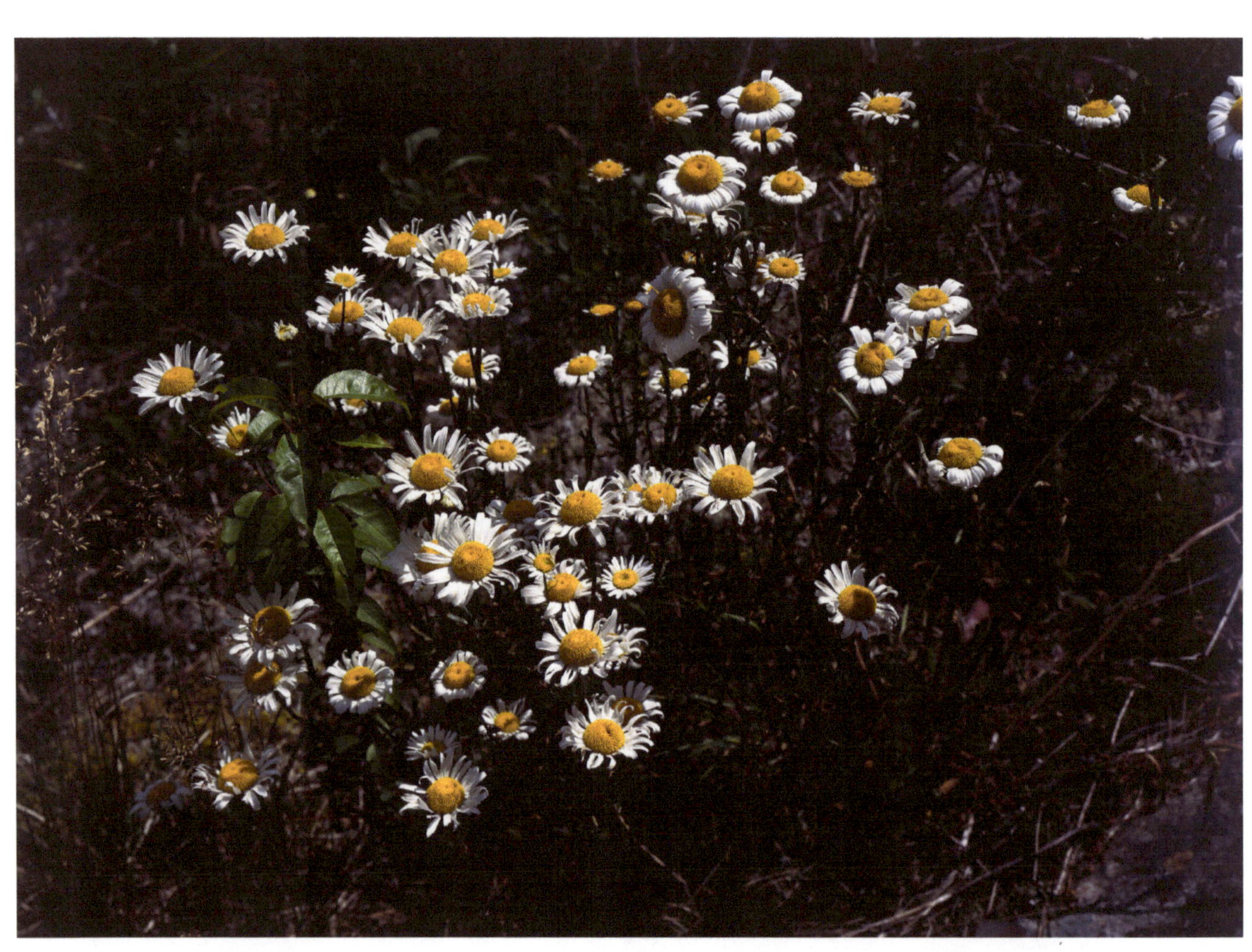

51   2100   Scanlon - Carlton, Minnesota

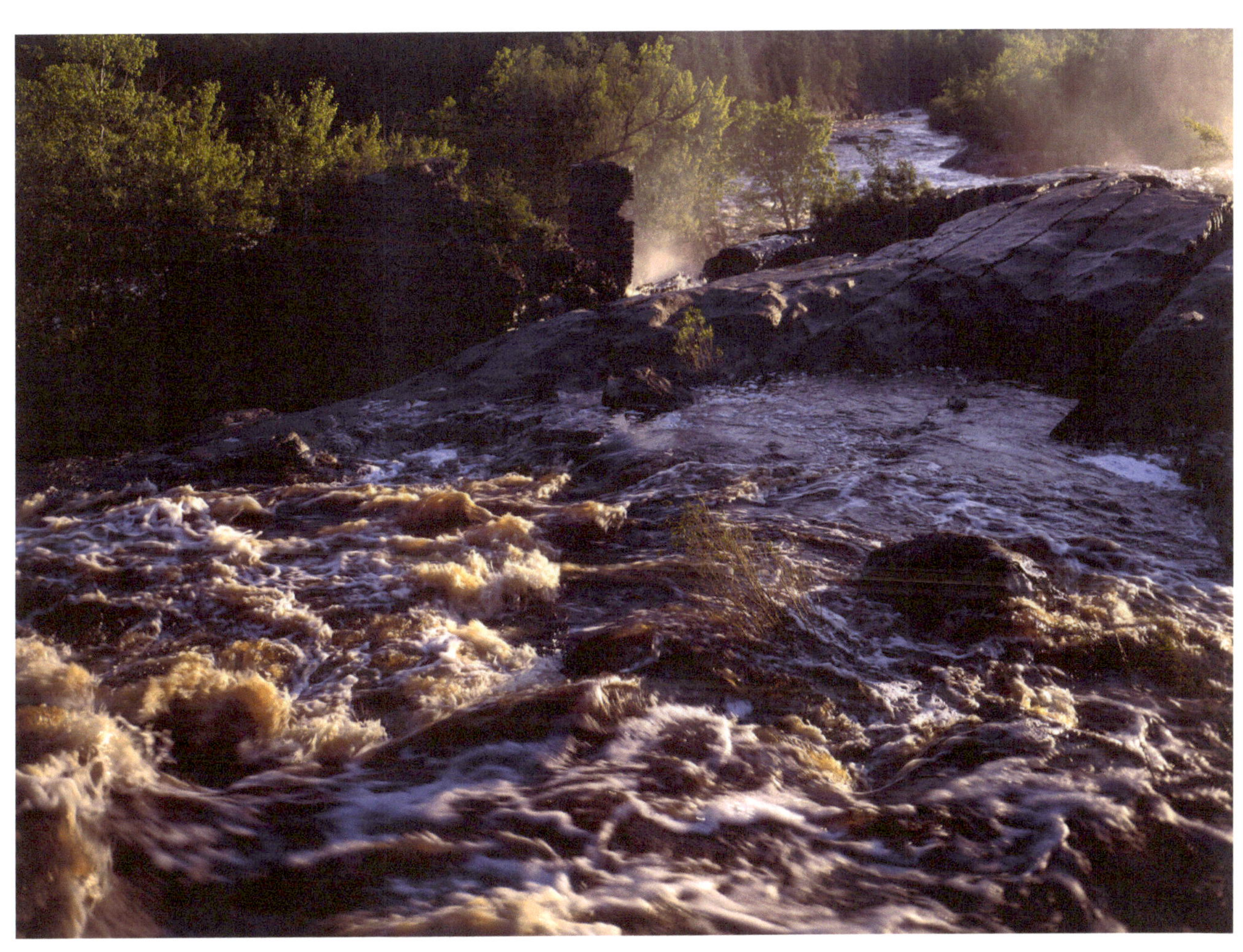

52   2166   Thomson, Minnesota

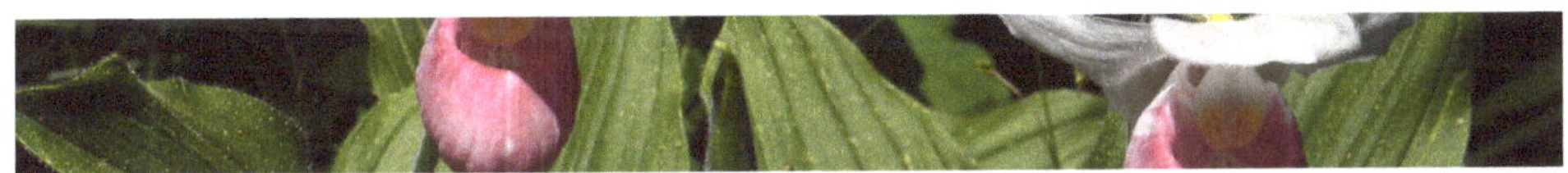

Each wildflower has its time to bloom, and most bloom in the summer. I feel the most beautiful are the orchids, like yellow ladyslipper flowers, common in Jay Cooke, and the showy ladyslipper flowers, uncommon, the Minnesota state flower. All wildflowers in the park are legally protected from disturbance, and rightfully so. Ladyslipper flowers cannot even be dug and planted elsewhere; they will expire. Wild flowers in our north region do not bunch together, unlike flowers in the western mountains that solidly carpet their fields. So I constantly look for close groups of flowers, but such are hard to find.

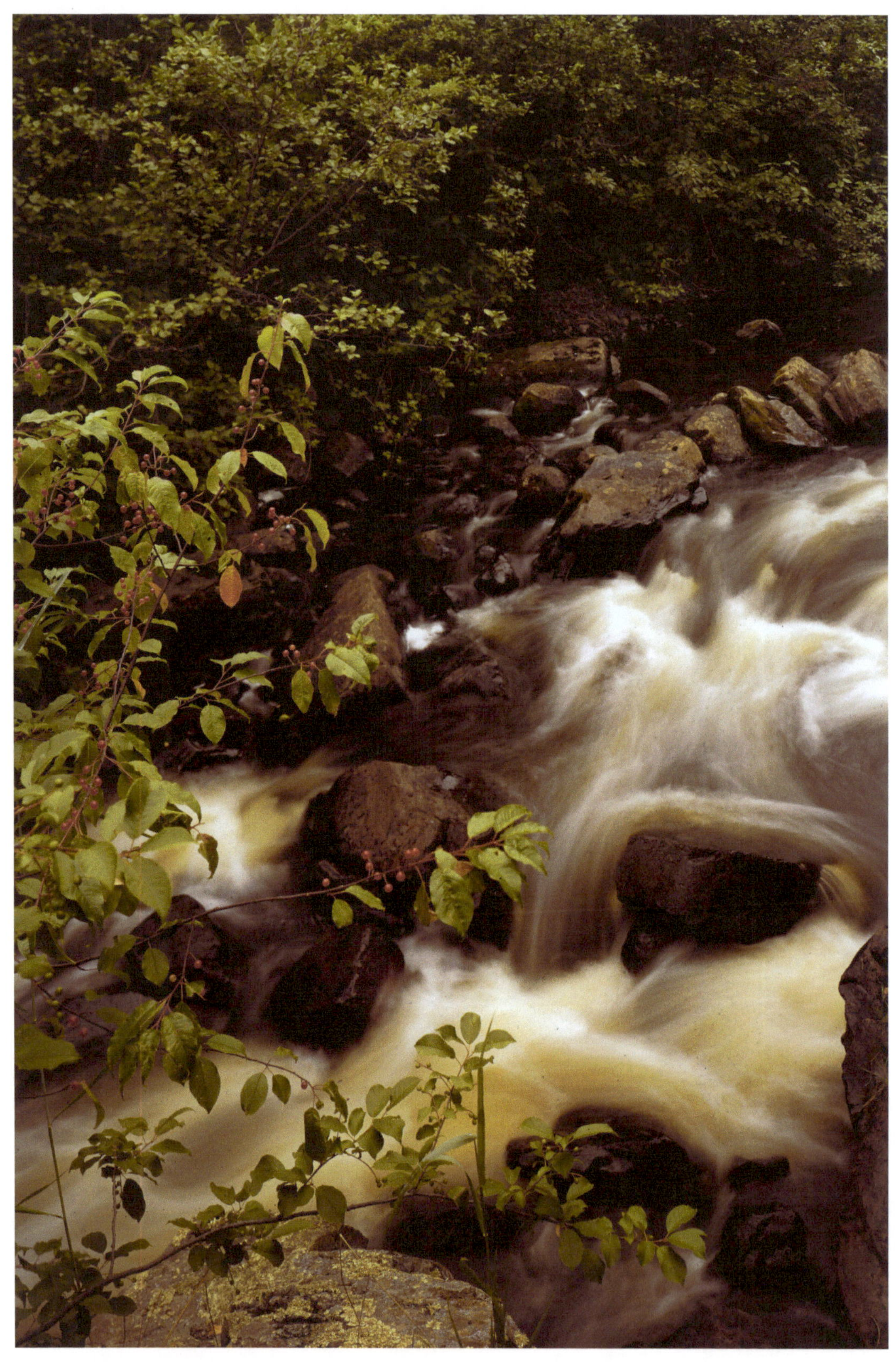

Carlton, Minnesota

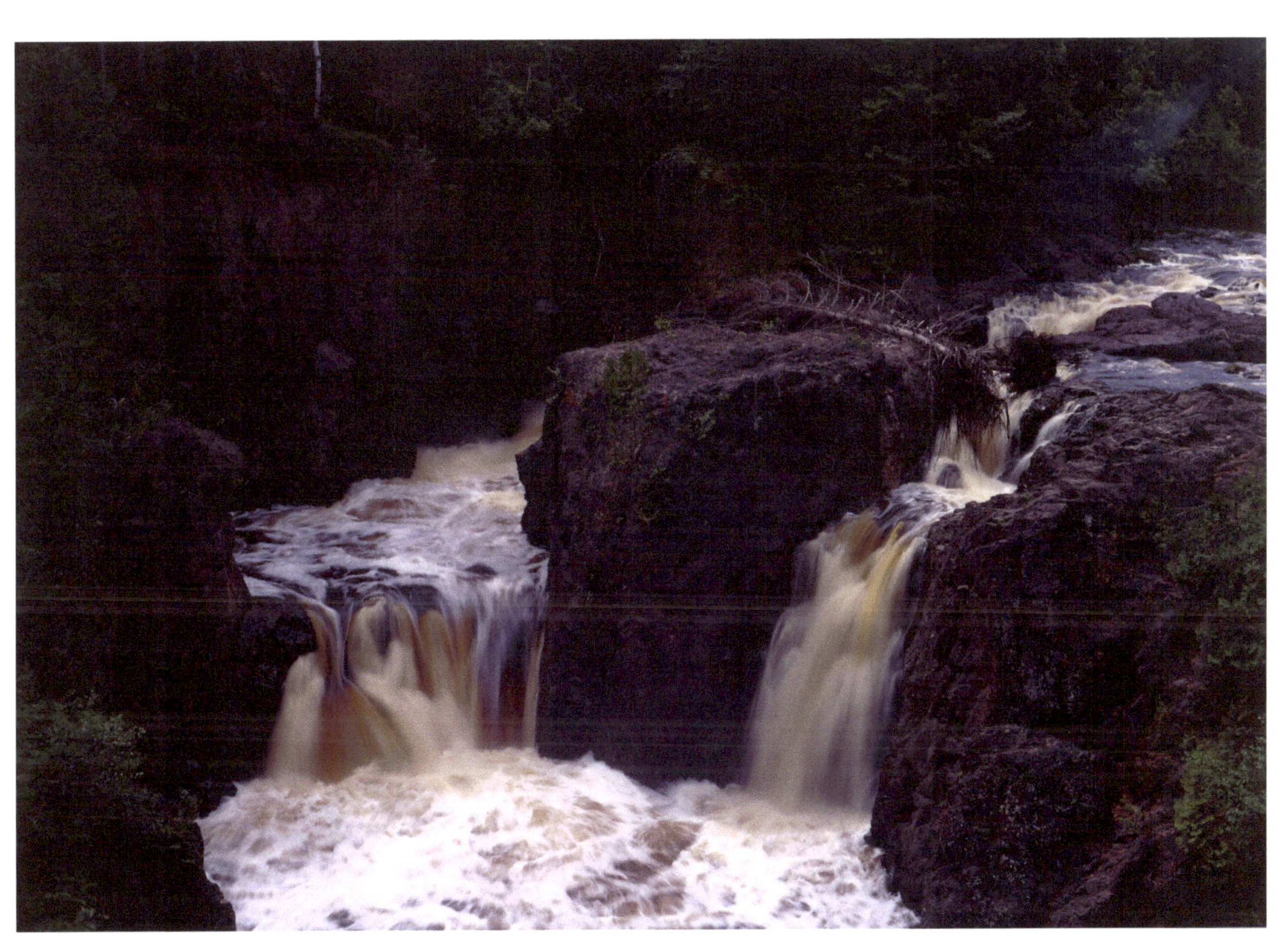

54   428   Copper Falls State Park, Wisconsin

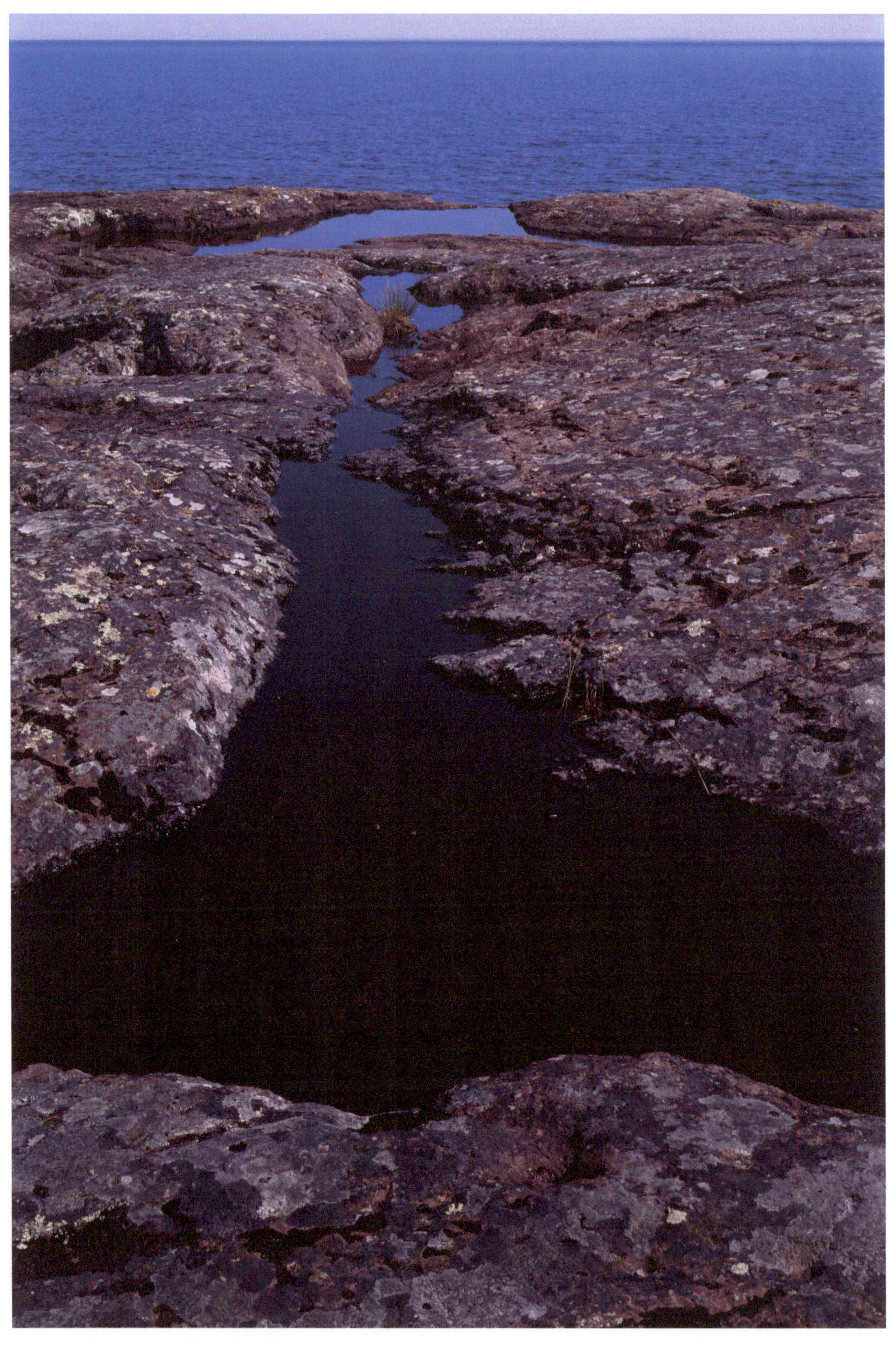

55   472   Gooseberry Falls State Park, Minnesota

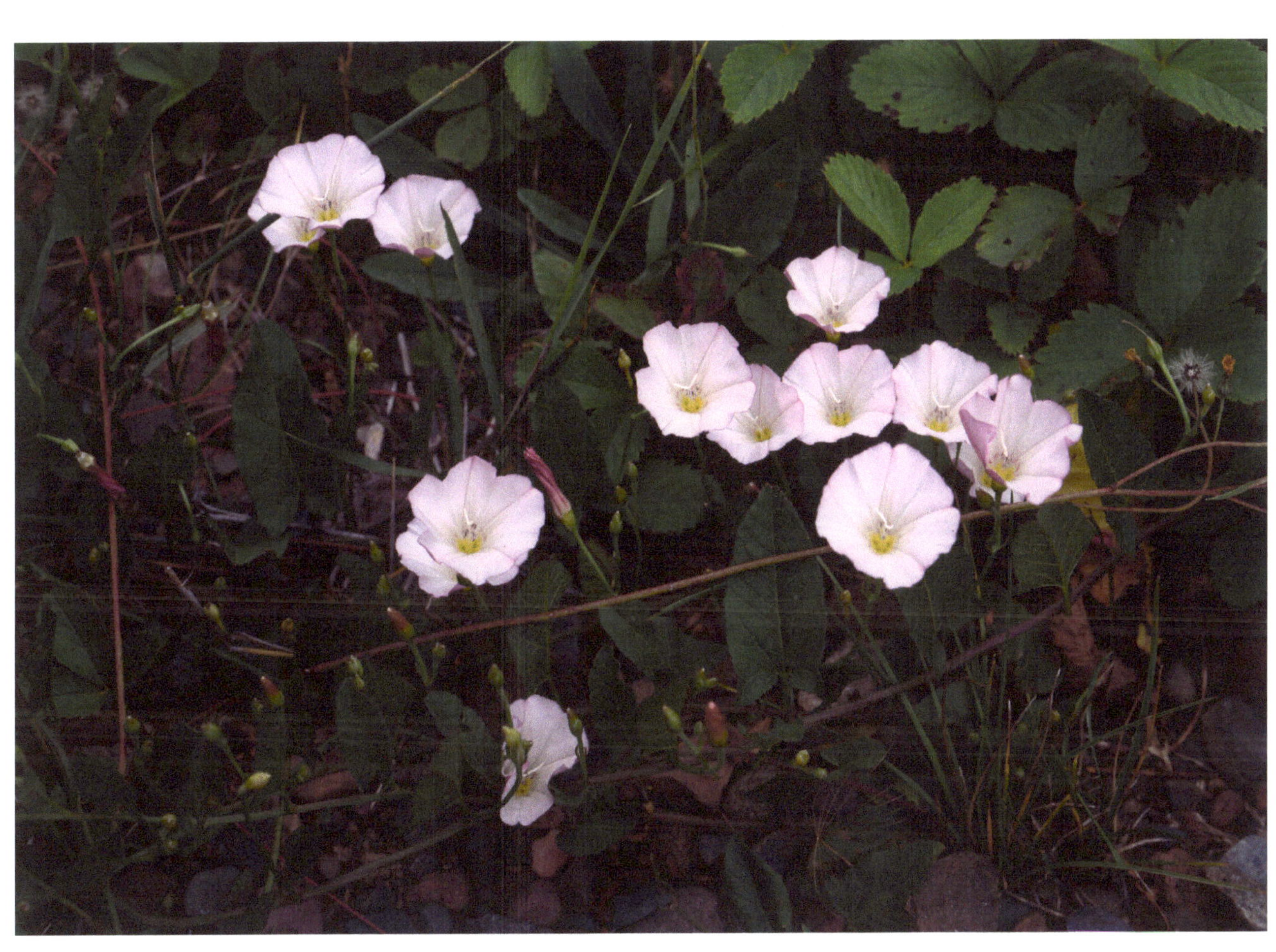

     Munger Trail, Carlton, Minnesota

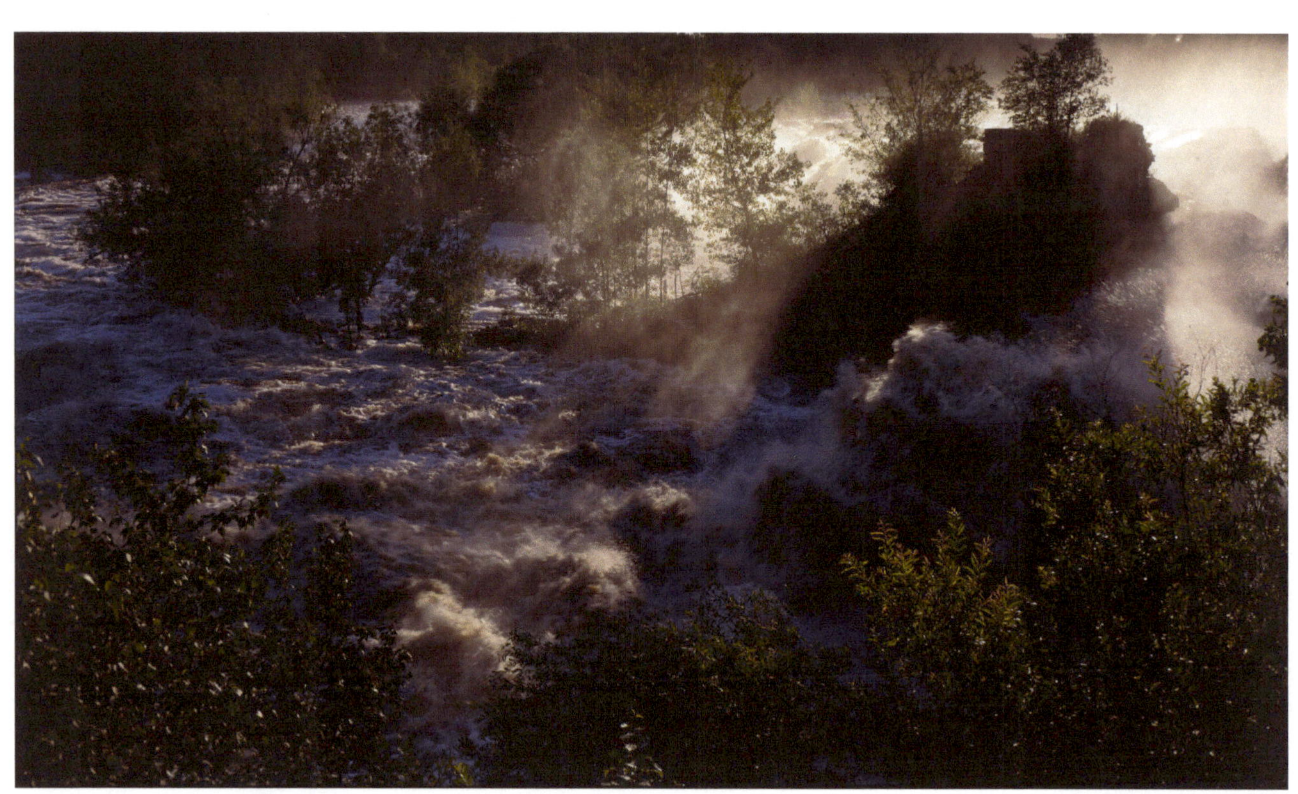

57   768   Thomson, Minnesota

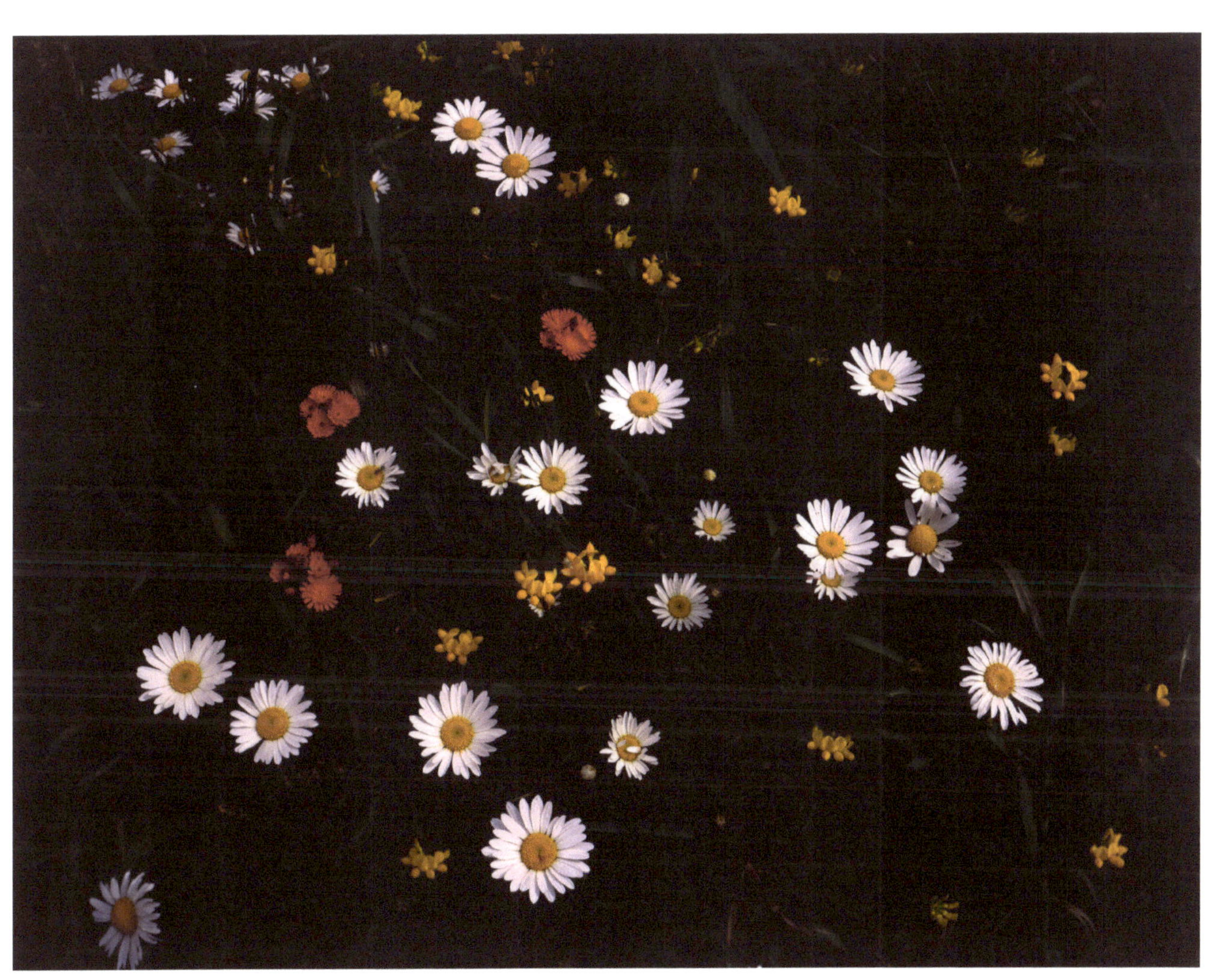

58   1493   Jay Cooke State Park, Minnesota

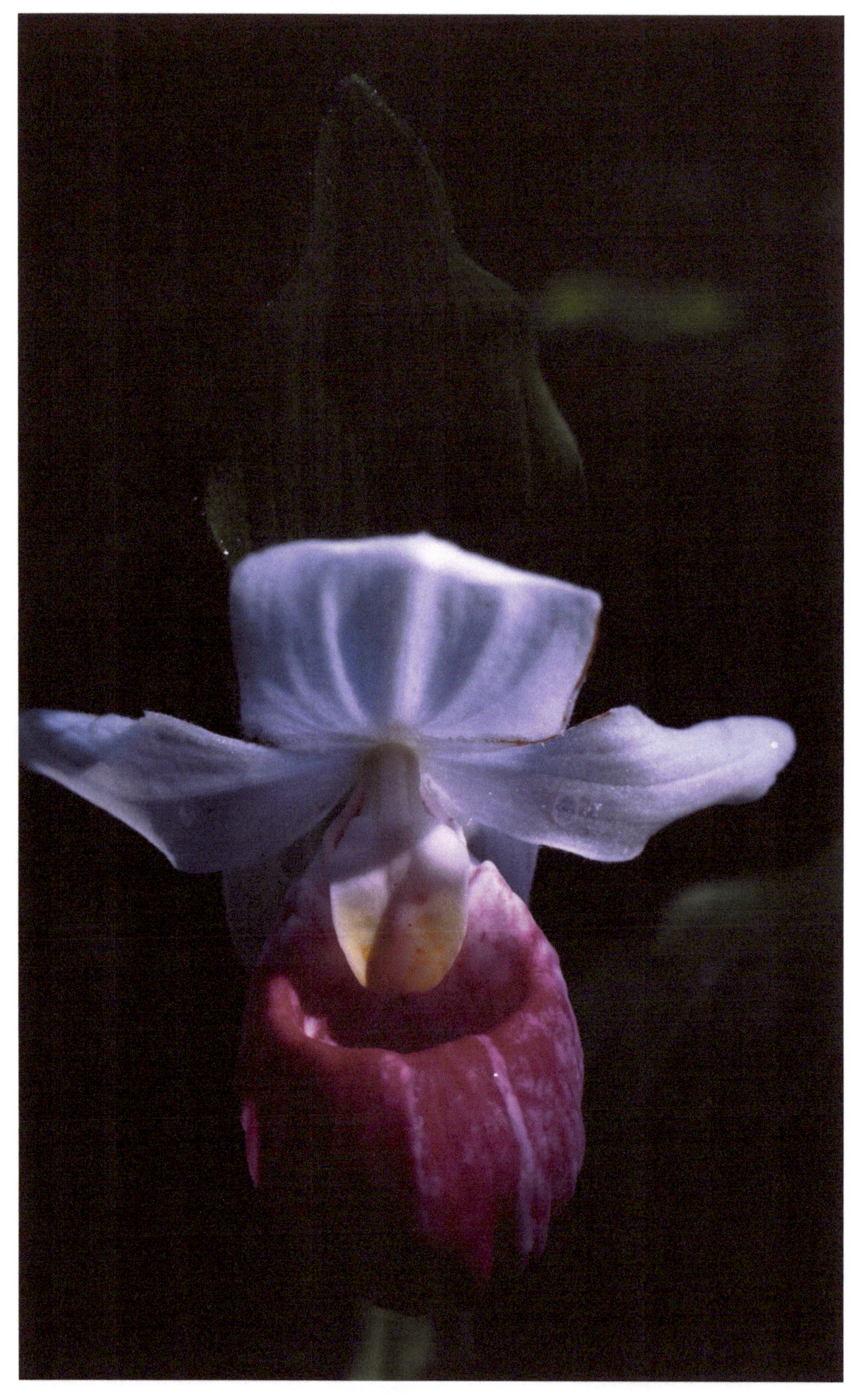

59   1495   Jay Cooke State Park, Minnesota

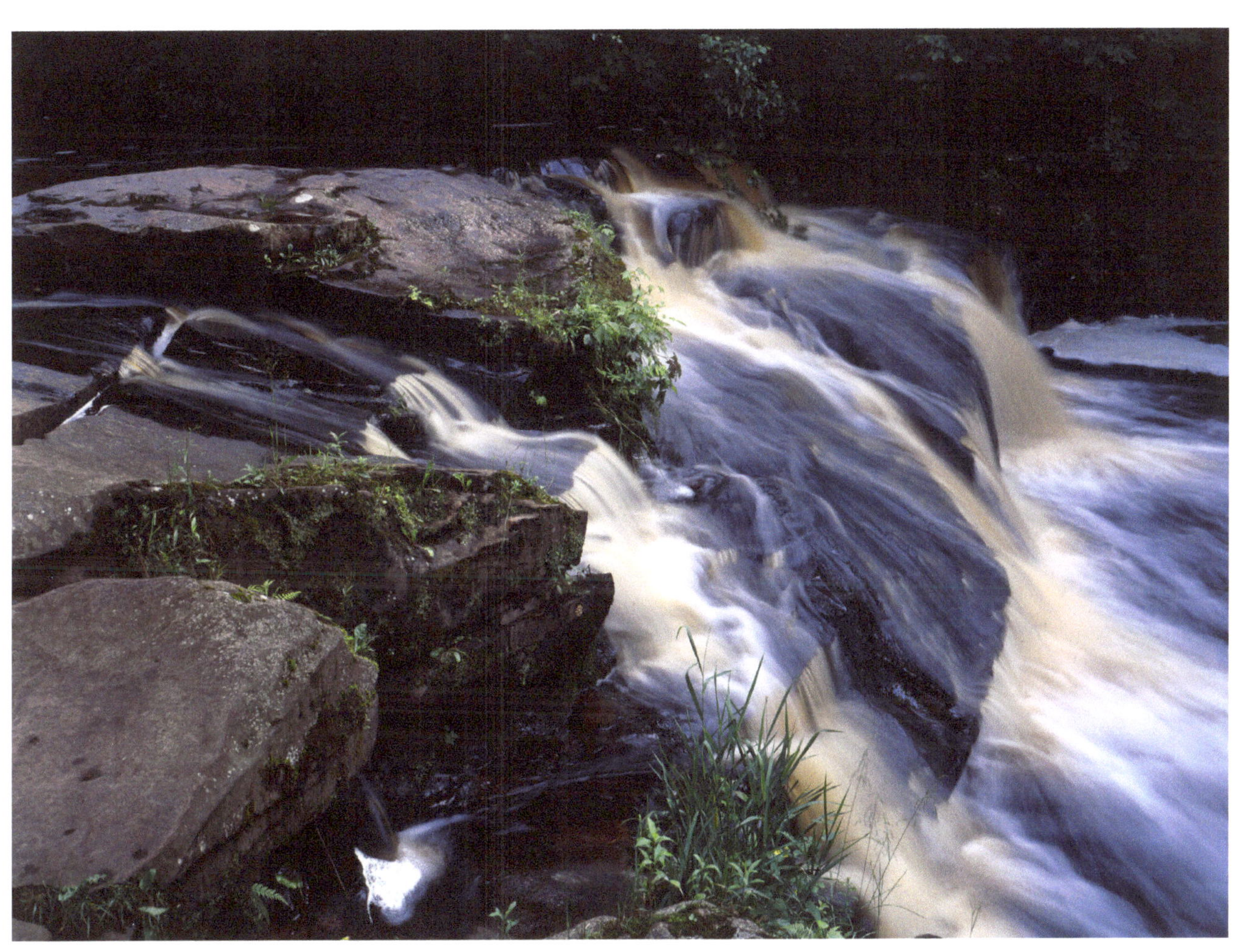

    2012   Net River, Holyoke, Minnesota

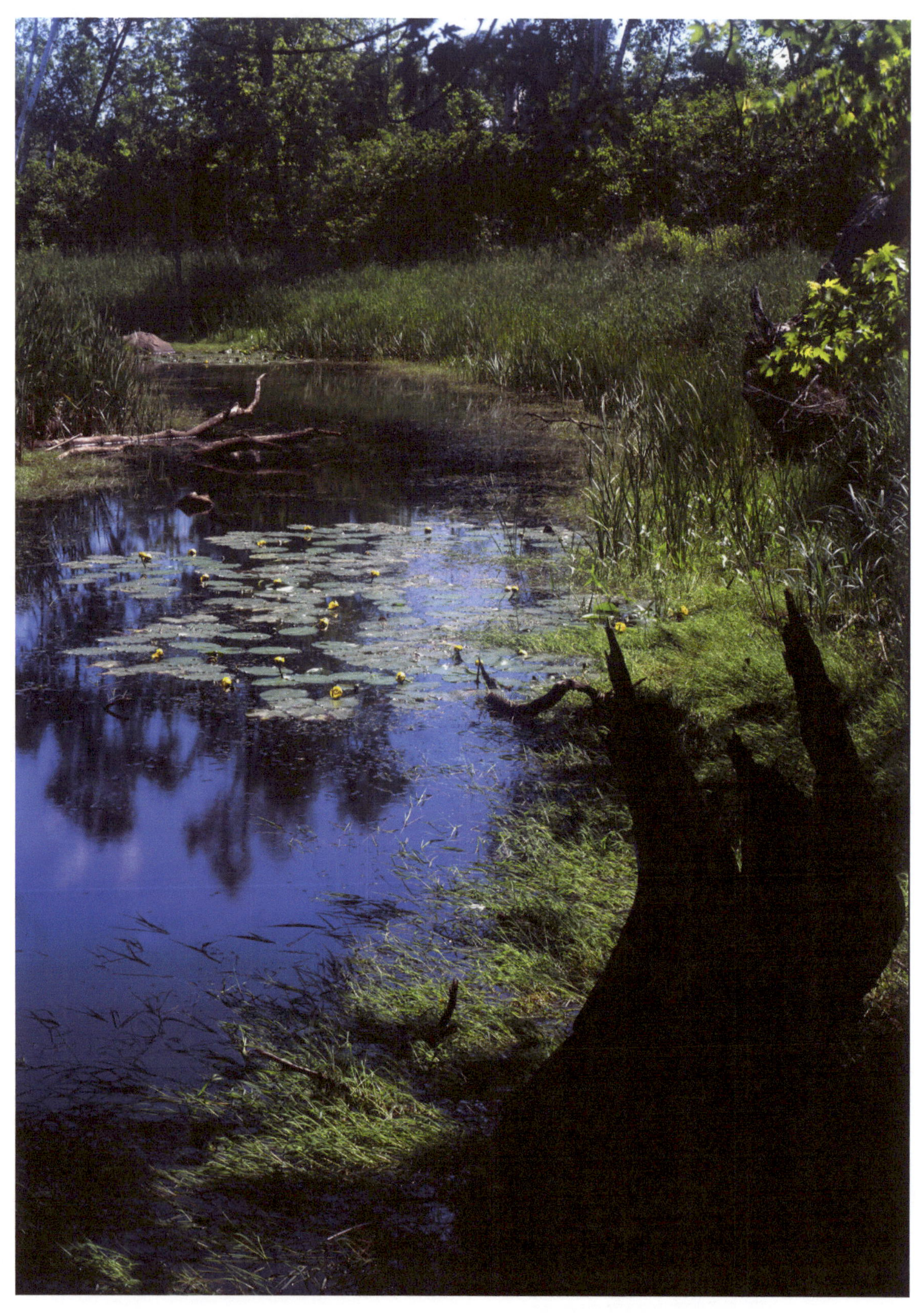

    Scanlon - Carlton, Minnesota

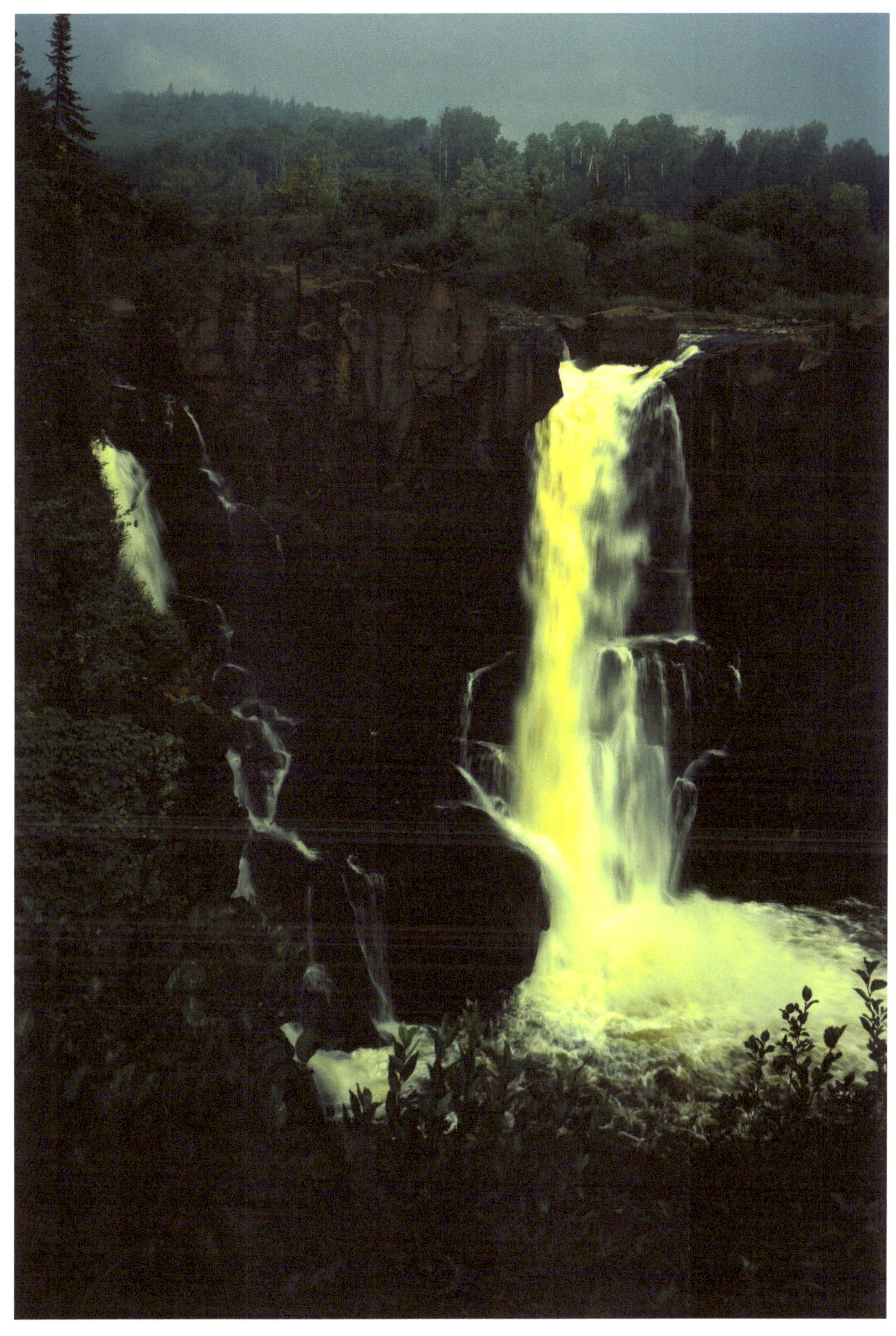

    Pigeon River, Minnesota

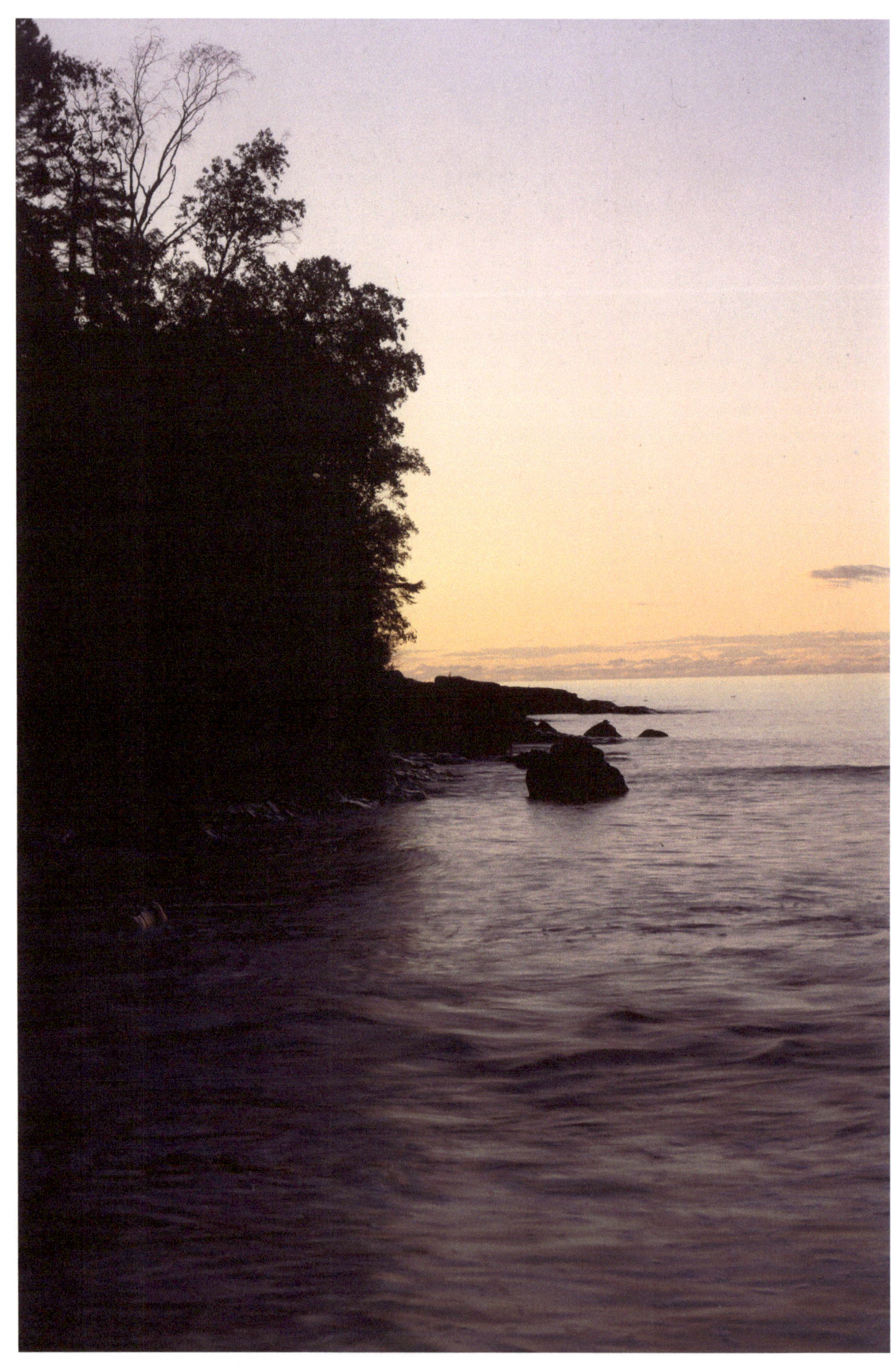

63   378   Cascade River State Park, Minnesota

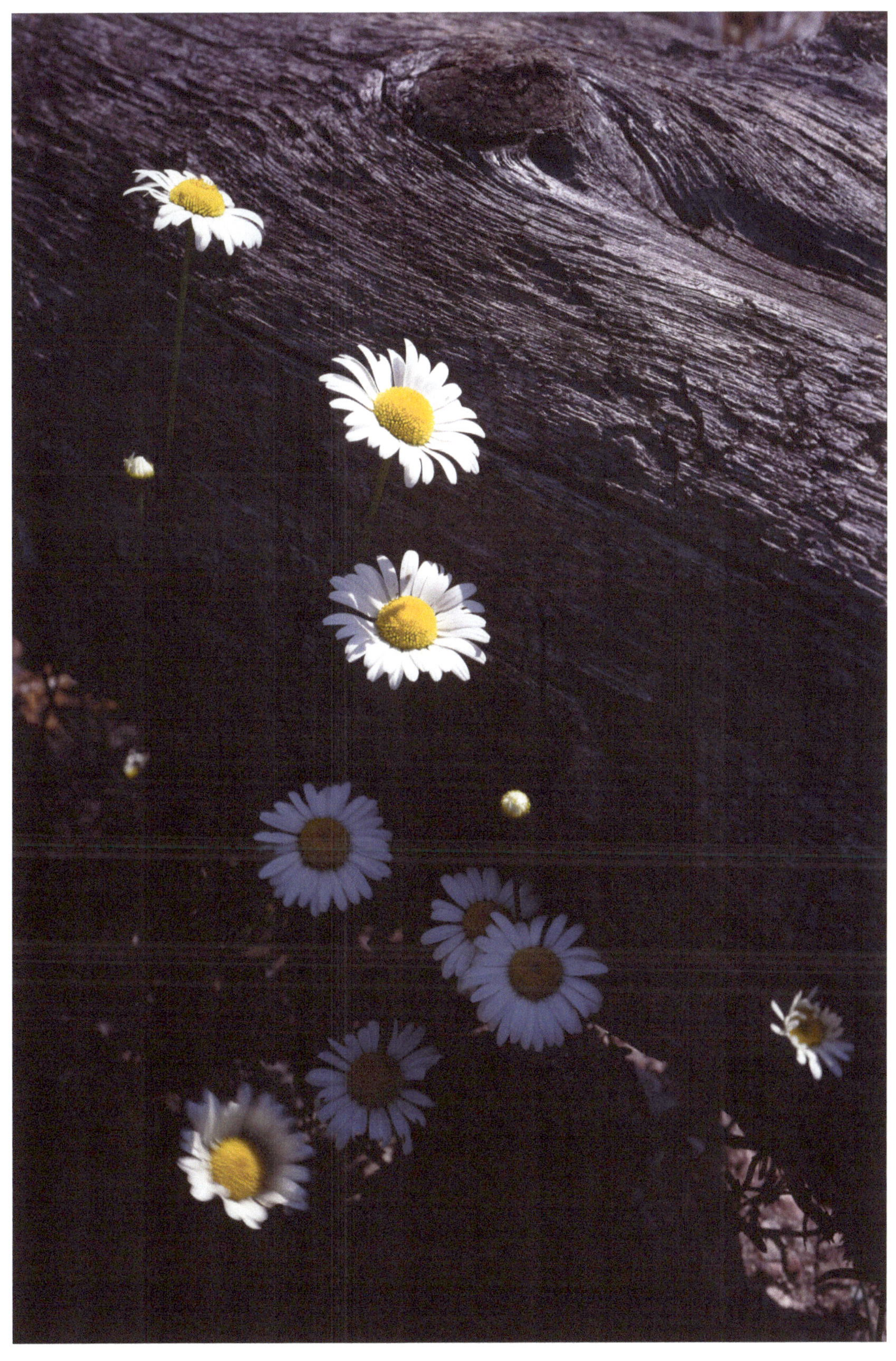

East Beaver Bay, Minnesota

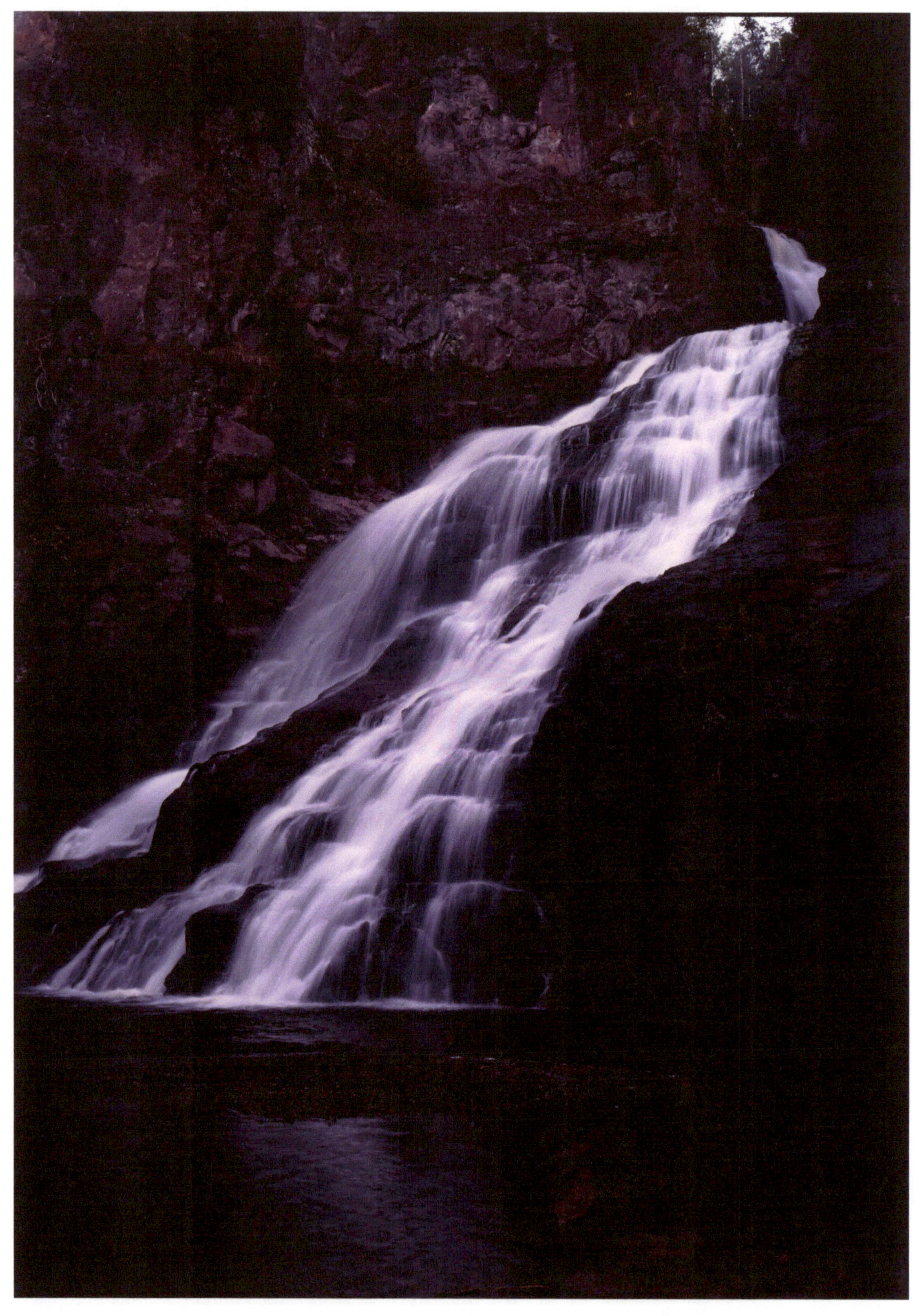

     Caribou River, Minnesota

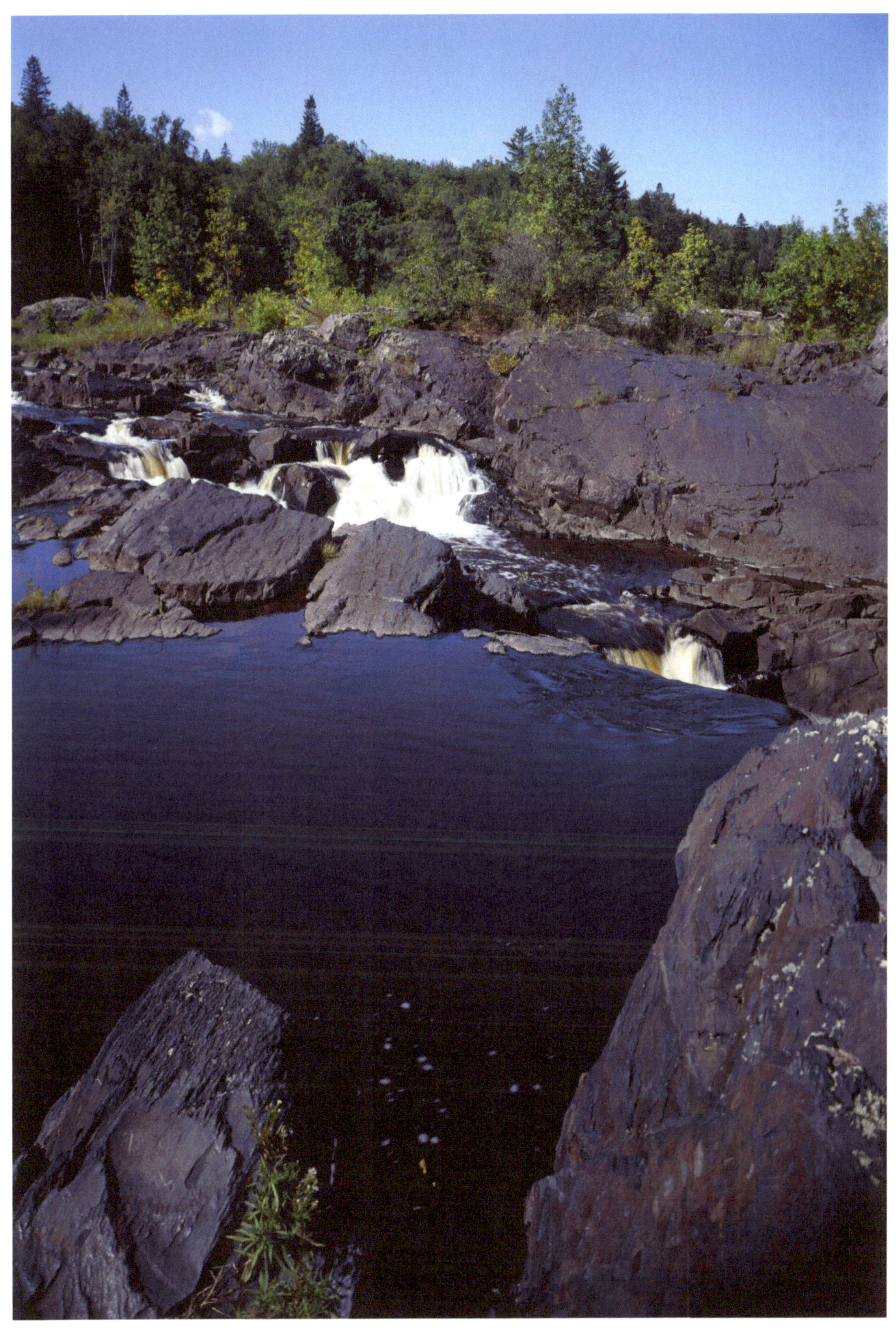

66   1401   Jay Cooke State Park, Minnesota

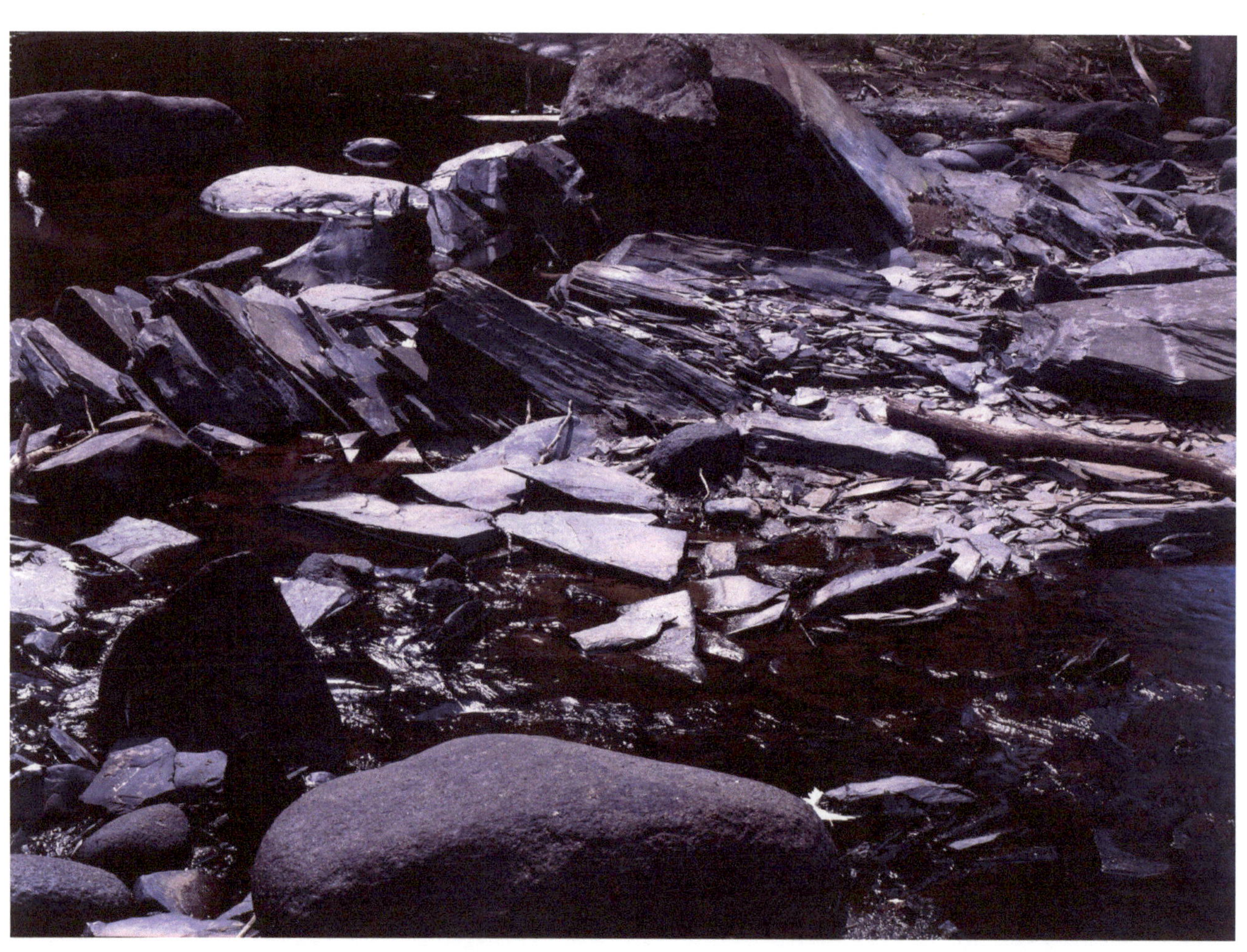

67   1572   Scanlon - Carlton, Minnesota

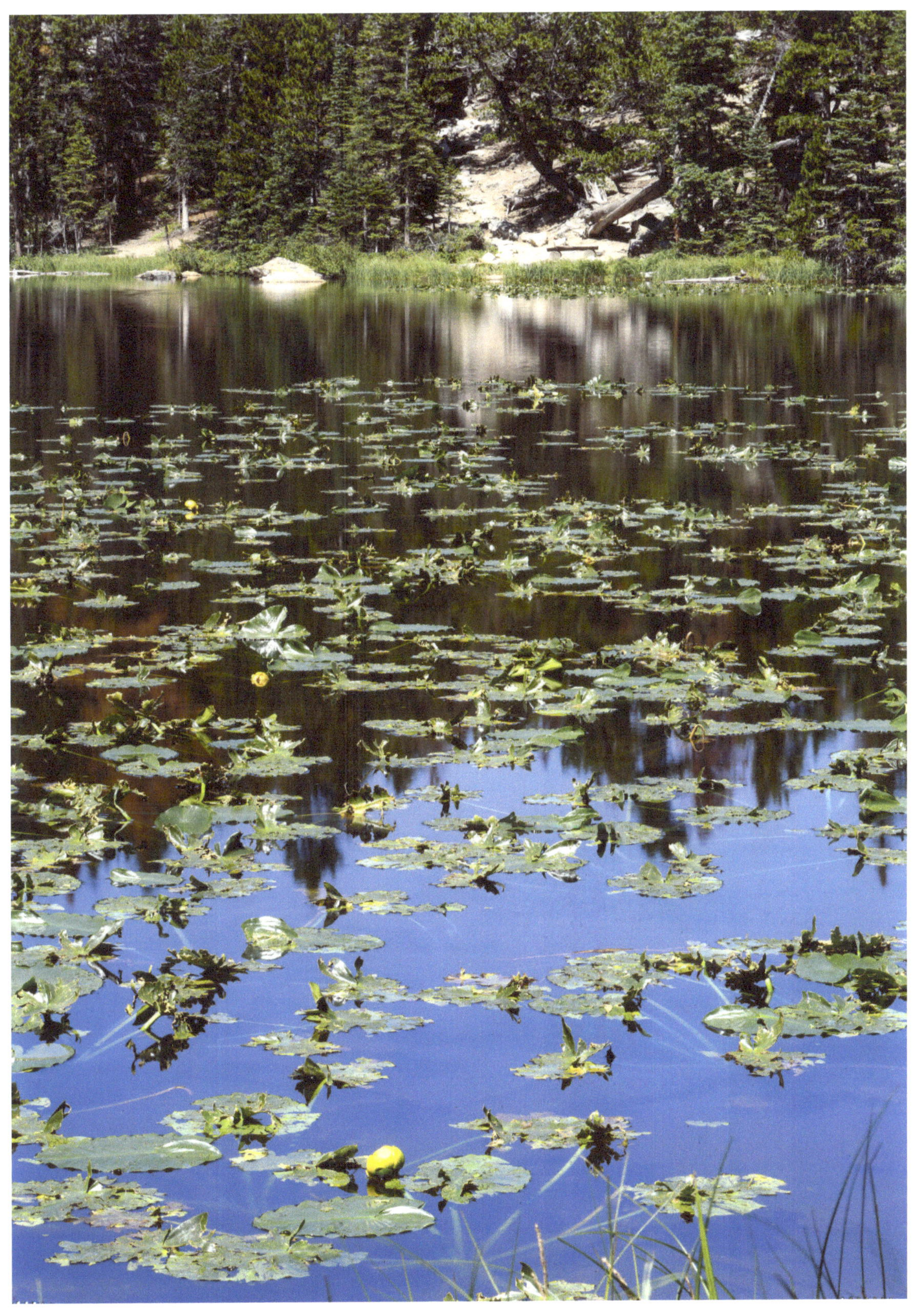

68   1839   Rocky Mountain National Park, Colorado

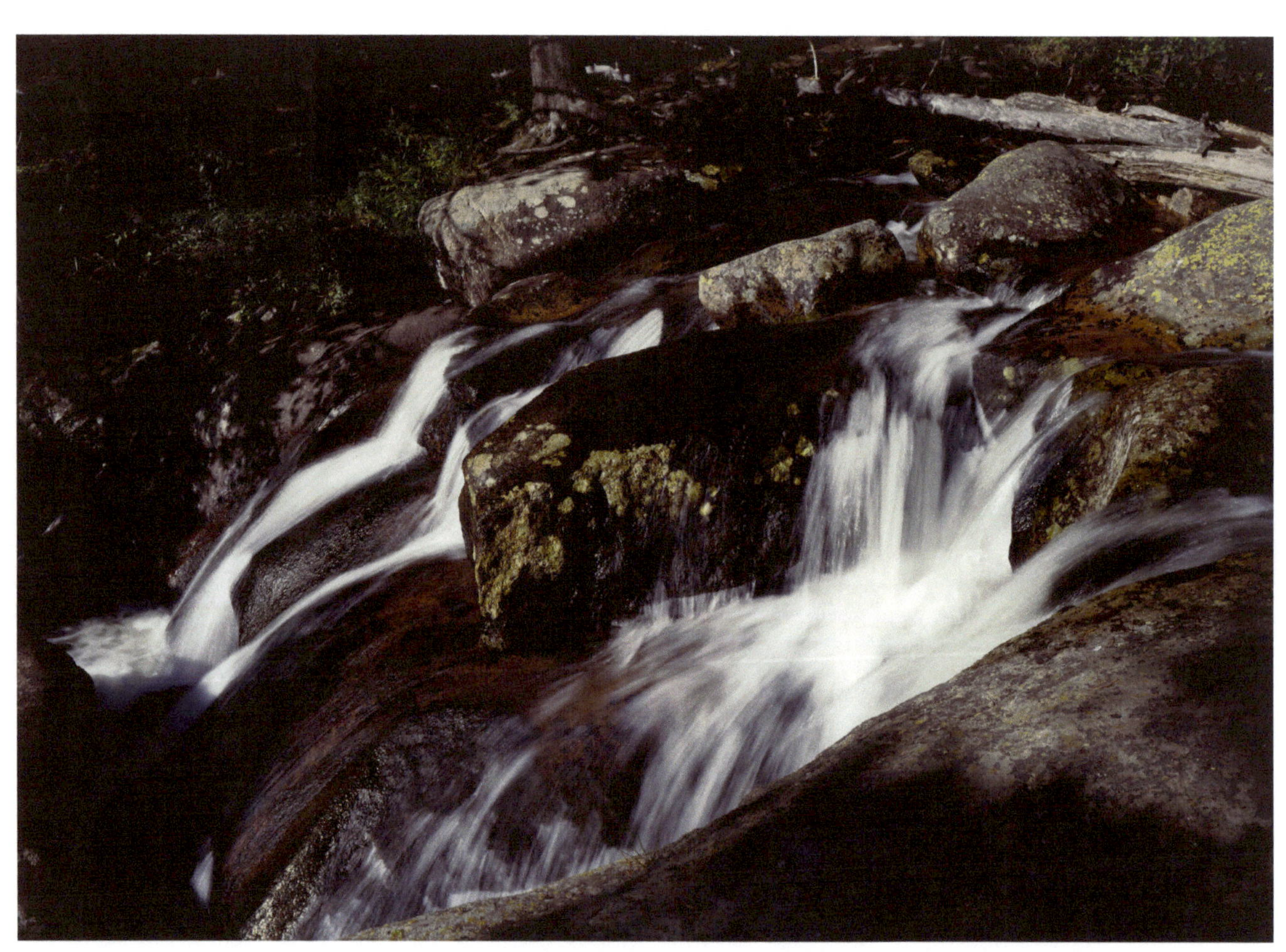

69   1842   Rocky Mountain National Park, Colorado

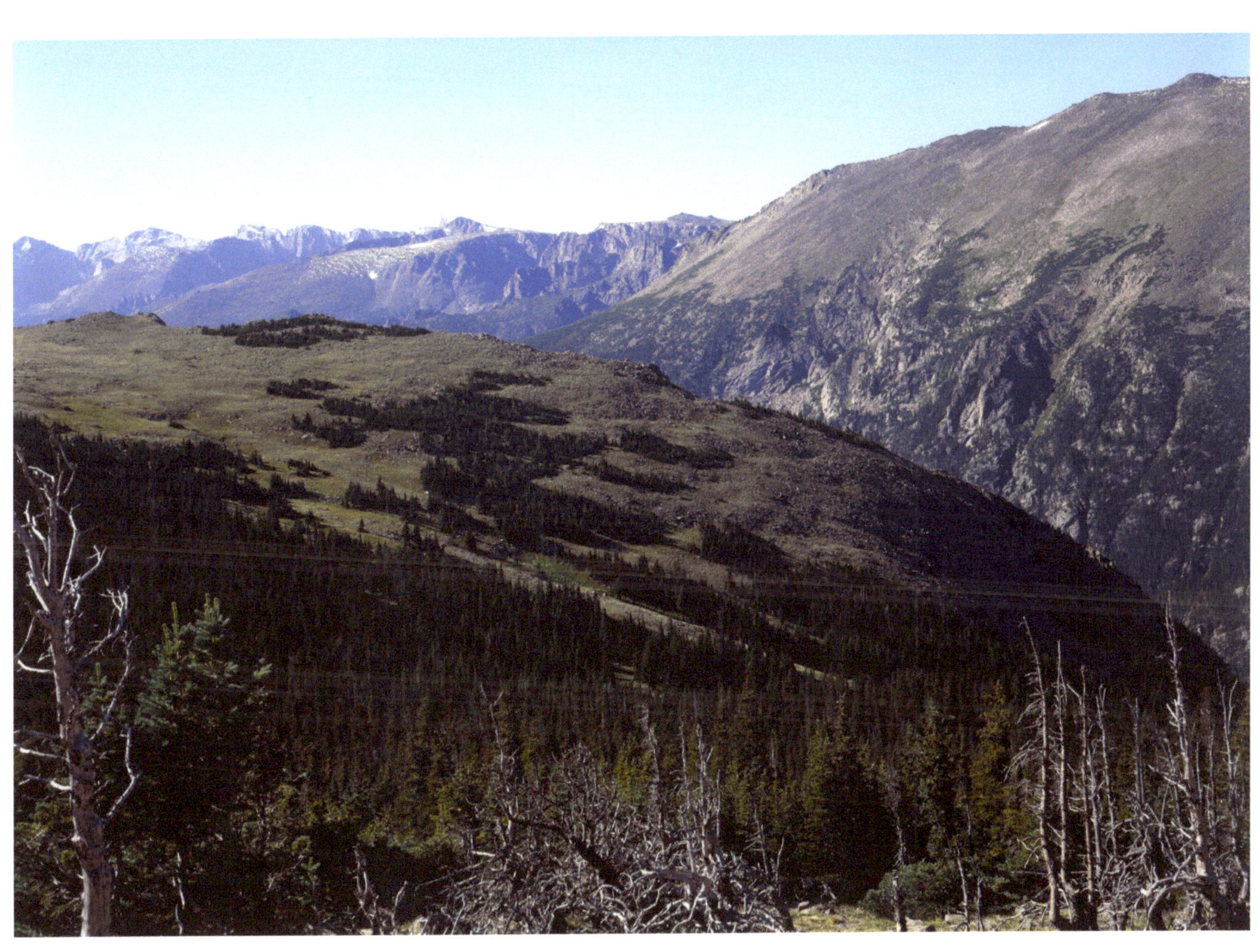

70   1843   Rocky Mountain National Park, Colorado

AUTUMN 71–100

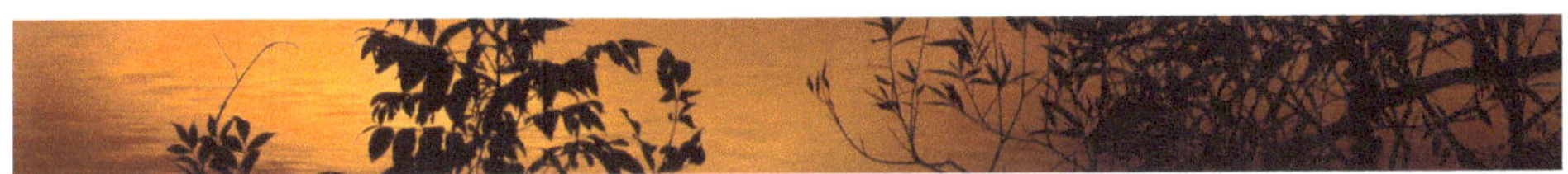

Fall season brings beautiful leaves for two weeks, but for calendar pictures one may stretch time to show them for 3 months. Although I claim all seasons are fit for photography, it seems easy in the colorful leaf season to point the camera in any direction of colorful leaf trees and come up with a delightful picture. Different areas have different weeks for maximum color. Geographical altitude is important to determine early or late for the color. Cooling temperatures suppress the annoying bugs, and the shorter days help display a deep blue sky after sunset.

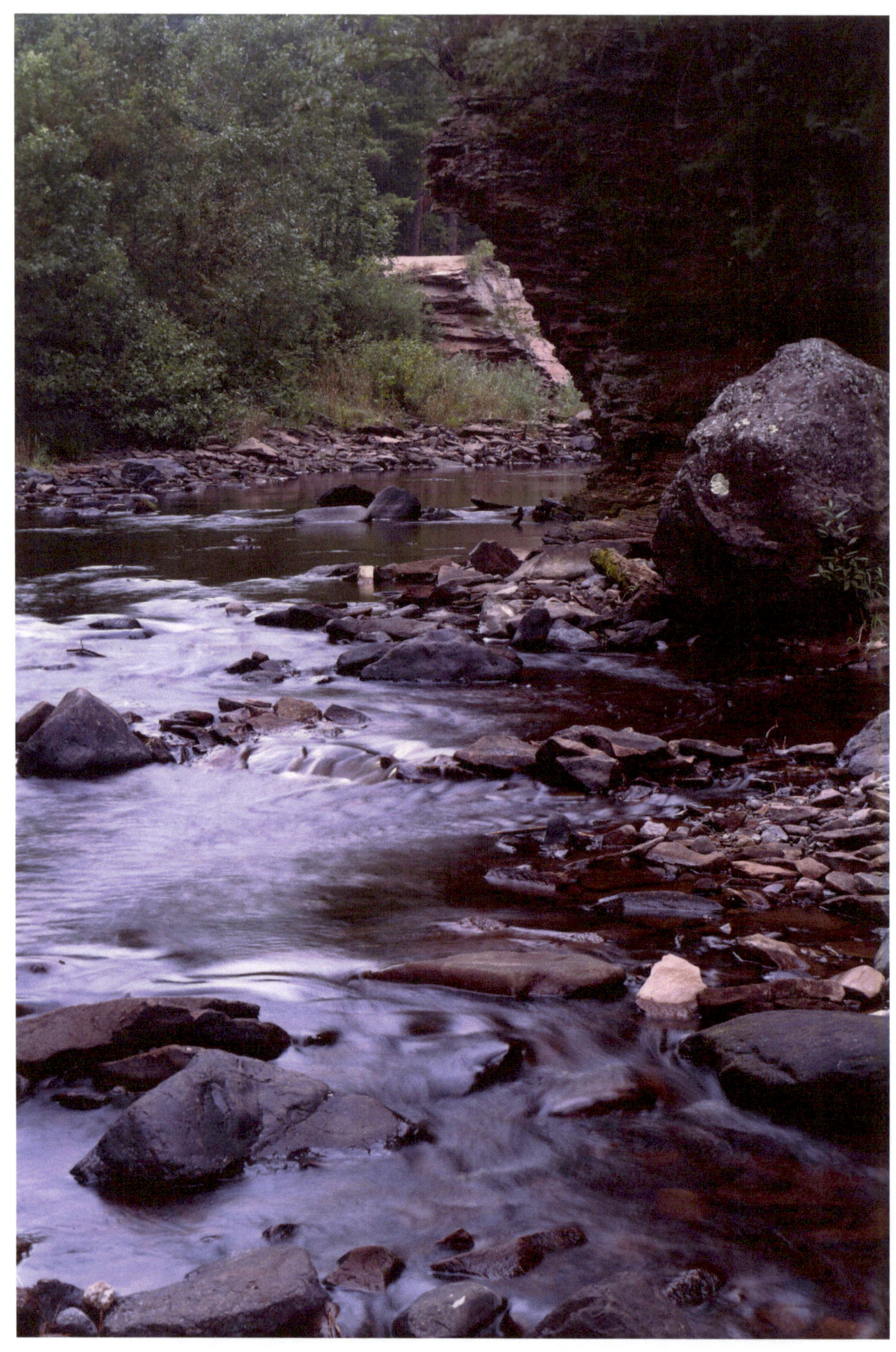

71   394   Amnicon Falls State Park, Wisconsin

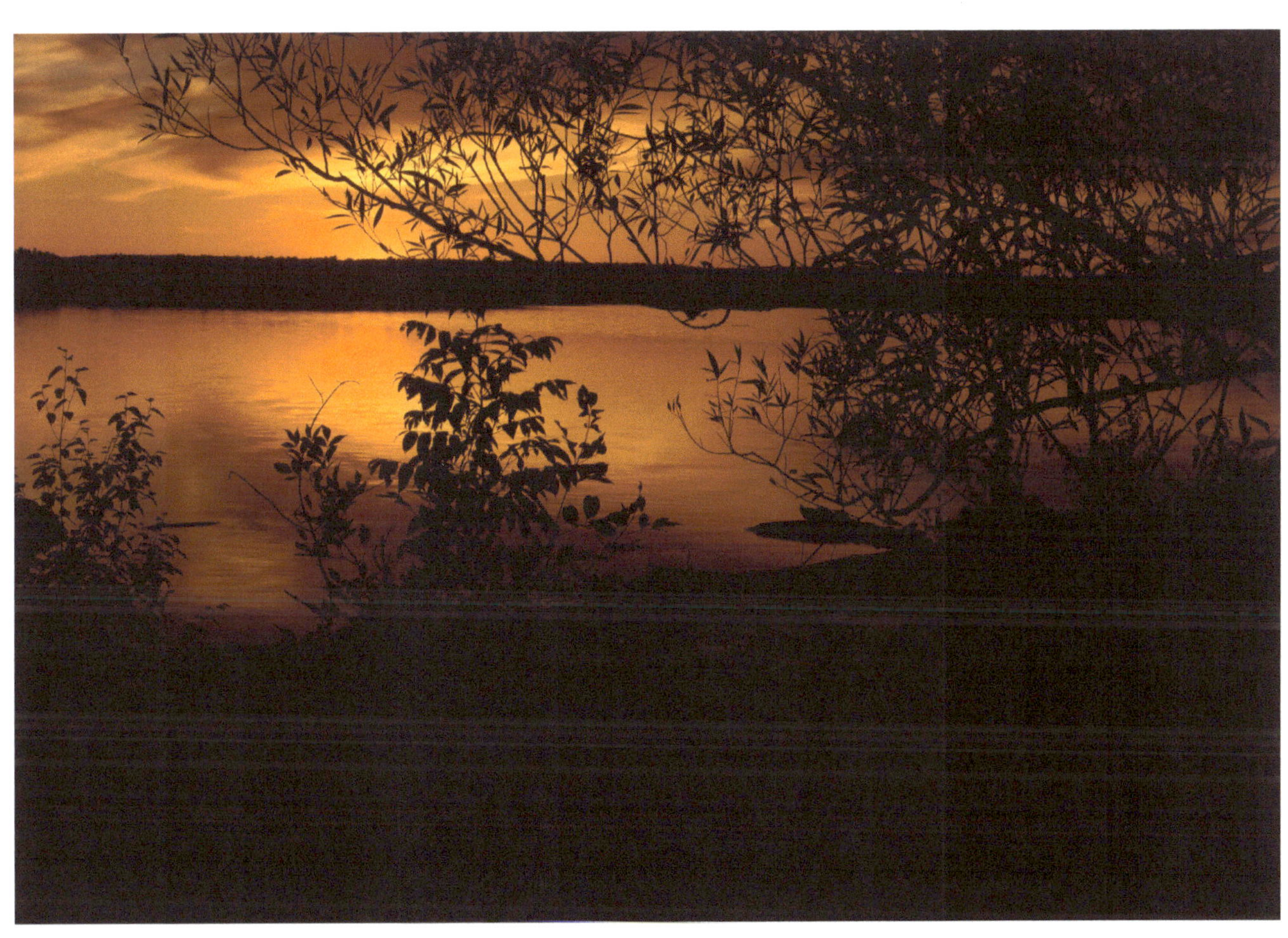

72   481   Thomson, Minnesota

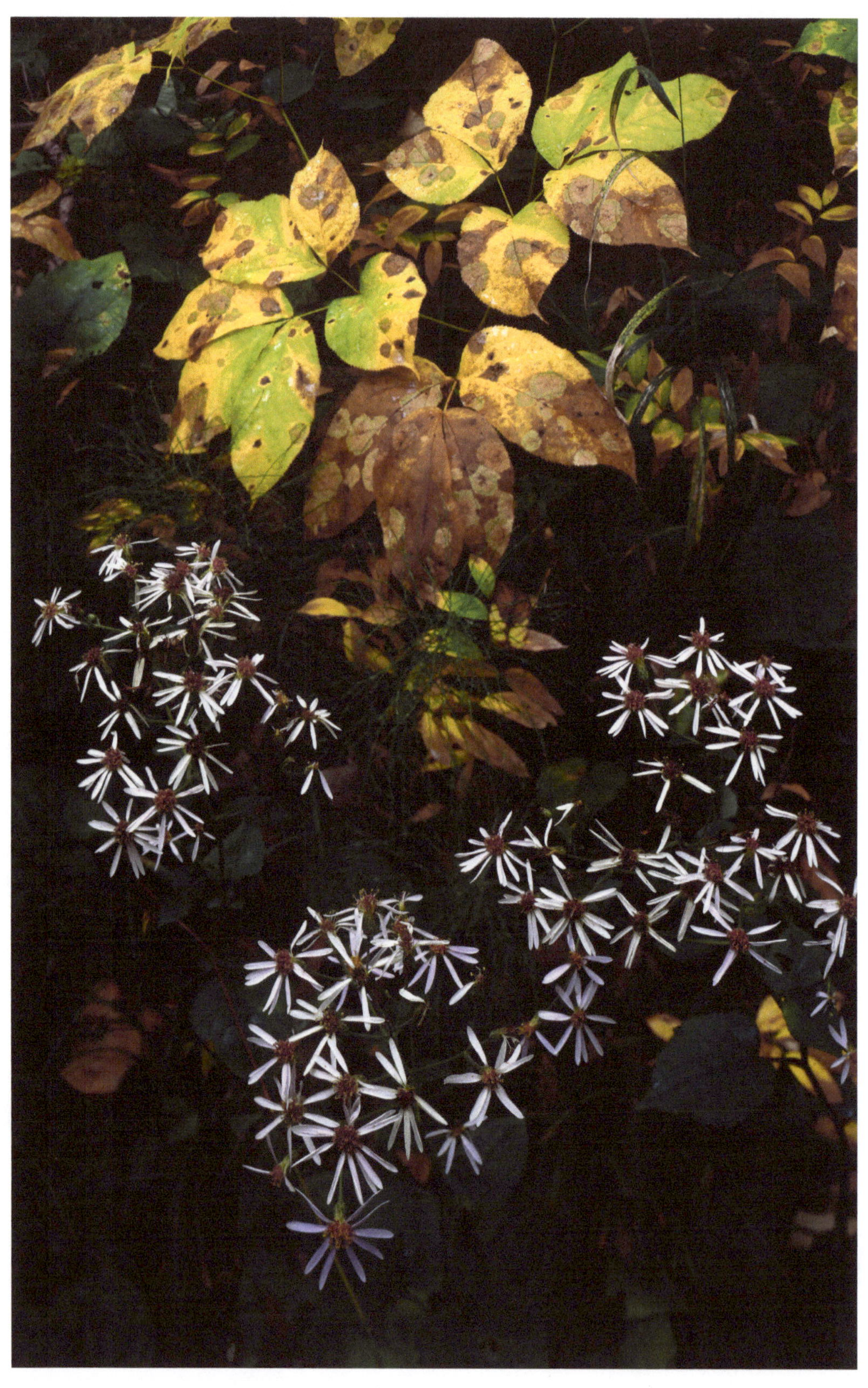

73   1412   Jay Cooke State Park, Minnesota

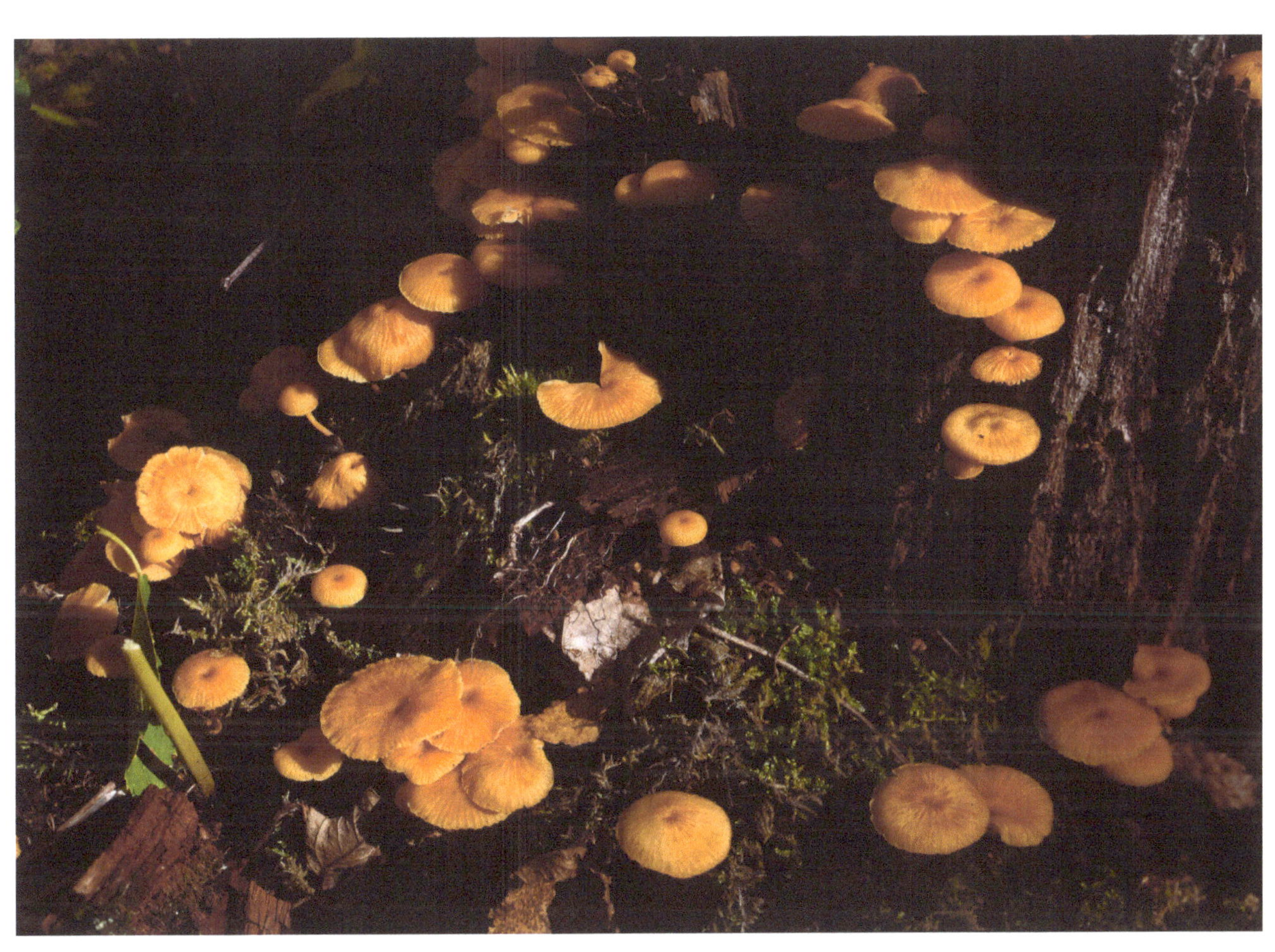

74   1504   Jay Cooke State Park, Minnesota

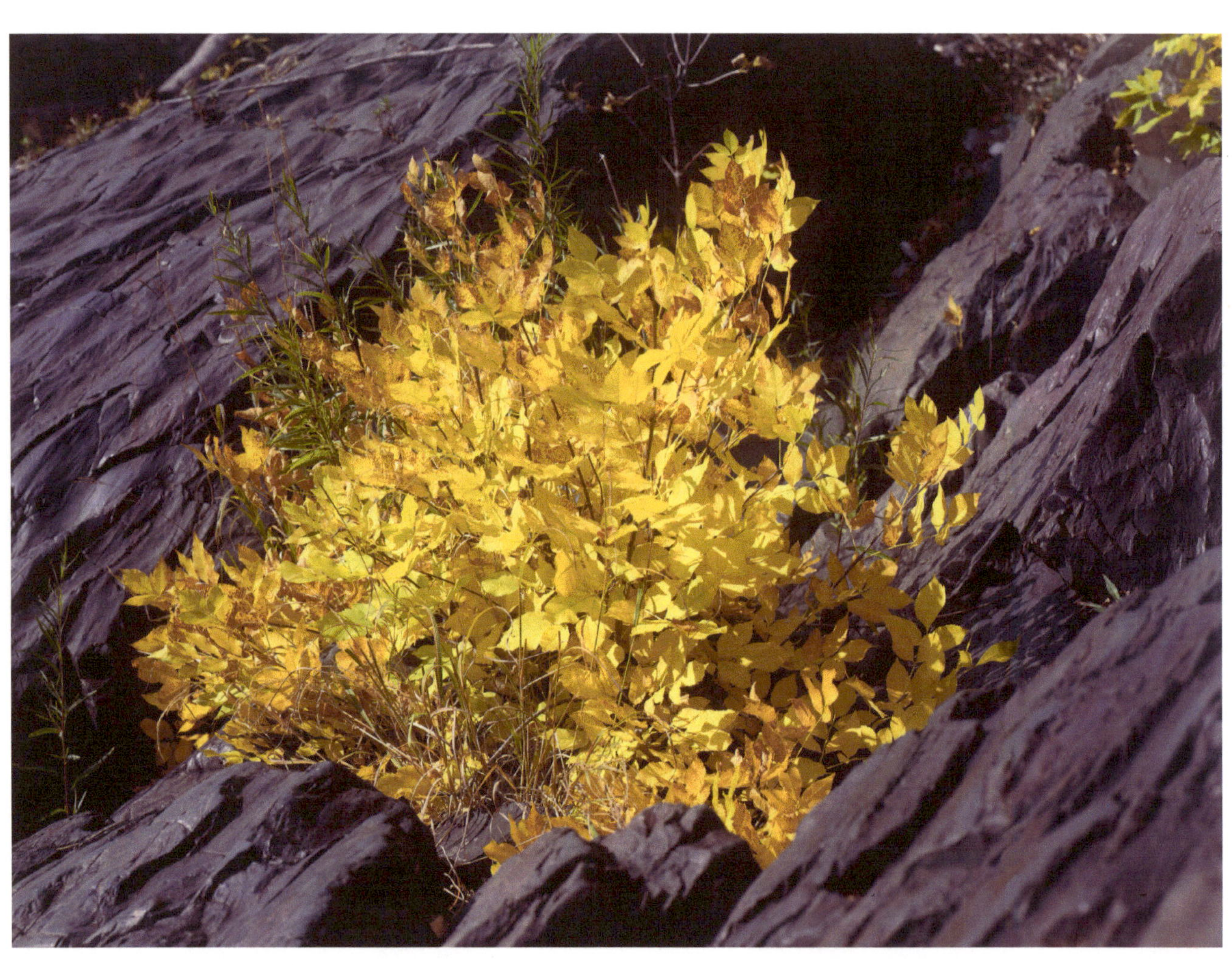

75   1662   Jay Cooke State Park, Minnesota

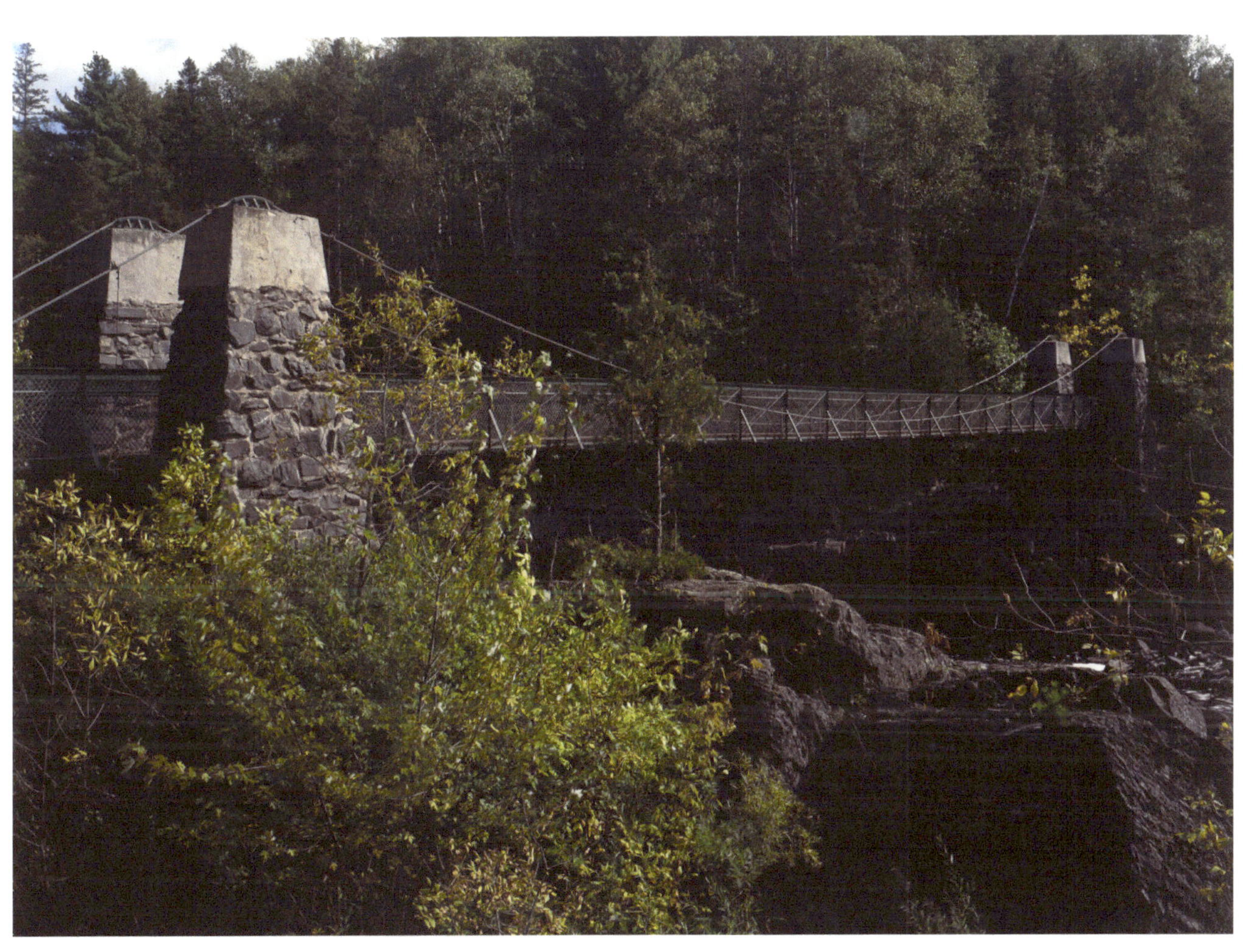

76   2027   Jay Cooke State Park, Minnesota

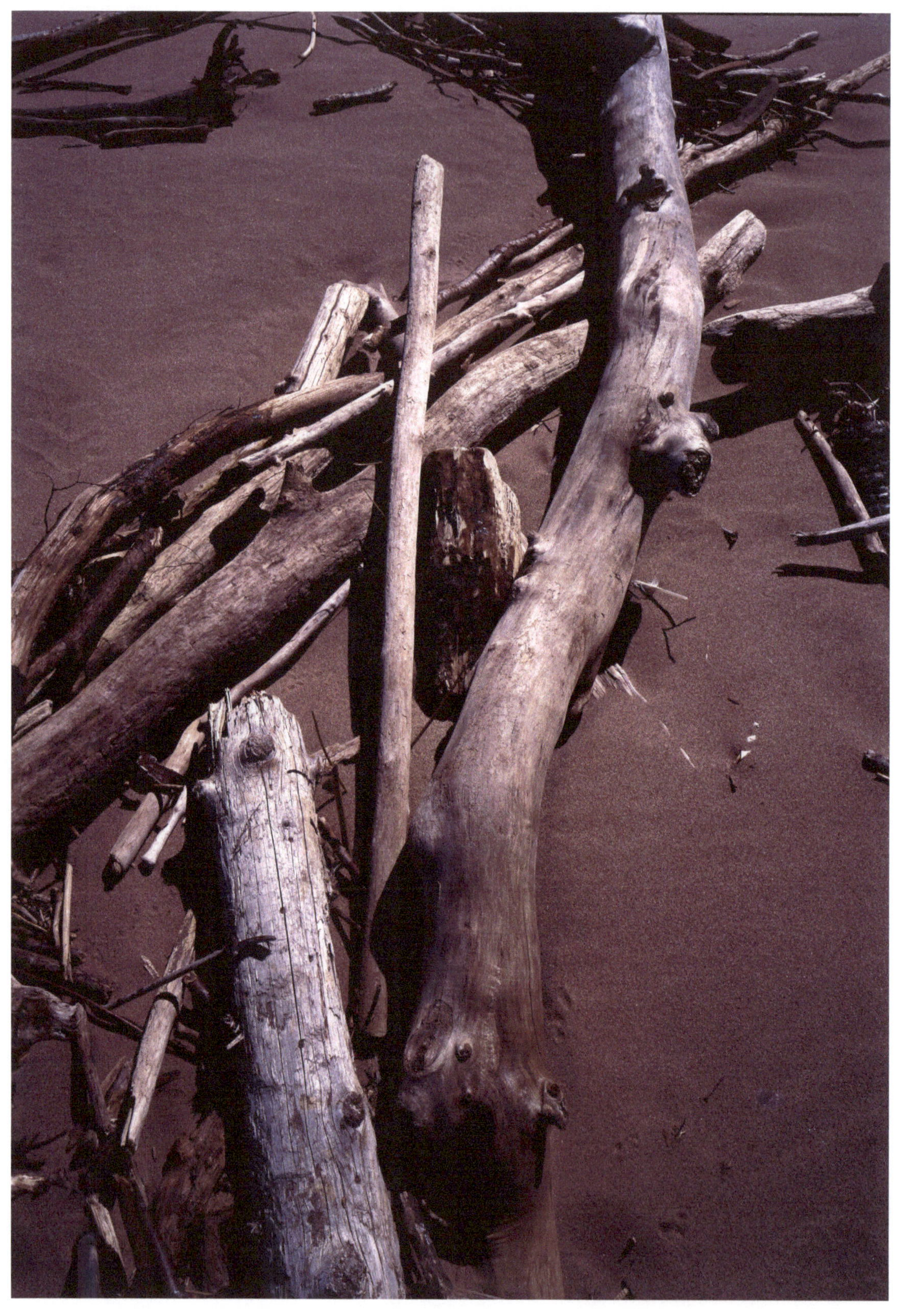

77   2030   Dutchman Creek, Superior, Wisconsin

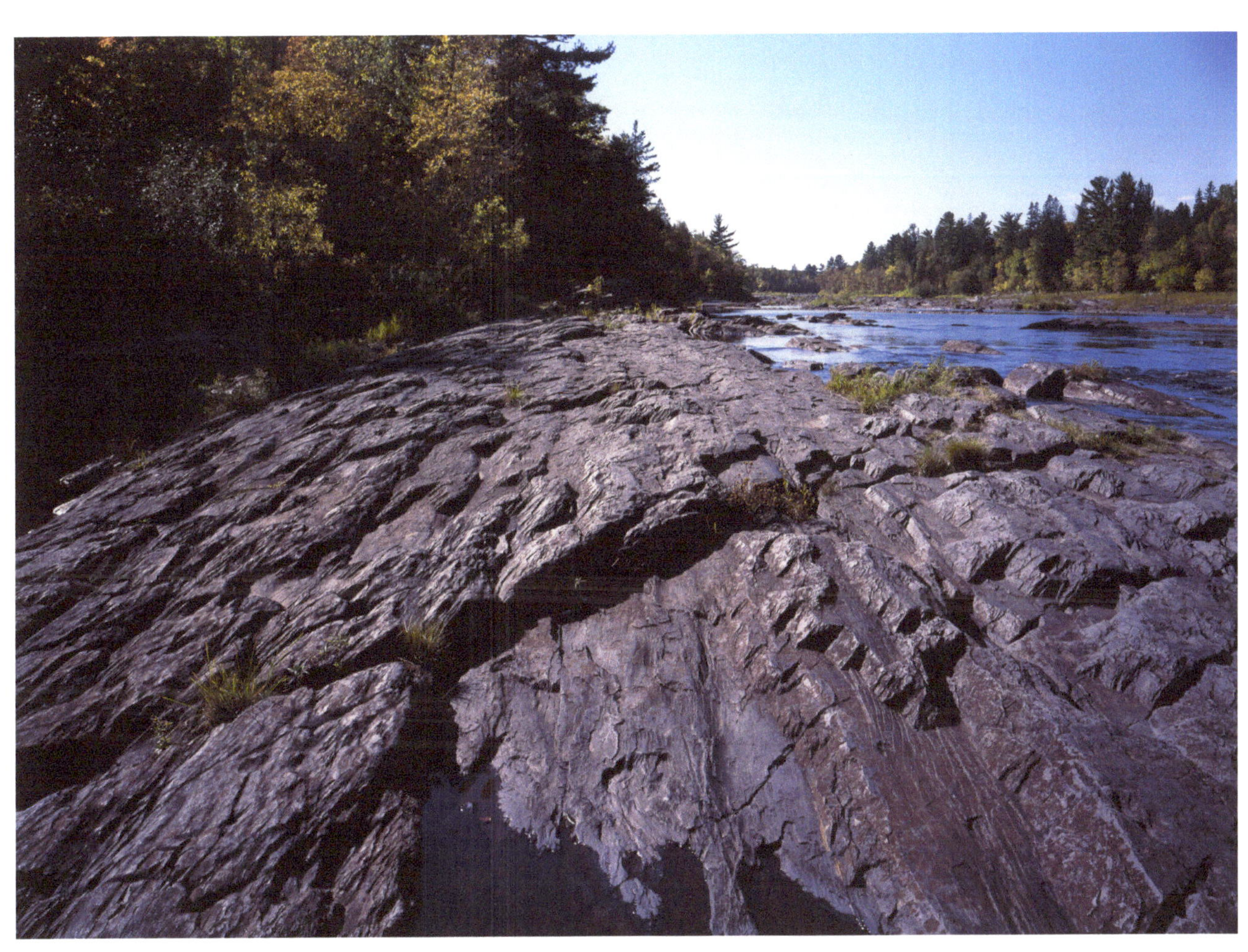

78   2037   Jay Cooke State Park, Minnesota

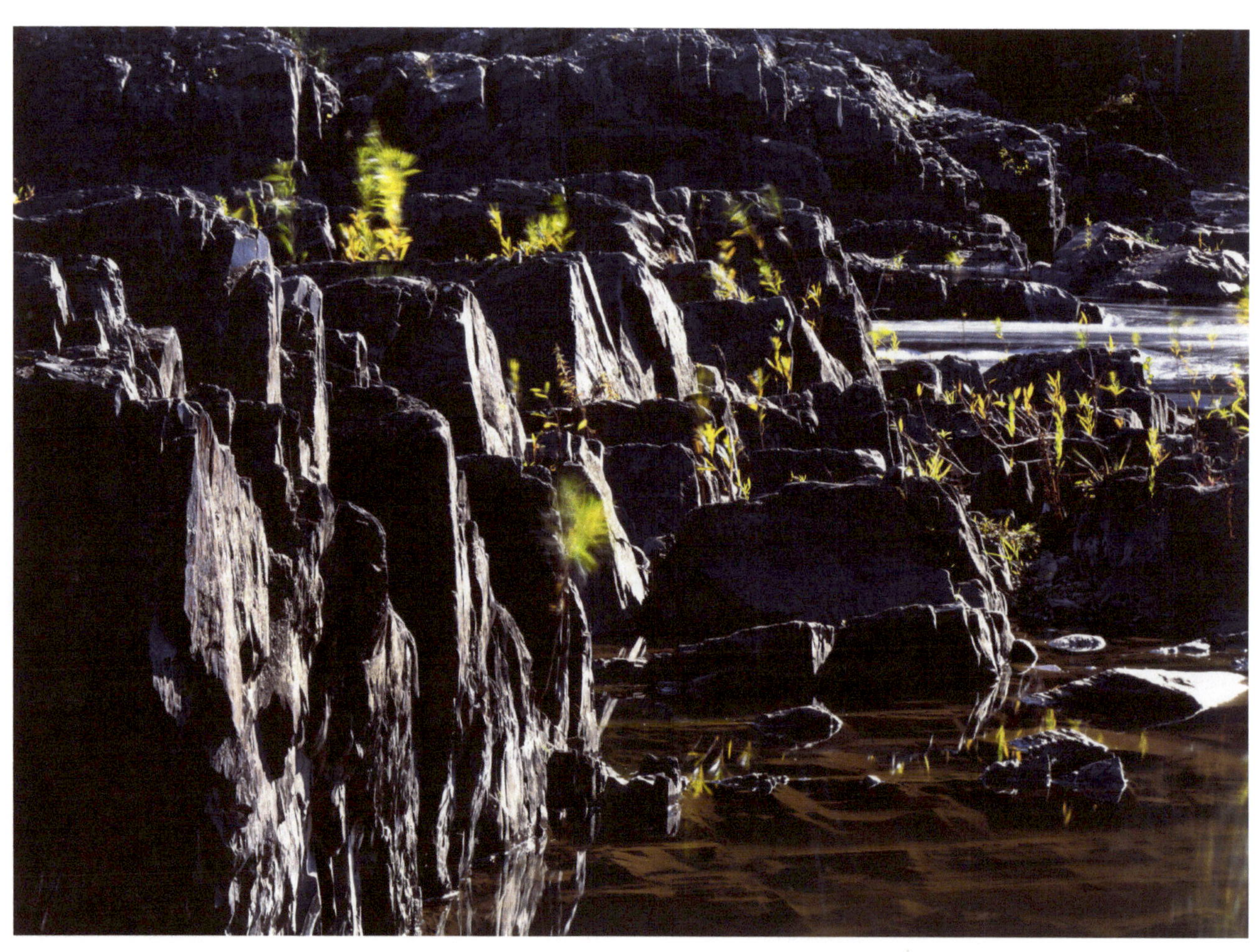

79   2043   Jay Cooke State Park, Minnesota

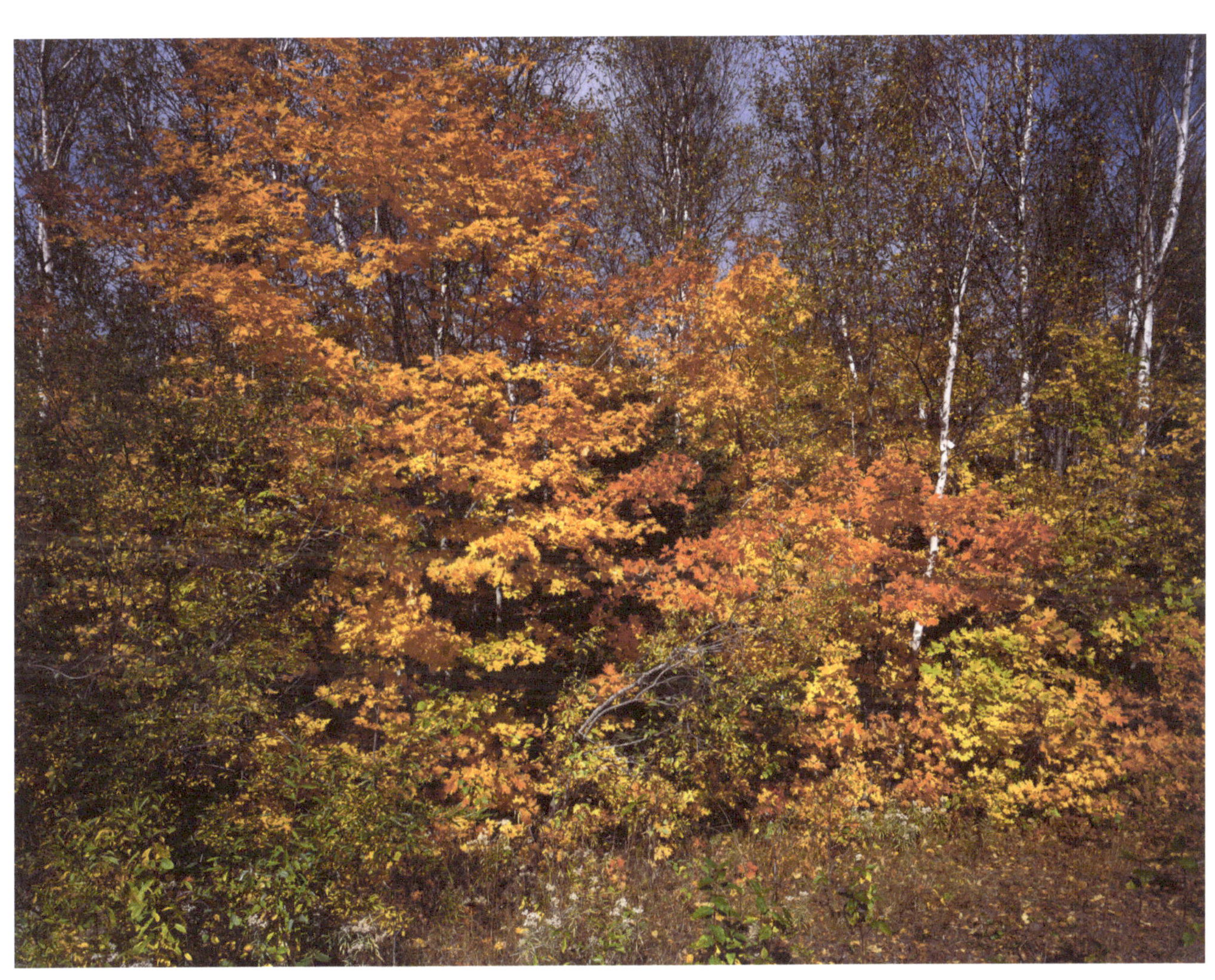

80   2118   Cook County 164, Minnesota

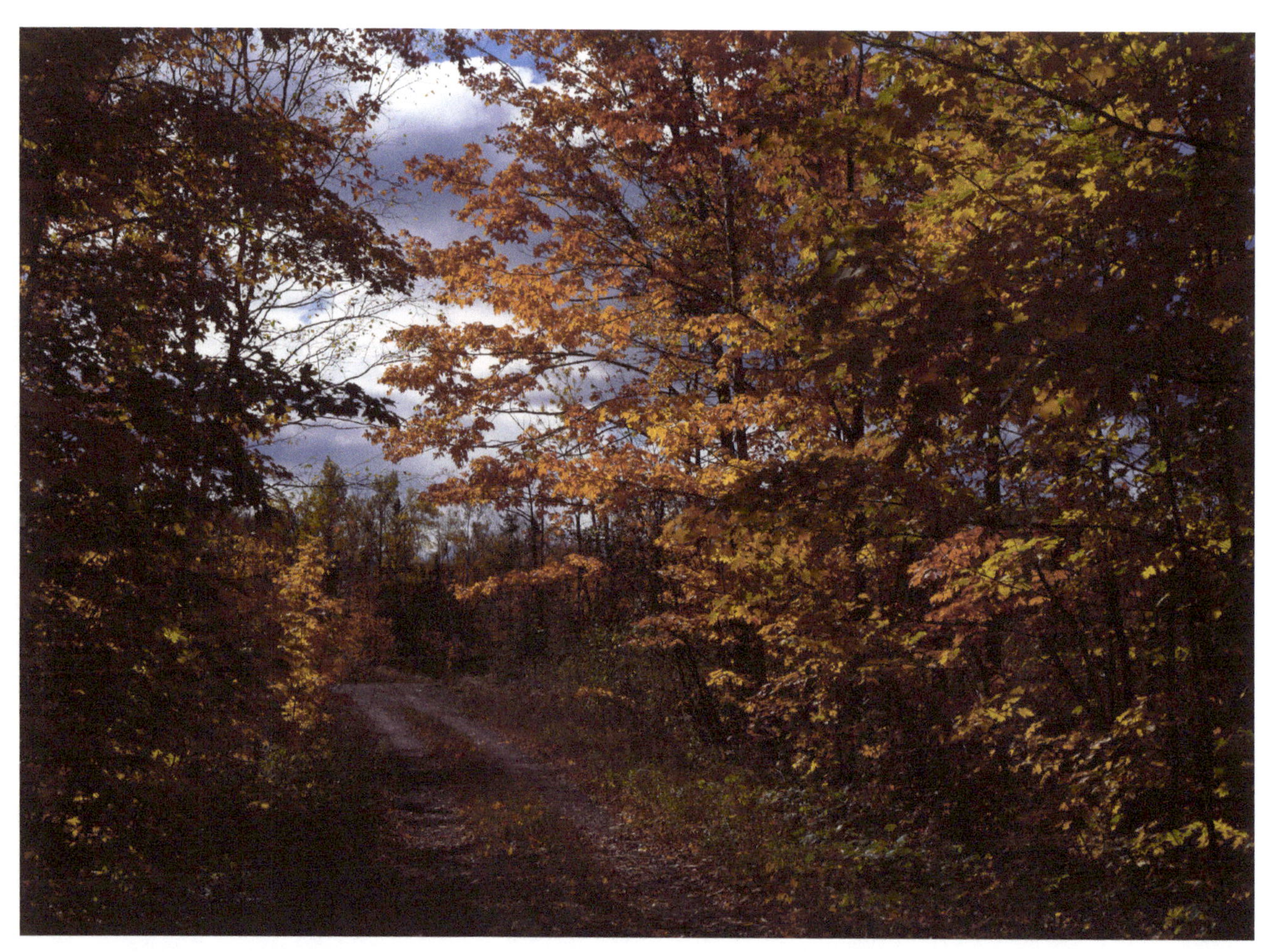

81   2119   Cook County 164, Minnesota

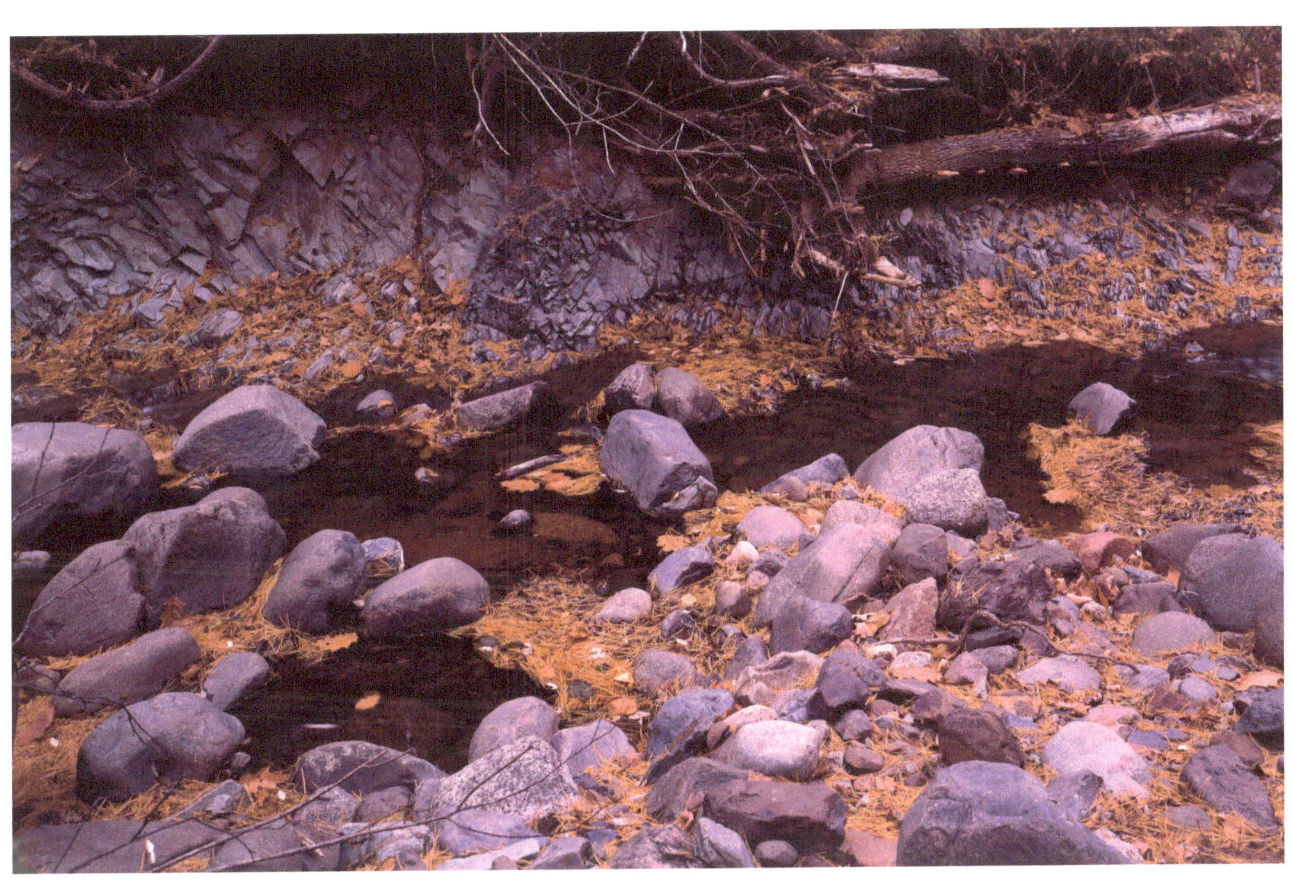

    Jay Cooke State Park, Minnesota

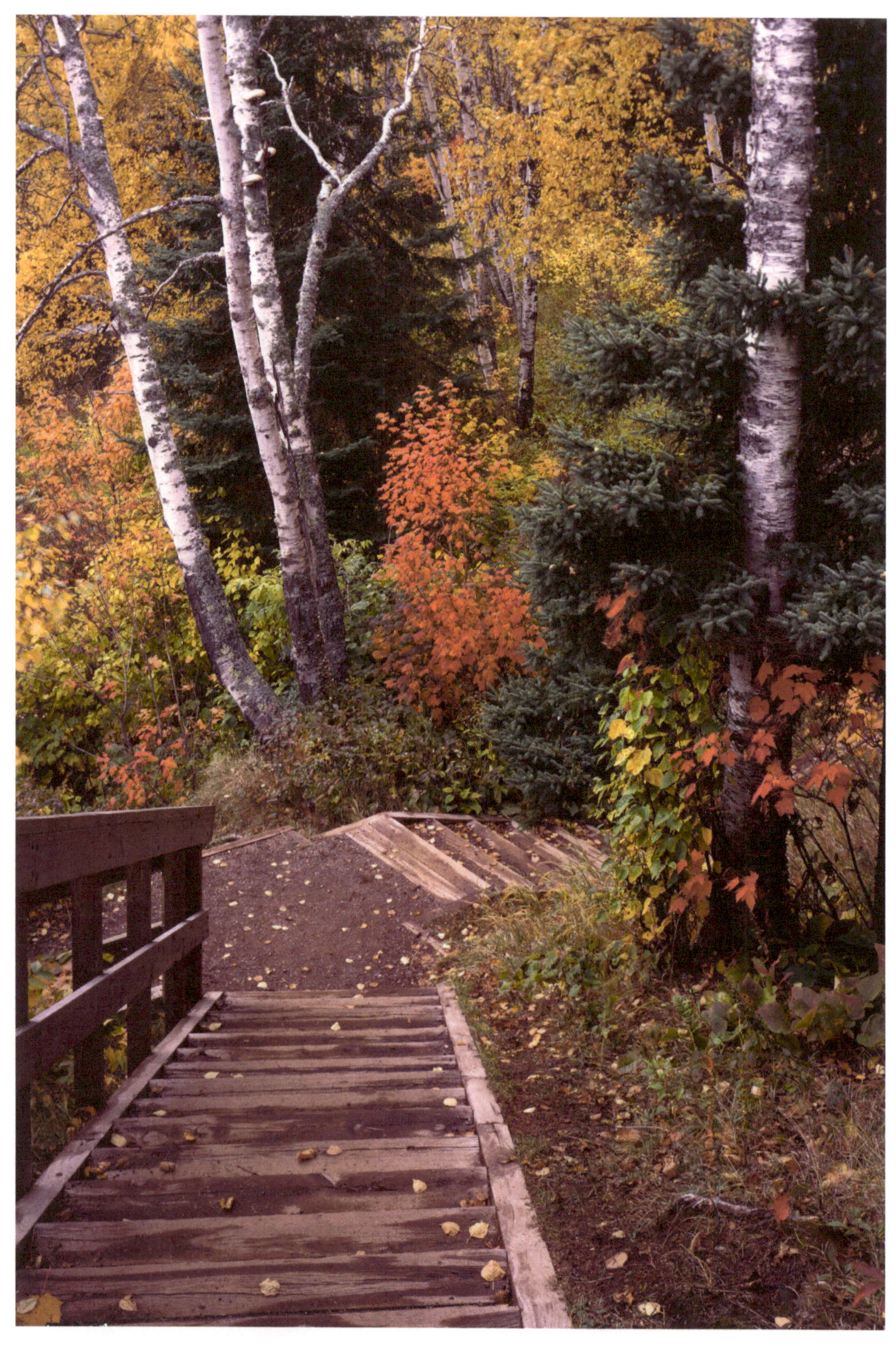

83   453   Tettagouche State Park, Minnesota

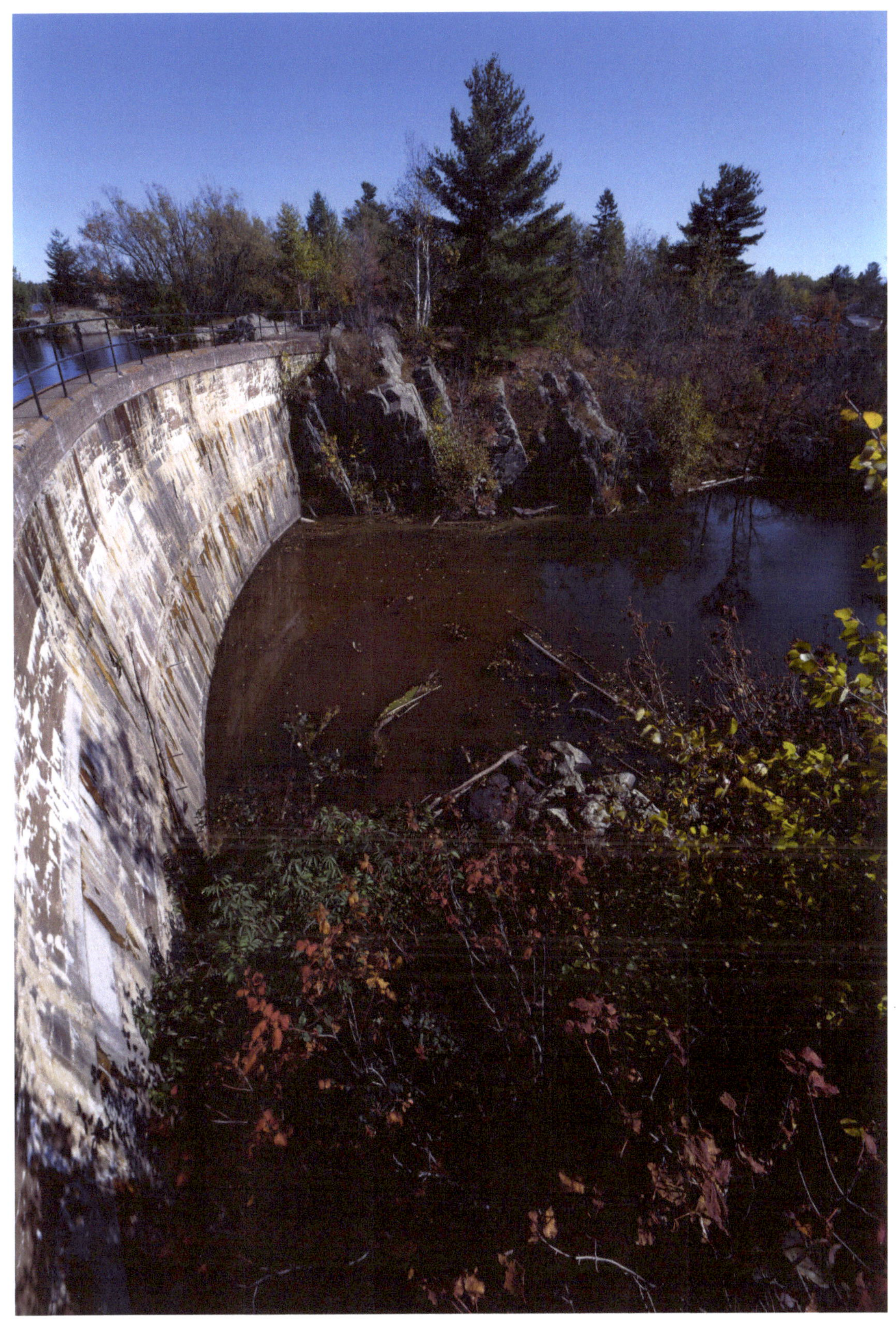

84   1417   Thomson, Minnesota

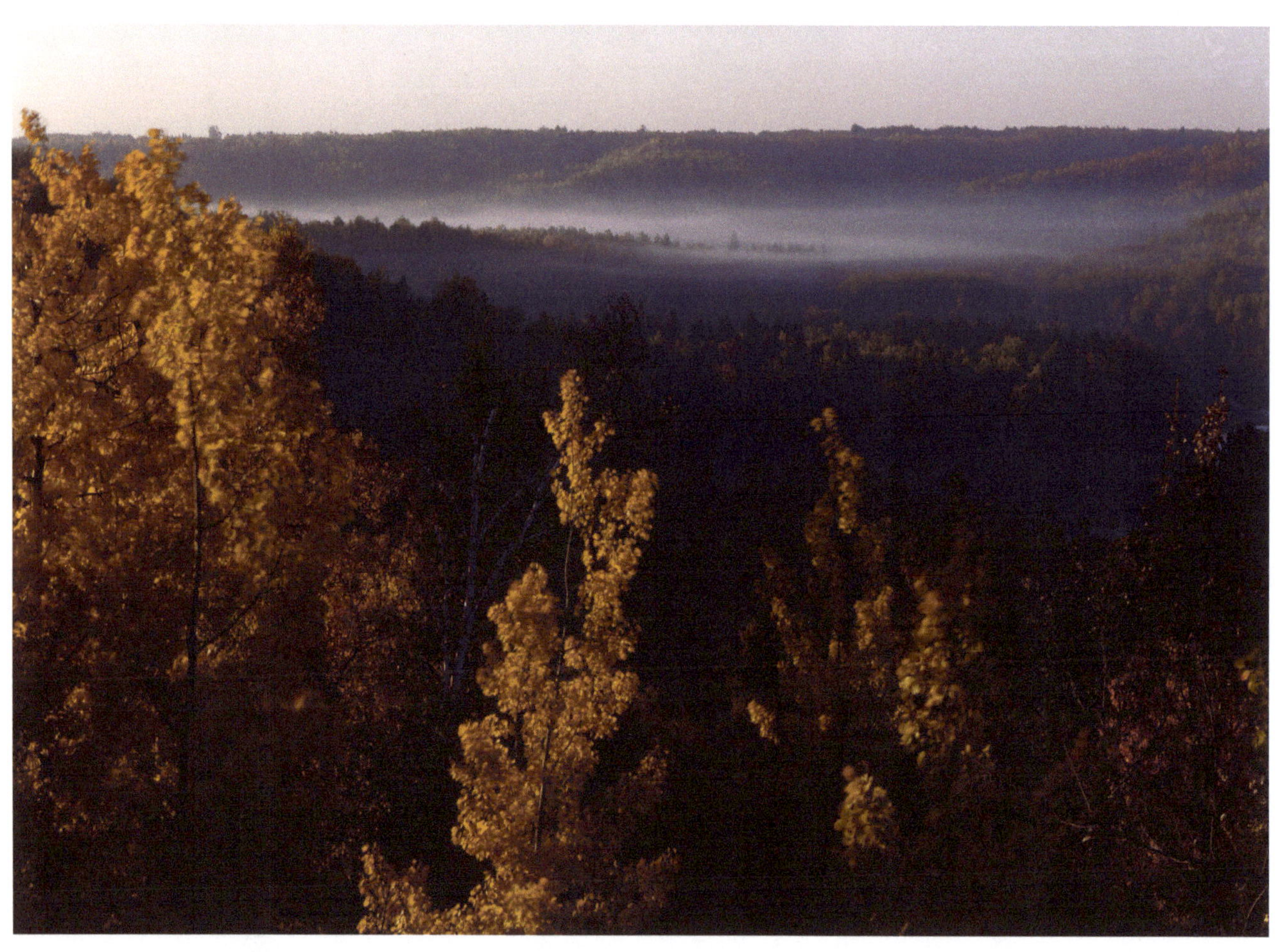

85   1429   Jay Cooke State Park, Minnesota

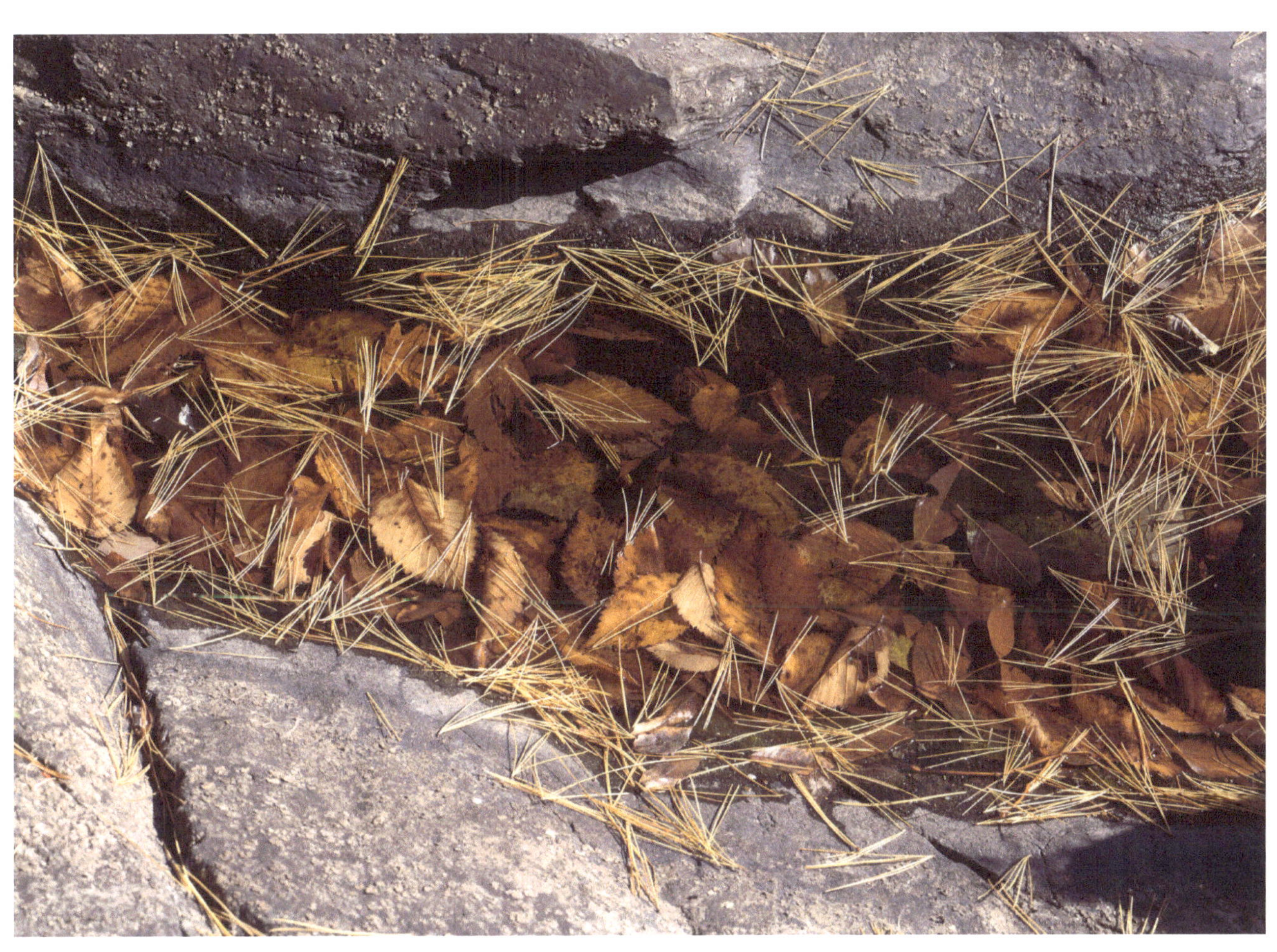

86   1435   Jay Cooke State Park, Minnesota

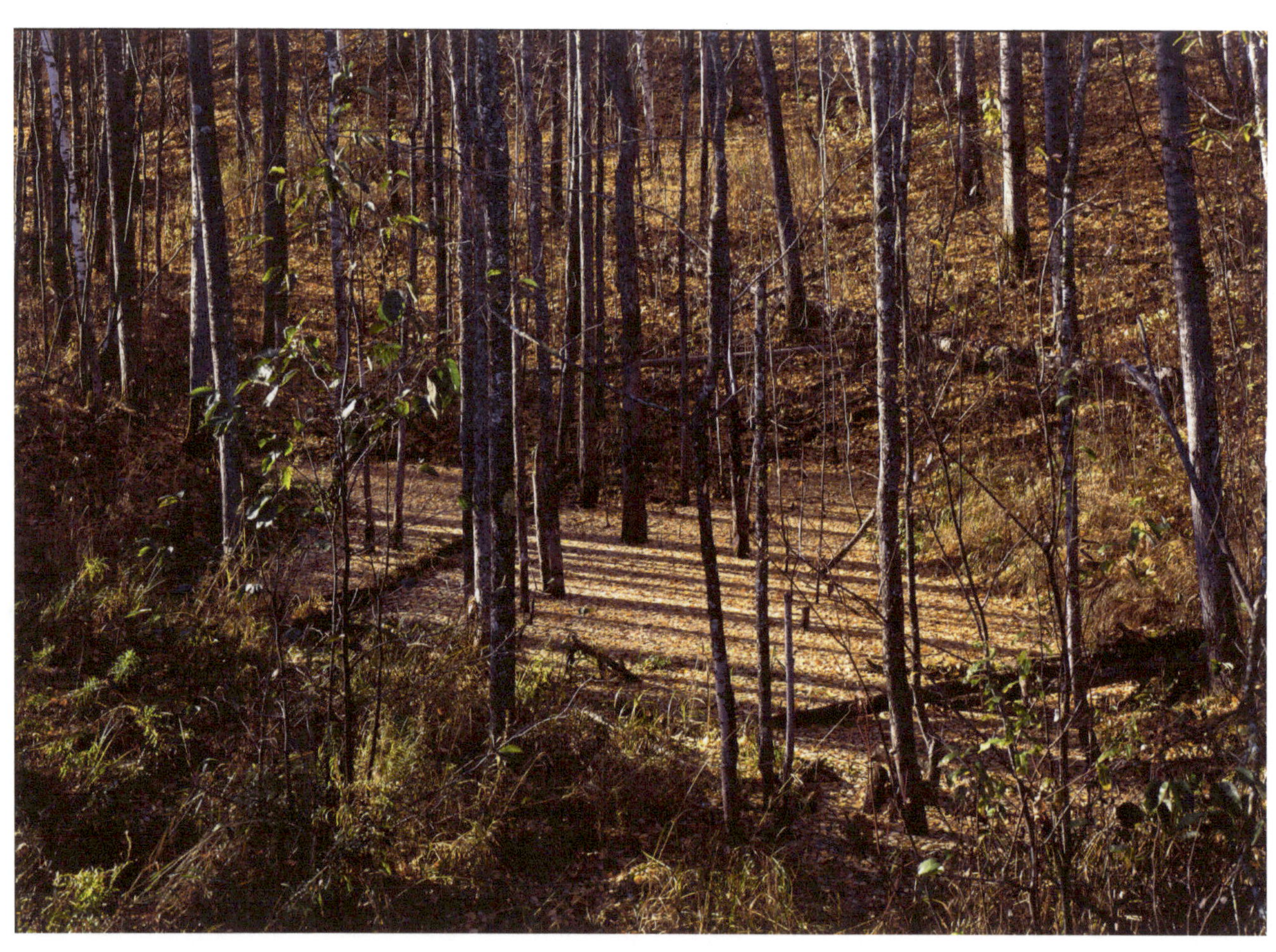

87   1439   Harding Road, Oliver, Wisconsin

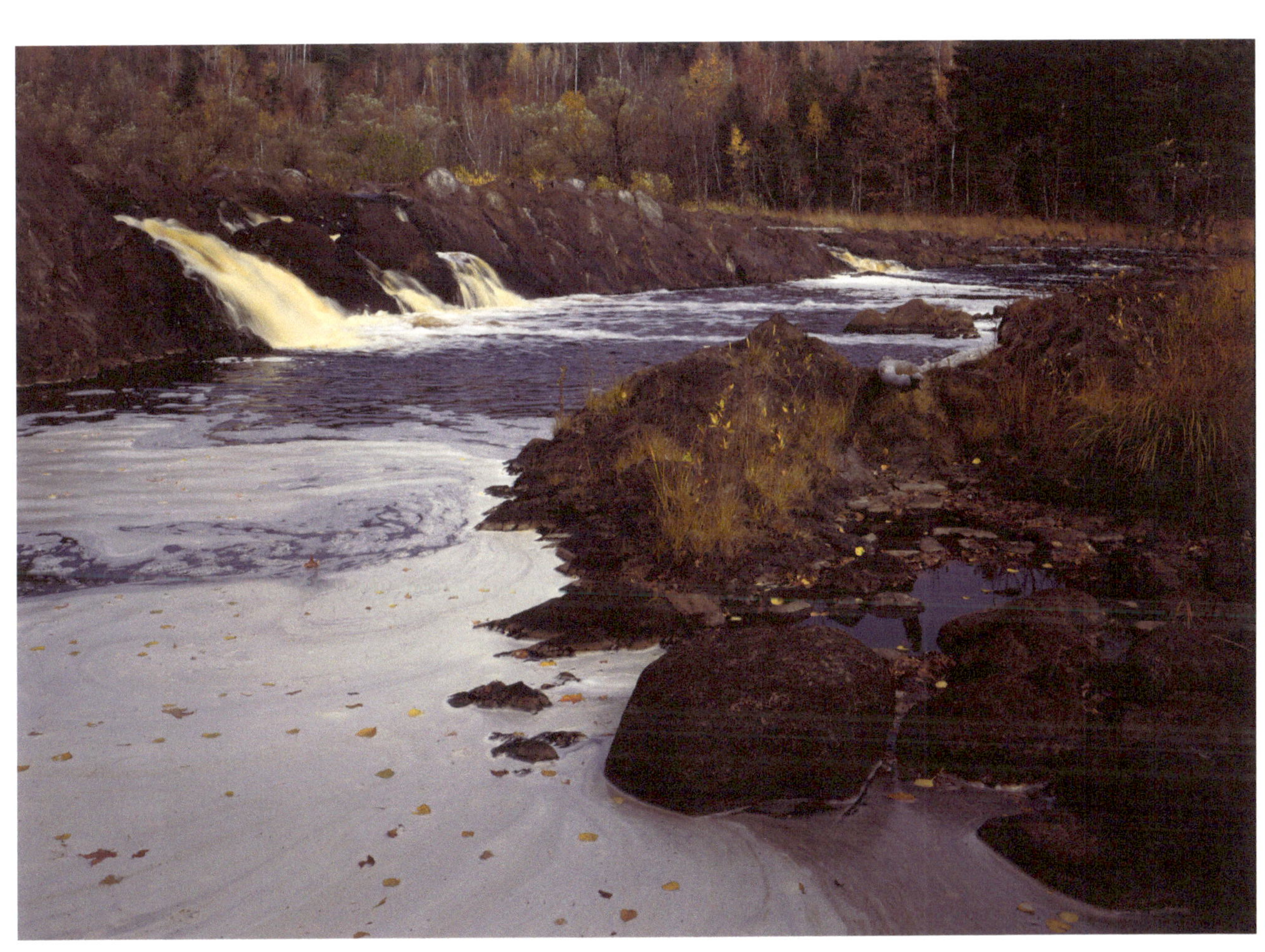

88   1869   Jay Cooke State Park, Minnesota

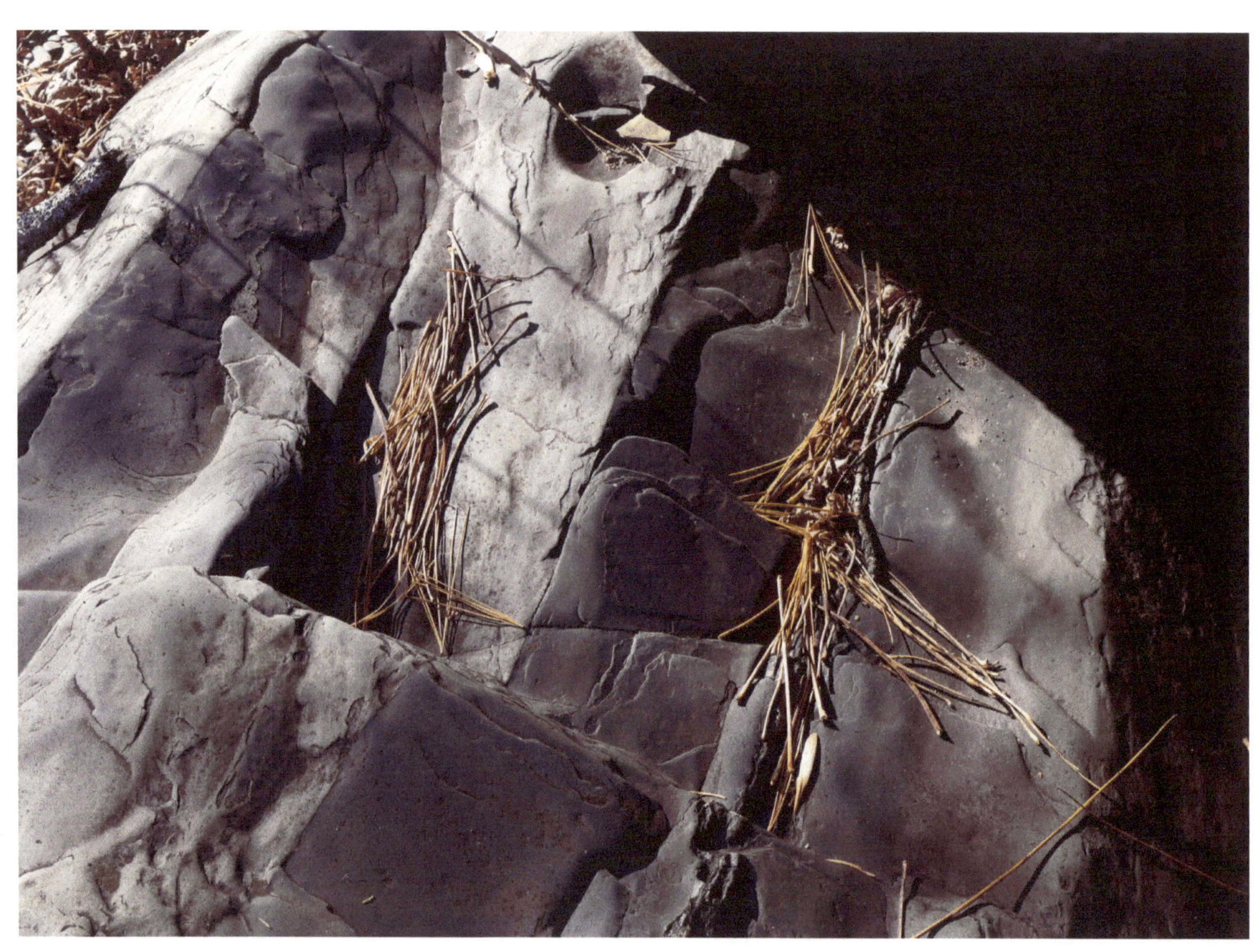

89   1872   Jay Cooke State Park, Minnesota

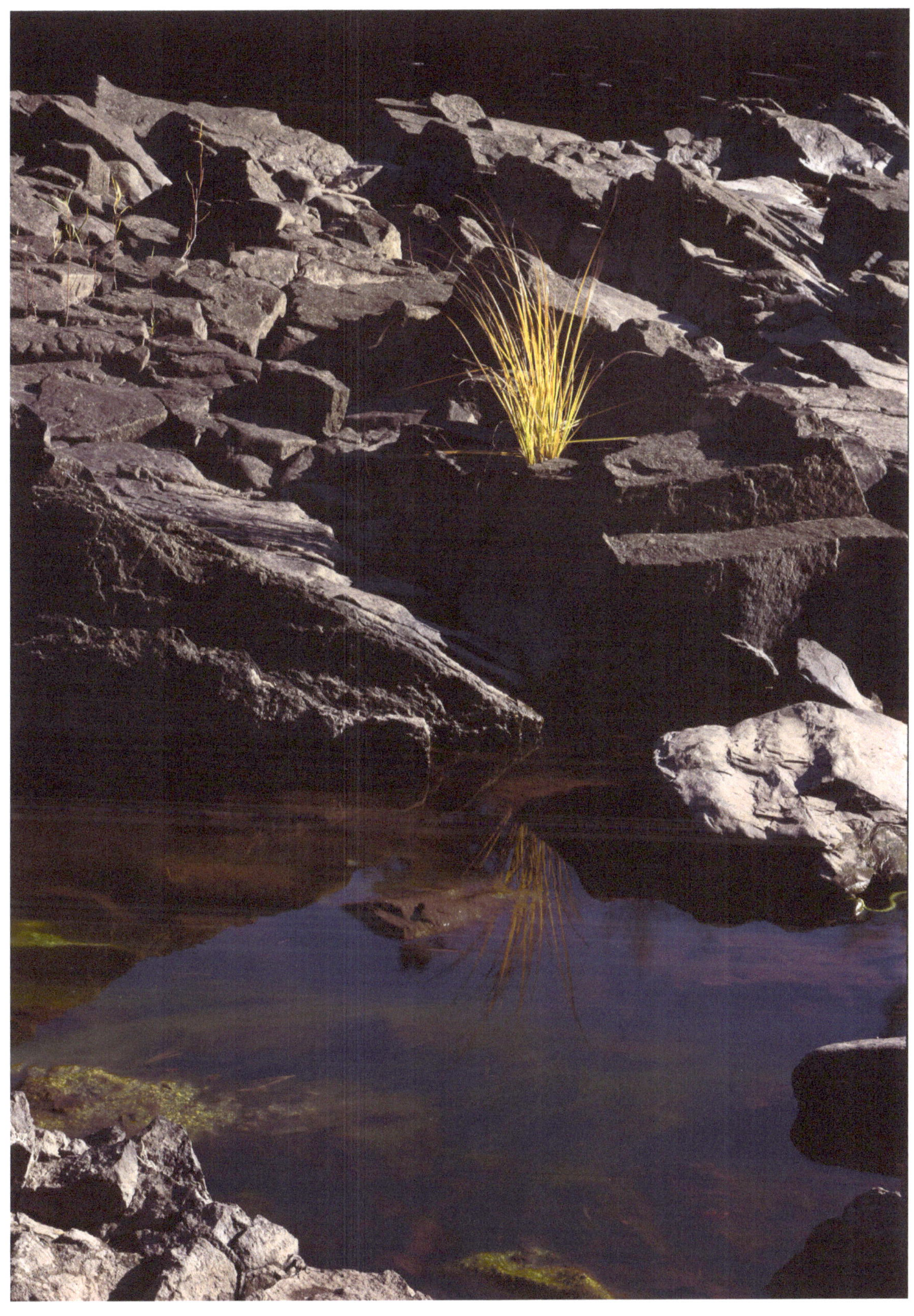

90   1874   Jay Cooke State Park, Minnesota

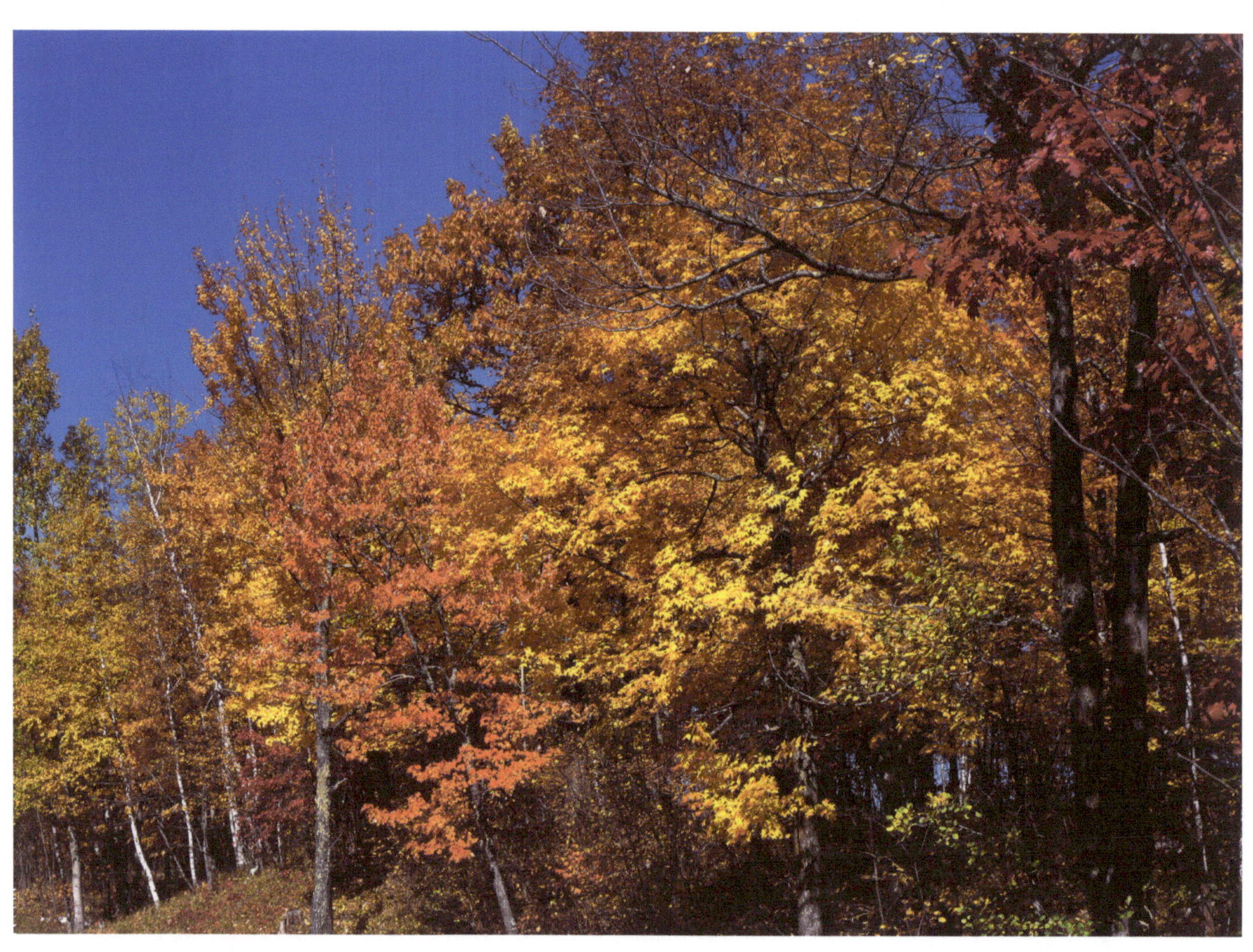

91   2044   Highway 210, Minnesota

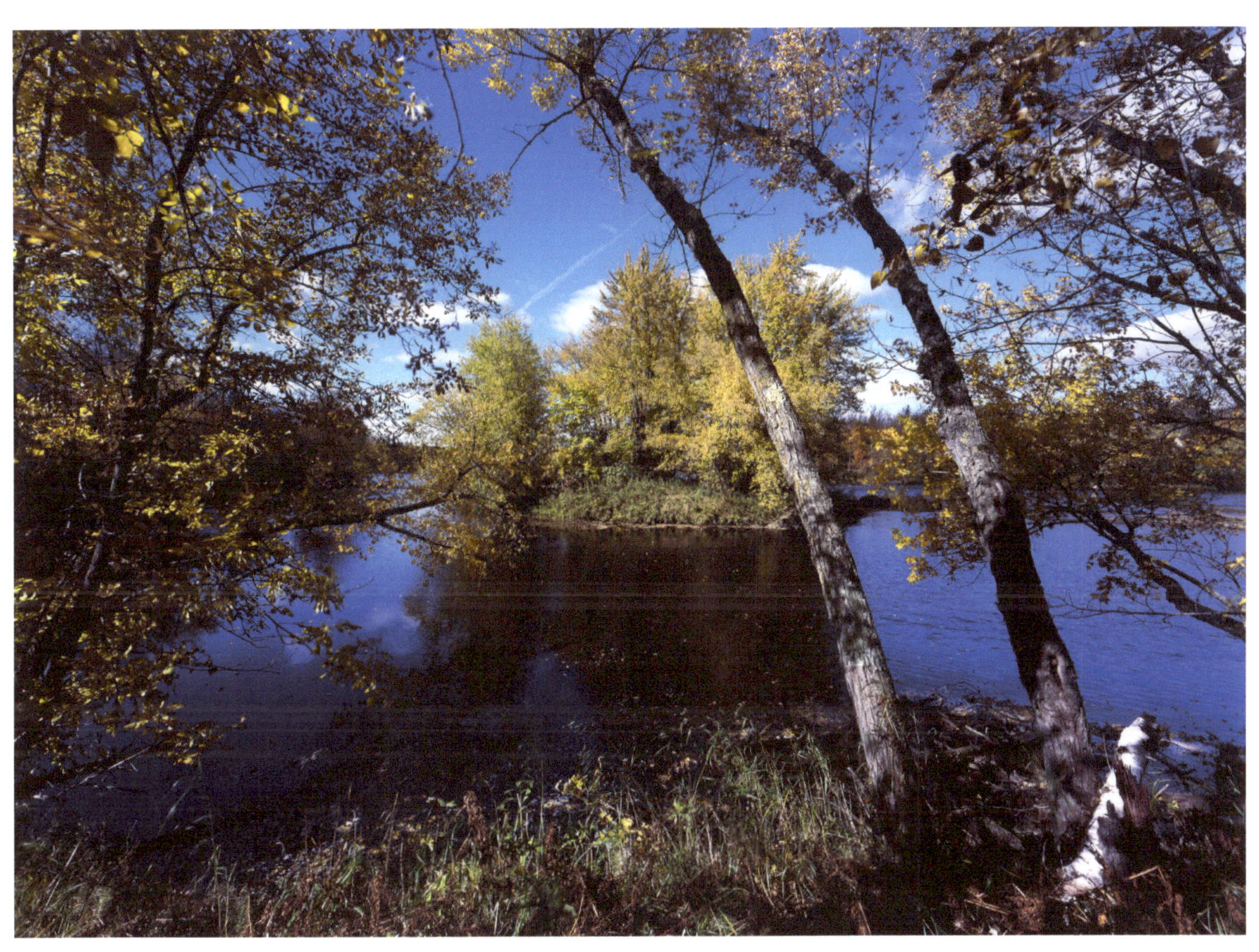

92   2046   Scanlon - Carlton, Minnesota

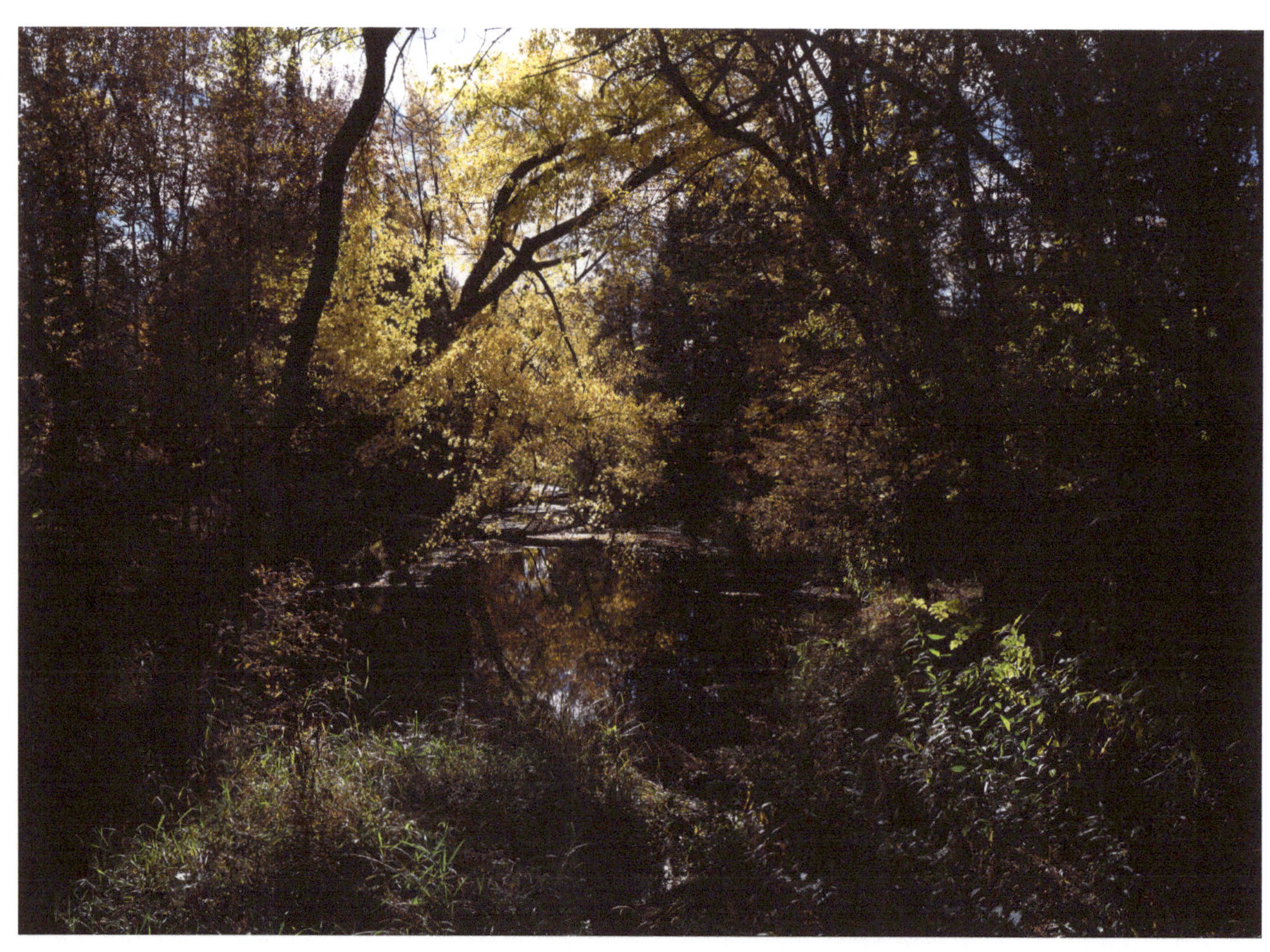

93   2048   Scanlon - Carlton, Minnesota

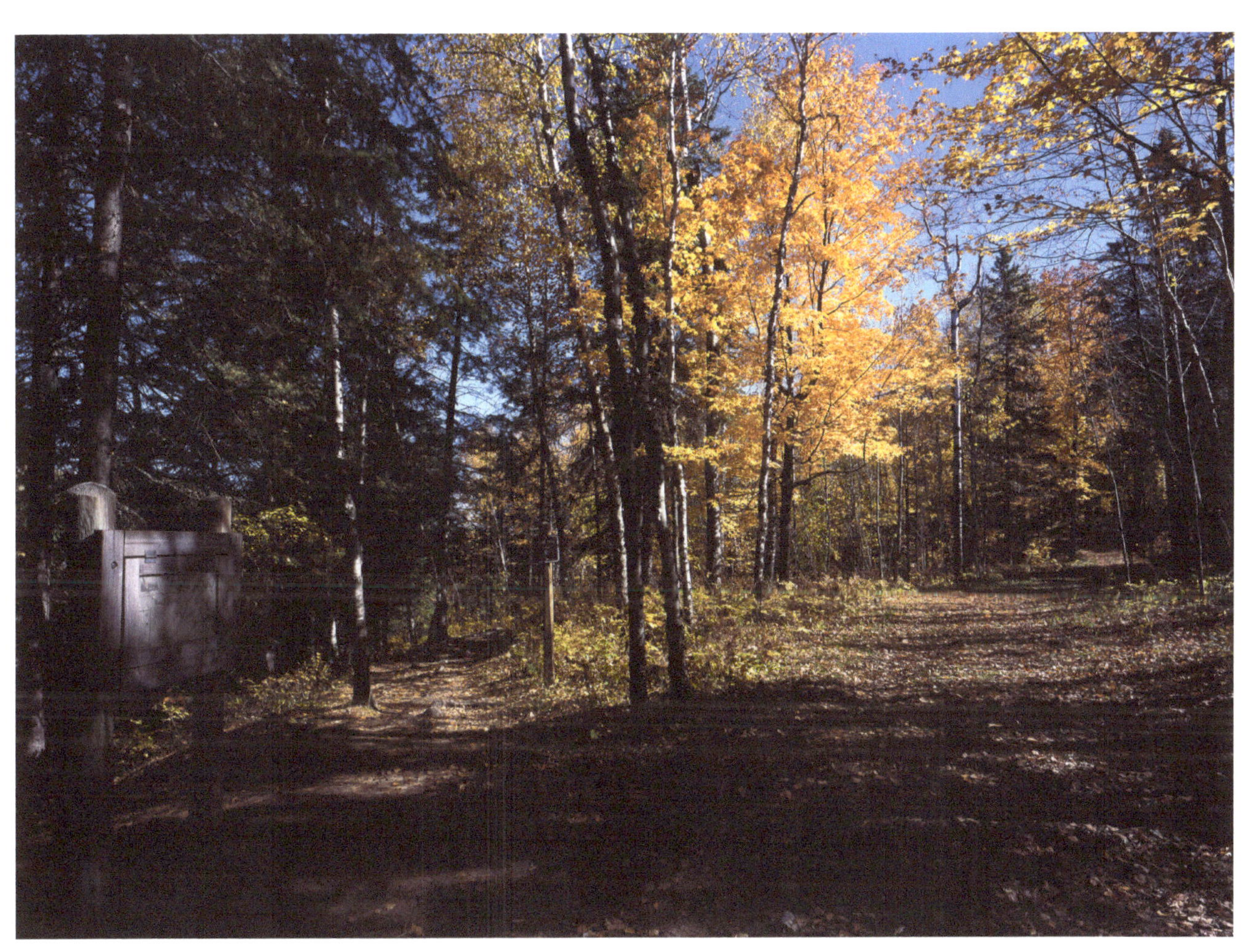

94   2049   Jay Cooke State Park, Minnesota

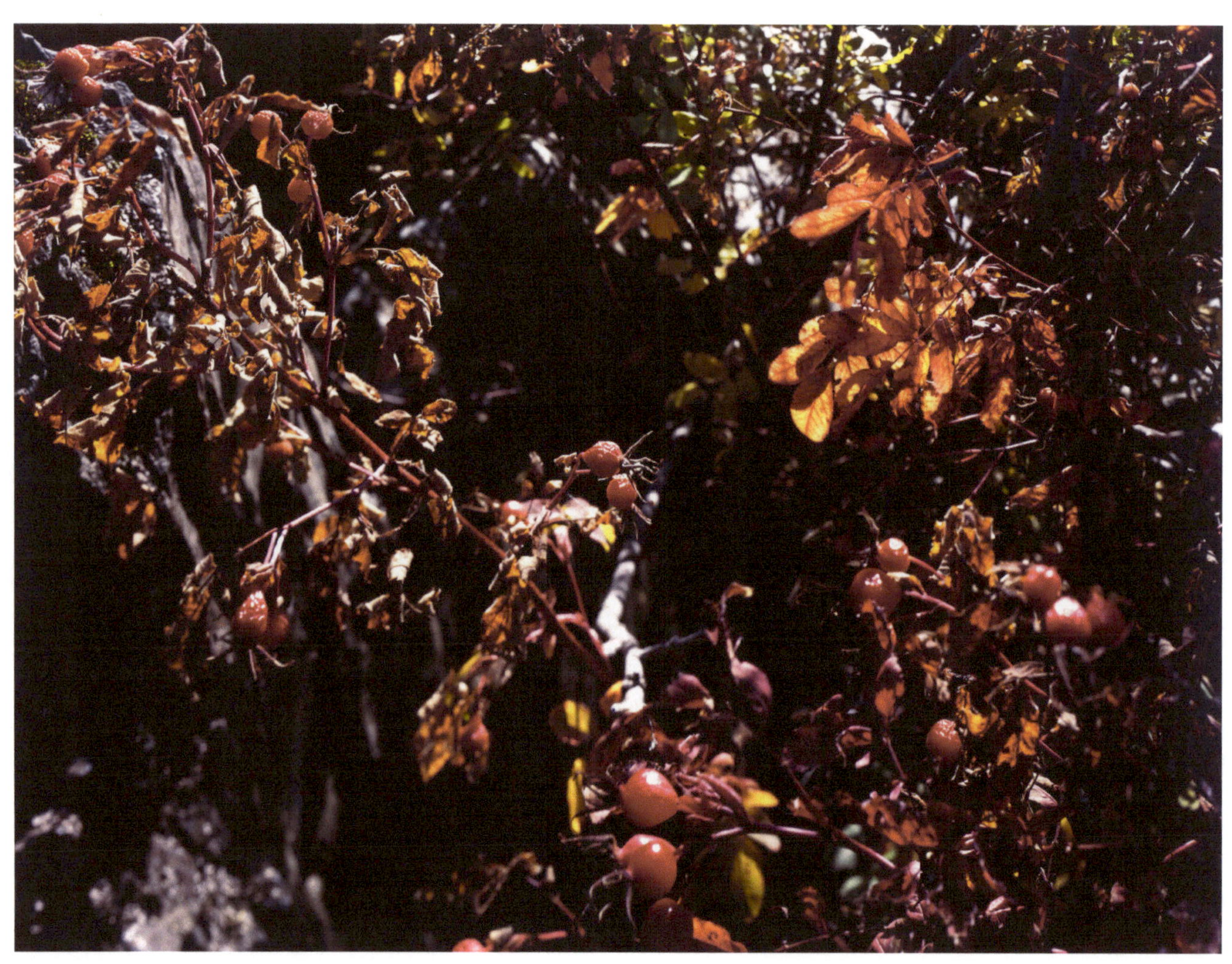

95   2050   Jay Cooke State Park, Minnesota

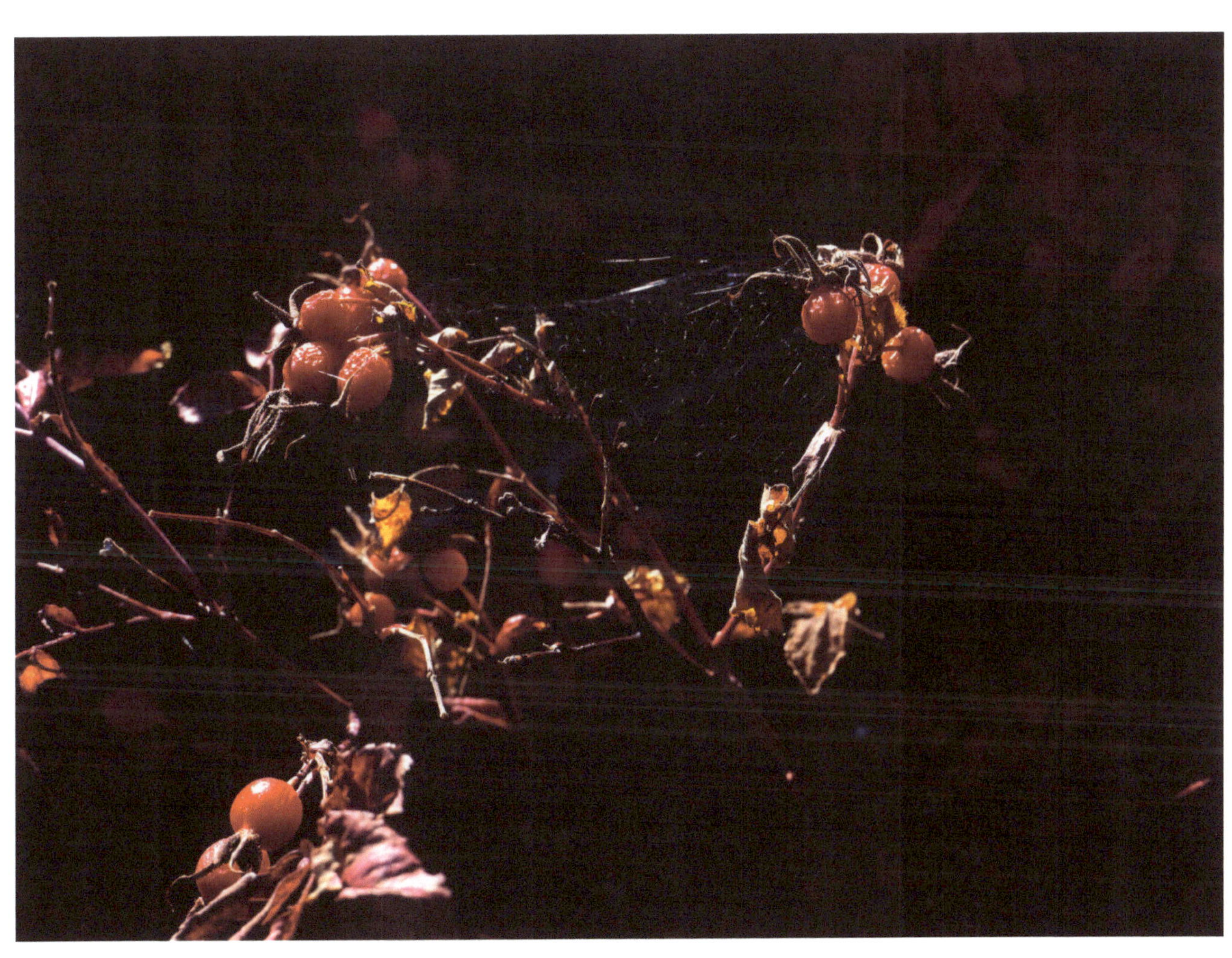

    Jay Cooke State Park, Minnesota

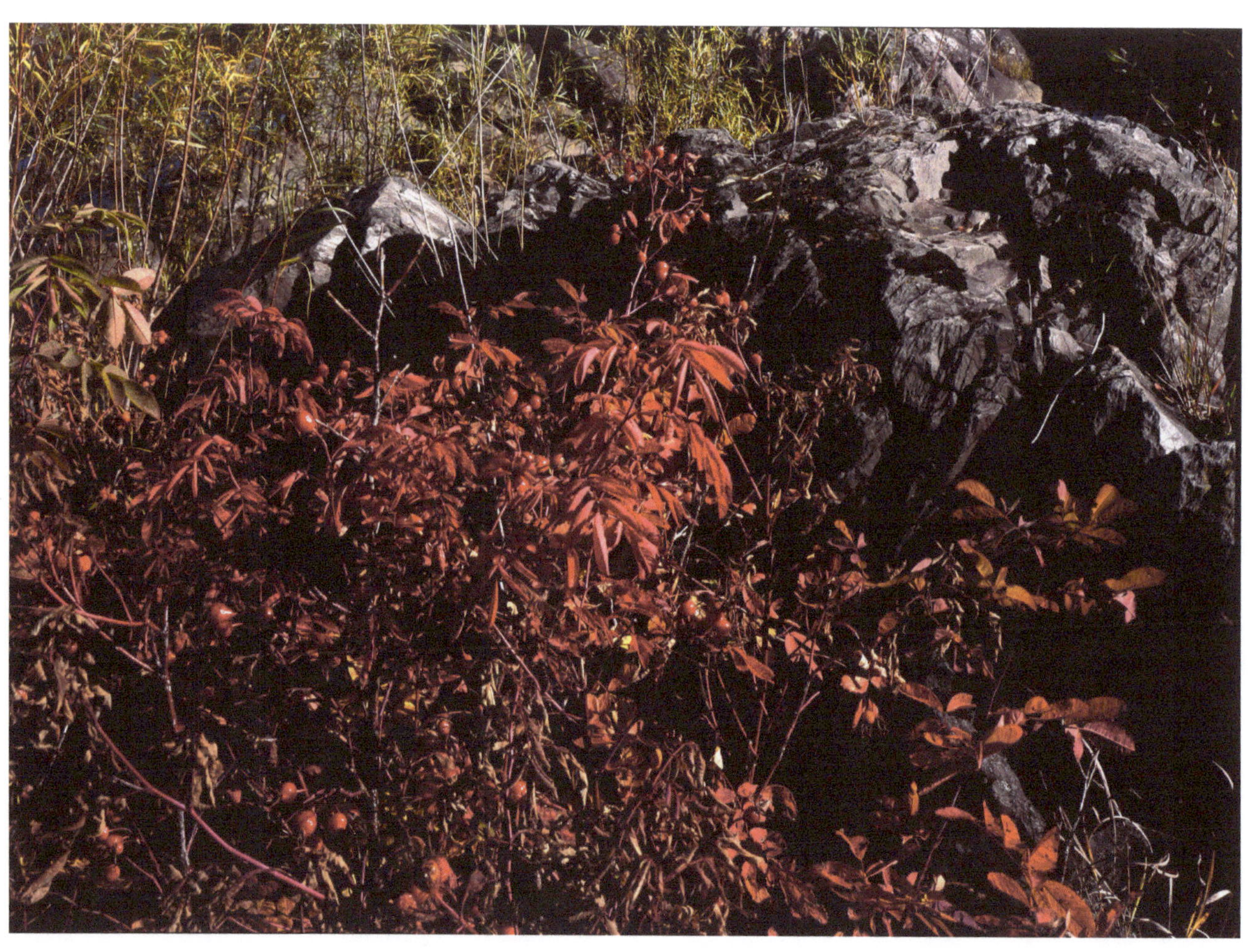

97   2054   Jay Cooke State Park, Minnesota

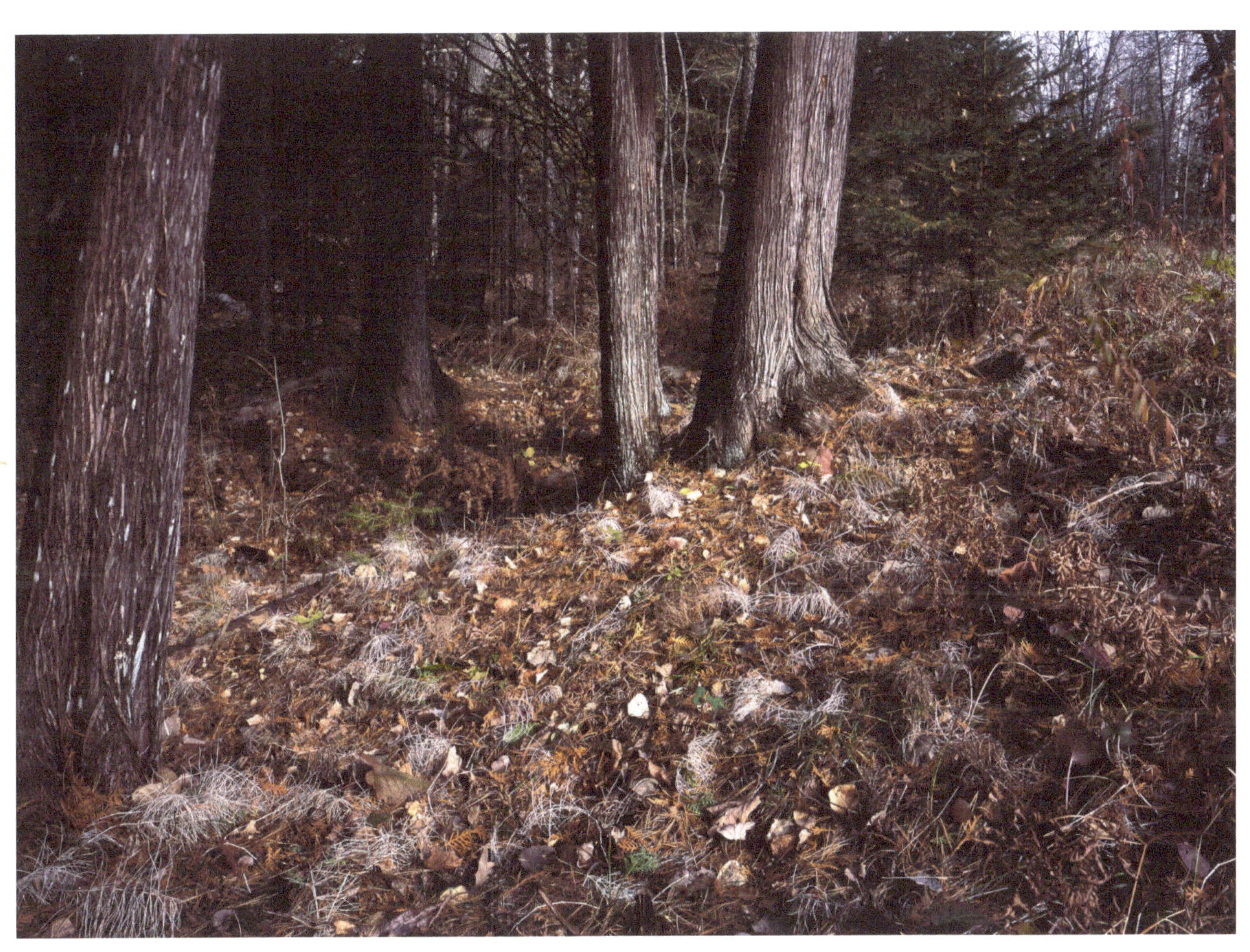

98   2059   Jay Cooke State Park, Minnesota

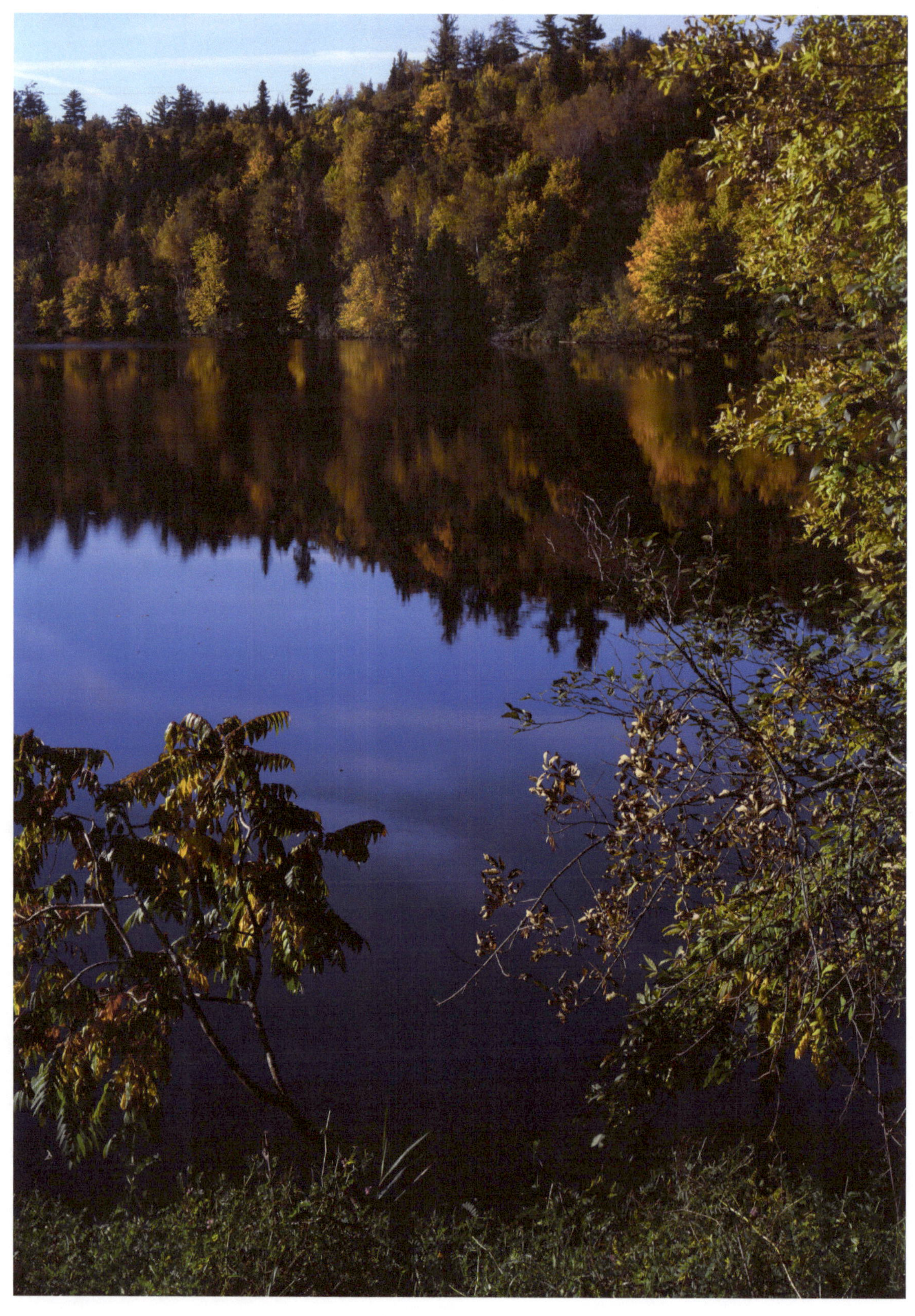

Jay Cooke State Park, Minnesota

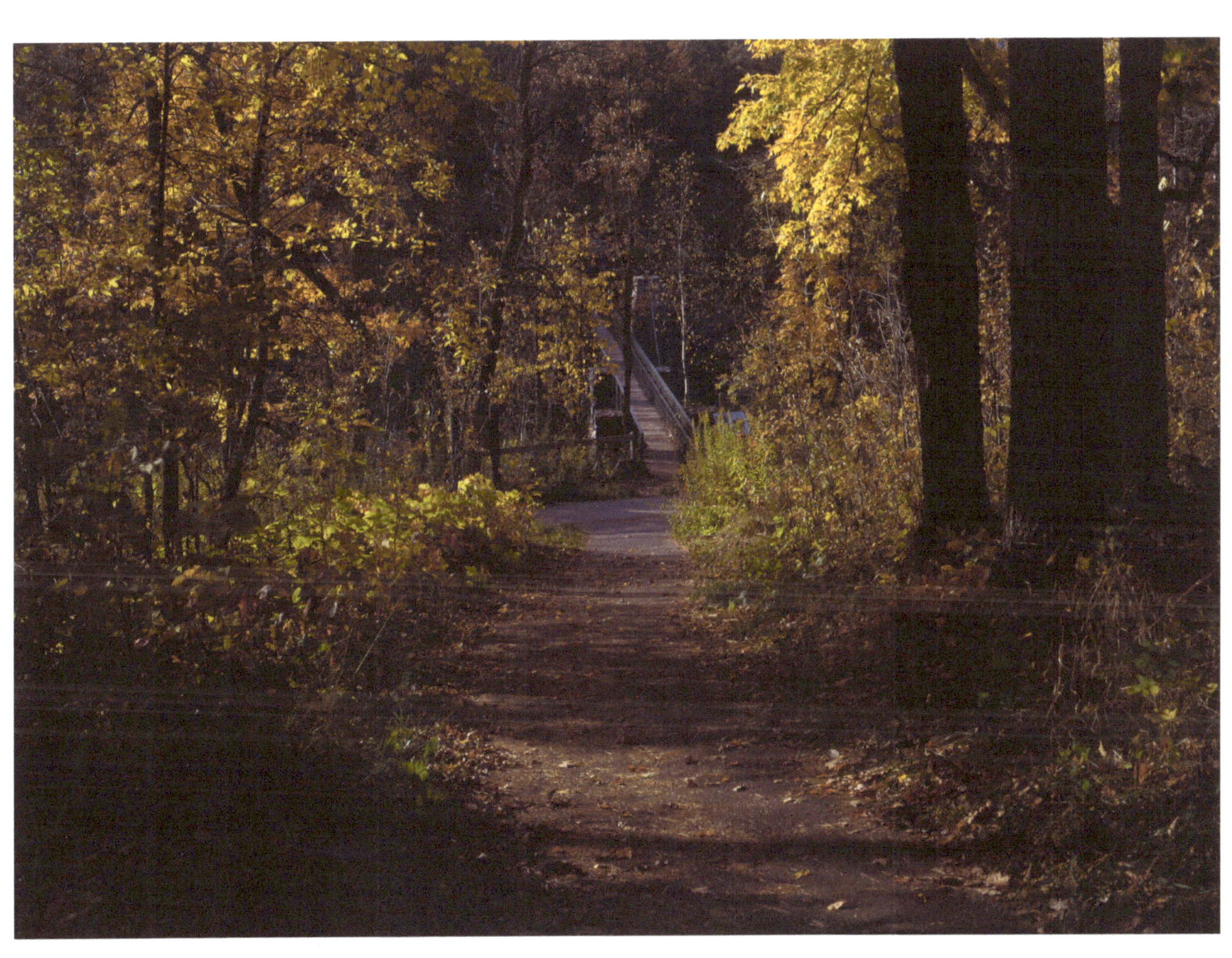

100   2126   Jay Cooke State Park, Minnesota

Appendix I

The Scheimpflug Principle

proof by Allen Anway.   This theorem shows that any plane, even at an unusual angle, may focus onto another plane, here the film, if the lens is adjusted properly. This gives the view camera its flexible focus compared with ordinary cameras.

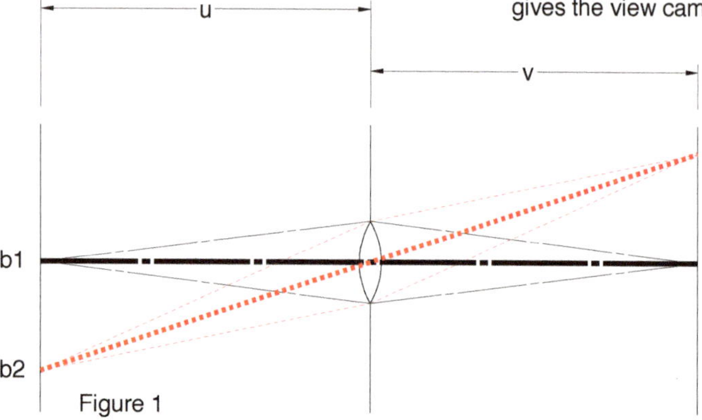

Assumptions: Figure 1
(1) A lens is an optical machine which can bring light rays originating at a point to intersections at another point. This is called focussing.
(2) $1/f = 1/u + 1/v$ thin lens focussing relation. f is a constant of the lens, the focal length.
(3) Flat field: The locus of off-axis focussing points is a plane perpendicular to the lens axis. The same focussing equation holds with the same distances u and v.
(4) Rays through lens center are undeviated even if not parallel to the axis (oblique ray shown in red color).

Construction to change the figure:
(5) Move b2 of Figure 1 toward lens, Figure 2.
(6) Figure 2, extend b1-b2 to intersect at b3.
(7) Draw b3-b4 and b3-b5 lines to focus points.

Question: Find b3-b4 relationship to b3-b5.

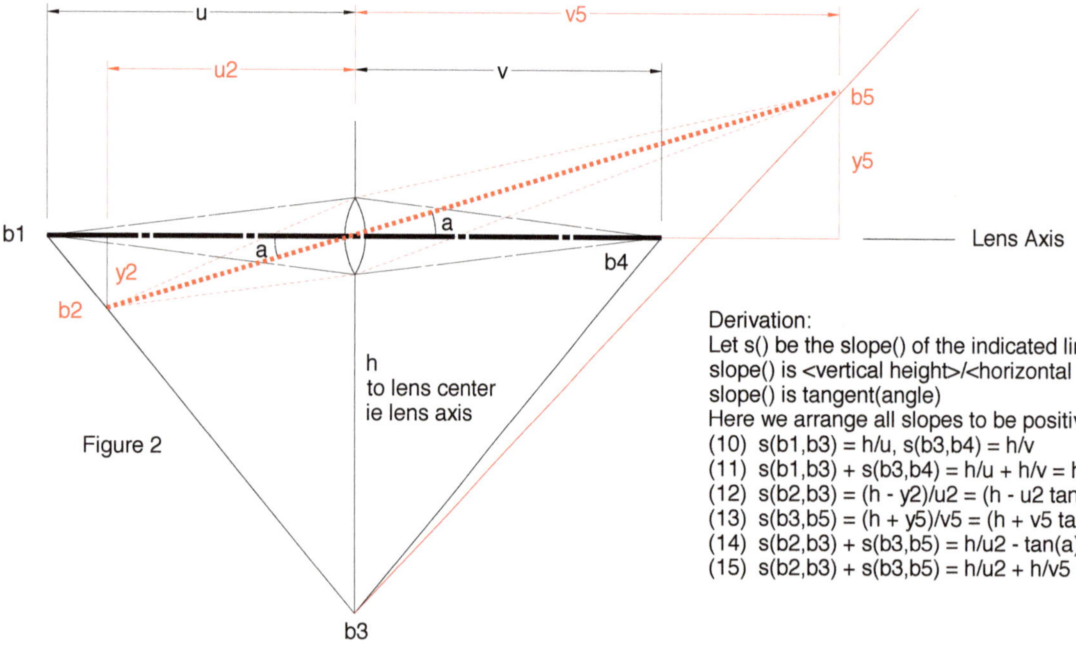

Derivation:
Let s() be the slope() of the indicated line.
slope() is <vertical height>/<horizontal distance>
slope() is tangent(angle)
Here we arrange all slopes to be positive.
(10) $s(b1,b3) = h/u$, $s(b3,b4) = h/v$
(11) $s(b1,b3) + s(b3,b4) = h/u + h/v = h/f$, a constant
(12) $s(b2,b3) = (h - y2)/u2 = (h - u2\,\tan(a))/u2$
(13) $s(b3,b5) = (h + y5)/v5 = (h + v5\,\tan(a))/v5$
(14) $s(b2,b3) + s(b3,b5) = h/u2 - \tan(a) + h/v5 + \tan(a)$
(15) $s(b2,b3) + s(b3,b5) = h/u2 + h/v5 = h/f$, a constant

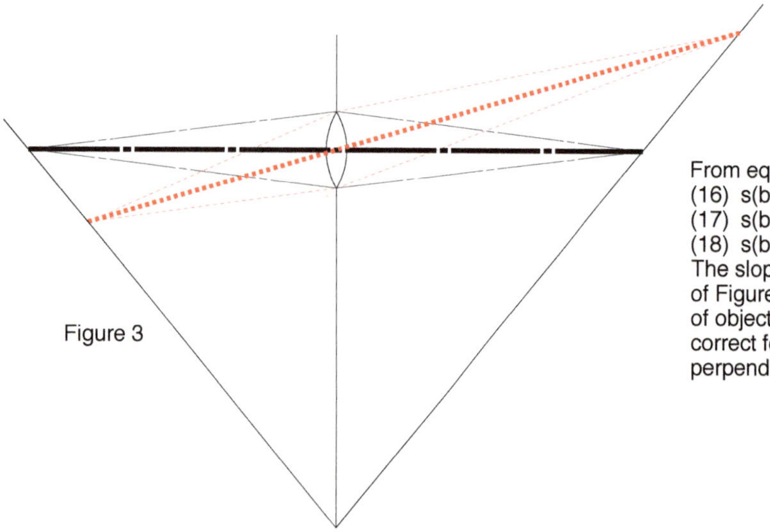

From equations (11) and (15) we get
(16) $s(b1,b3) + s(b3,b4) = s(b2,b3) + s(b3,b5)$,
(17) $s(b1,b3) = s(b2,b3)$ the left side slopes are alike, so,
(18) $s(b3,b4) = s(b3,b5)$.
The slopes drawn differently on the right hand side of Figure 2 are really the same. Thus the three planes of object, lens, and film meet at a common point for correct focus when the object or the film is not perpendicular to the lens axis, Figure 3.

Appendix 2

Technical Information About the Photographs

I used 5×7 cameras:
 a (1940s vintage) Burke & James Grover Monorail,
 b (1999) K B Canham T657 wood,
 c (2014) K B Canham T657 wood, and
 d (1970s?) Peter Gowland 5x7 Monorail.

I also purchased a bag bellows for the T657, useful for short focal length lenses. I used the Gowland when visiting my son-in-law, Keith, out west. I found his lending 5×7 cameras and lenses to visitors to be the mark of an exceptional host. Upon first receiving the Gowland, Keith modified the camera front lens holder so that we could both use Canham lens boards on it for interchangeable lenses.

Some photographers love the grand old lenses, but I assure the reader that the new ones are the good ones. The recent surge in digital camera technology has greatly reduced view camera lens manufacture. The Copal Shutter Company—all my lenses have Copal shutters—ceased their manufacture, also. I foresee that these newer lenses and shutters will become collectables. However, view camera manufacture still thrives, with amateur photographers still purchasing them.

no.	serial #		lens	date	place
1	321	h	305mm f/4.5 Carl Meyer Anastigmat	01-Nov-81	MN Duluth Fond du Lac W
2	324	h	180mm f/5.6 Symmar Convertible	01-Nov-81	MN Duluth Fond du Lac
3	1443	h	450mm f/9 Nikkor-M	08-Nov-03	MN JCSP swinging bridge N E
4	1448	h	300mm f/5.6 Symmar Convertible	19-Nov-03	MN JCSP swinging bridge N E
5	2066	h	240mm f/5.6 Sironar-N	07-Nov-10	MN JCSP CCC Trail
6	1696	h	240mm f/5.6 Sironar-N	09-Dec-06	MN JCSP swinging bridge N E
7	1700	h	135mm f/5.6 Apo-Sironar-S	10-Dec-06	MN JCSP swinging bridge N W
8	2068	h	240mm f/5.6 Sironar-N	27-Dec-10	WI Superior Dutchman Creek
9	1461	h	180mm f/5.6 Symmar Convertible	26-Feb-04	MN JCSP swinging bridge N W
10	884	h	180mm f/5.6 Symmar Convertible	12-Mar-00	MN JCSP Fond du Lac spillway
11	1884	v	300mm f/5.6 Symmar Convertible	14-Mar-09	MN Duluth Lester River, Lake Superior
12	2074	h	240mm f/5.6 Sironar-N	19-Mar-11	MN Scanlon - Carlton
13	2075	h	450mm f/9 Nikkor-M	23-Mar-11	MN Gooseberry Falls State Park
14	2076	h	450mm f/9 Nikkor-M	27-Mar-11	MN JCSP opposite Thomson Cemetery
15	2077	h	240mm f/5.6 Sironar-N	27-Mar-11	MN JCSP opposite Thomson Cemetery
16	2078	h	135mm f/5.6 Apo-Sironar-S	27-Mar-11	MN JCSP opposite Thomson Cemetery
17	2153	h	450mm f/9 Nikkor-M	18-Mar-12	MN Cascade River S P
18	106	h	180mm f/5.6 Symmar Convertible	12-Apr-75	WI Superior Superior Entry
19	914	v	180mm f/5.6 Symmar Convertible	29-Apr-00	MN Duluth Fond du Lac W
20	1468	h	240mm f/5.6 Sironar-N	10-Apr-04	MN JCSP Silver Creek Trail
21	1471	h	600mm f/9 Nikkor T*ED	17-Apr-04	MN JCSP St. Louis R opposite Little River
22	1728	v	240mm f/5.6 Sironar-N	22-Apr-07	MN JCSP White Pine Trail
23	2082	v	180mm f/5.6 Symmar Convertible	08-Apr-11	MN JCSP Little River tributary 44'
24	2083	h	300mm f/5.6 Symmar Convertible	09-Apr-11	MN Scanlon - Carlton
25	2085	h	180mm f/5.6 Symmar Convertible	24-Apr-11	MN JCSP swinging bridge N E
26	67	h	180mm f/5.6 Symmar Convertible	26-May-73	WI Superior Dutchman Creek
27	330	h	180mm f/5.6 Symmar Convertible	21-May-82	MN JCSP swinging bridge S W
28	335	v	180mm f/5.6 Symmar Convertible	30-May-82	MN Split Rock Lighthouse SP
29	366	h	180mm f/5.6 Symmar Convertible	21-May-85	MN Duluth arena
30	426	v	180mm f/5.6 Symmar Convertible	29-May-93	MN JCSP 210 East entrance
31	919	v	300mm f/5.6 Symmar Convertible	07-May-00	MN Scanlon - Carlton
32	923	v	180mm f/5.6 Symmar Convertible	13-May-00	MN JCSP Little River tributary 44'
33	1900	h	72mm f/5.6 Super Angulon XL	03-May-09	MN JCSP amphitheater W River Inn
34	1987	h	90mm f/5.6 Super Angulon XL	09-May-10	MN JCSP Carlton Trail near Ridge T
35	1988	h	72mm f/5.6 Super Angulon XL	15-May-10	MN Carlton County Road 4
36	1994	v	240mm f/5.6 Sironar-N	18-May-10	MN JCSP Oldenburg Point
37	2091	v	180mm f/5.6 Symmar Convertible	07-May-11	MN JCSP camping area N N CCC Trail
38	2095	h	180mm f/5.6 Symmar Convertible	25-May-11	MN JCSP swinging bridge N
39	2096	v	180mm f/5.6 Symmar Convertible	28-May-11	MN St. Louis Cty Road 8
40	2160	h	135mm f/5.6 Apo-Sironar-S	22-May-12	MN JCSP Silver Creek Trail Gazebo
41	72	h	180mm f/5.6 Symmar Convertible	16-Jun-73	MN JCSP Thomson Hydro opposite
42	931	v	180mm f/5.6 Symmar Convertible	04-Jun-00	MN JCSP Silver Creek Trail
43	1073	h	300mm f/5.6 Symmar Convertible	27-Jun-01	MN JCSP River Inn W
44	1744	h	135mm f/5.6 Apo-Sironar-S	08-Jun-07	MN JCSP Silver Creek Trail Gazebo
45	1751	h	135mm f/5.6 Apo-Sironar-S	28-Jun-07	MN JCSP River Inn W

time	f/	camera	film
1/10	f/32	B&J Grover 5x7	64 ASA 6117
1 sec	f/32	B&J Grover 5x7	64 ASA 6117
1/8	f/54	Canham T657	100 6105 8x10
1/2	f/22	Canham T657	100 6105 8x10
20 sec	f/45	Canham bag bllws	Provia 100F
1/8	f/64	Canham T657	100 6105 8x10
1 sec	f/32	Canham T657	100 6105 8x10
1/15	f/32	Canham bag bllws	Provia 100F
1/15	f/38	Canham T657	100 6105 8x10
1/2	f/38	Canham T657	100 ASA 6105
1/15	f/64	Canham T657	100 6105 8x10
1/4	f/64	Canham T657	E100G 8x10
1/30	f/27	Canham T657	E100G 8x10
1/4	f/128	Canham T657	E100G 8x10
1/30	f/45	Canham T657	E100G 8x10
1/60	f/32	Canham T657	E100G 8x10
1/8	f/128	Canham T657	E100G 8x10
1 sec	f/45	B&J Grover 5x7	50 ASA 6115
1/2	f/64	Canham T657	100 ASA 6105
1 sec	f/27	Canham T657	100 6105 8x10
1 sec	f/64	Canham T657	100 6105 8x10
1 sec	f/32	Canham T657	100 6105 8x10
1/8	f/45	Canham bag bllws	E100G 8x10
1/4	f/64	Canham T657	E100G 8x10
1/15	f/45	Canham T657	E100G 8x10
1/4	f/32	B&J Grover 5x7	50 ASA 6115
1/2	f/38	B&J Grover 5x7	64 ASA 6117
1 sec	f/64	B&J Grover 5x7	64 ASA 6117
1 sec	f/16	B&J Grover 5x7	64 ASA 6117
1/15	f/32	B&J Grover 5x7	100 ASA 6105
1/4	f/32	Canham T657	100 ASA 6105
1/4	f/32	Canham T657	100 ASA 6105
1/8	f/32	Canham T657	100 6105 8x10
1/2	f/32	Canham bag bllws	100 6105 8x10
1/4	f/32	Canham bag bllws	100 6105 8x10
1/60	f/8	Canham bag bllws	100 6105 8x10
1/4	f/54	Canham T657	Provia 100F
1/8	f/45	Canham T657	Provia 100F
1/8	f/32	Canham T657	Provia 100F
1/2	f/19	Canham T657	E100G 8x10
1 sec	f/28	B&J Grover 5x7	50 ASA 6115
1 sec	f/32	Canham T657	100 ASA 6105
1/4	f/45	Canham T657	100 6105 8x10
1/4	f/16	Canham bag bllws	100 6105 8x10
15 sec	f/22	Canham bag bllws	100 6105 8x10

no.	serial #		lens	date	place
46	1829	v	300mm f/5.6 Symmar Convertible	15-Jun-08	MN Two Harbors Burlington Bay
47	1907	v	300mm f/9 Rodenstock Geronar	05-Jun-09	WA Olallie SP I90 Exit 38
48	1913	v	420mm f/8 Fujinon-L	08-Jun-09	WA Franklin Falls near I90
49	1918	h	210mm f/5.6 Fujinon-L	10-Jun-09	WA Snoqualmie
50	2001	v	420mm f/8 Fujinon-L	22-Jun-10	WA Olallie State Park
51	2100	h	240mm f/5.6 Sironar-N	28-Jun-11	MN Scanlon - Carlton
52	2166	h	180mm f/5.6 Symmar Convertible	05-Jun-12	MN Thomson Thomson Dam
53	78	v	180mm f/5.6 Symmar Convertible	28-Jul-73	MN Otter Creek by Carlton
54	428	h	305mm f/4.5 Carl Meyer Anastigmat	05-Jul-93	WI Copper Falls SP
55	472	v	180mm f/5.6 Symmar Convertible	23-Jul-95	MN Gooseberry Falls SP
56	674	h	180mm f/5.6 Symmar Convertible	05-Jul-98	MN Carlton Munger Trail E
57	768	h	180mm f/5.6 Symmar Convertible	07-Jul-99	MN Thomson W
58	1493	h	180mm f/5.6 Symmar Convertible	10-Jul-04	MN JCSP swinging bridge N parking lot
59	1495	v	135mm f/5.6 Apo-Sironar-S	13-Jul-04	MN JCSP swinging bridge N E across 210
60	2012	h	180mm f/5.6 Symmar Convertible	11-Jul-10	MN Holyoke Net River
61	2101	v	300mm f/5.6 Symmar Convertible	02-Jul-11	MN Scanlon - Carlton
62	360	v	180mm f/5.6 Symmar Convertible	21-Aug-84	MN Pigeon River high falls
63	378	v	305mm f/4.5 Carl Meyer Anastigmat	05-Aug-90	MN Cascade River SP
64	381	v	180mm f/5.6 Symmar Convertible	10-Aug-91	MN East Beaver Bay
65	443	v	180mm f/5.6 Symmar Convertible	20-Aug-94	MN Caribou River
66	1401	v	135mm f/5.6 Apo-Sironar-S	30-Aug-03	MN JCSP swinging bridge S
67	1572	h	300mm f/5.6 Symmar Convertible	14-Aug-05	MN Scanlon - Carlton
68	1839	v	450mm f/9 Nikkor-M	19-Aug-08	CO Rky Mtn N Pk Nymph Lake
69	1842	h	150mm f/5.6 Fuginon-W	20-Aug-08	CO Rky Mtn N Pk one-way dirt road
70	1843	h	210mm f/5.6 Fujinon-W	21-Aug-08	CO Rky Mtn N Pk Hy 36
71	394	v	305mm f/4.5 Carl Meyer Anastigmat	02-Sep-91	WI Amnicon Falls SP
72	481	h	305mm f/4.5 Carl Meyer Anastigmat	08-Sep-95	MN Thomson Thomson Reservoir
73	1412	v	180mm f/5.6 Symmar Convertible	13-Sep-03	MN JCSP West Ridge Trail
74	1504	h	180mm f/5.6 Symmar Convertible	16-Sep-04	MN JCSP Little River
75	1662	h	300mm f/5.6 Symmar Convertible	30-Sep-06	MN JCSP swinging bridge N E
76	2027	h	180mm f/5.6 Symmar Convertible	11-Sep-10	MN JCSP swinging bridge N W
77	2030	v	135mm f/5.6 Apo-Sironar-S	13-Sep-10	WI Superior Dutchman Creek
78	2037	h	135mm f/5.6 Apo-Sironar-S	19-Sep-10	MN JCSP swinging bridge S W
79	2043	h	450mm f/9 Nikkor-M	26-Sep-10	MN JCSP swinging bridge N E
80	2118	h	115mm f/6.8 Grandagon	30-Sep-11	MN Cook Cty 164, tower road off of
81	2119	h	210mm f/5.6 Fujinon-L	30-Sep-11	MN Cook Cty 164, tower road off of
82	397	h	180mm f/5.6 Symmar Convertible	20-Oct-91	MN JCSP Little River Grand Portage Trail
83	453	v	180mm f/5.6 Symmar Convertible	08-Oct-94	MN Tettagouche SP
84	1417	v	72mm f/5.6 Super Angulon XL	05-Oct-03	MN Thomson Thomson Dam
85	1429	h	450mm f/9 Nikkor-M	08-Oct-03	MN JCSP Oldenburg Point
86	1435	h	300mm f/5.6 Symmar Convertible	12-Oct-03	MN JCSP Silver Creek Trail
87	1439	h	300mm f/5.6 Symmar Convertible	18-Oct-03	WI Oliver Harding Road
88	1869	h	180mm f/5.6 Symmar Convertible	18-Oct-08	MN JCSP Silver Creek Trail
89	1872	h	180mm f/5.6 Symmar Convertible	29-Oct-08	MN JCSP swinging bridge N E
90	1874	v	450mm f/9 Nikkor-M	29-Oct-08	MN JCSP swinging bridge N E

time	f/	camera	film
1/8	f/45	Canham T657	100 6105 8x10
1/8	f/64	Gowland 5x7	100 6105 8x10
1/15	f/45	Gowland 5x7	100 6105 8x10
1/8	f/27	Gowland 5x7	100 6105 8x10
1/15	f/54	Gowland 5x7	Provia 100F
1/15	f/45	Canham T657	Provia 100F
1/30	f/11	Canham bag bllws	E100G 8x10
1 sec	f/40	B&J Grover 5x7	50 ASA 6115
1/5	f/32	B&J Grover 5x7	100 ASA 6105
1/8	f/45	B&J Grover 5x7	100 ASA 6105
1/2	f/32	B&J Grover 5x7	100 ASA 6105
1/60	f/9.5	Canham T657	100 ASA 6105
1/8	f/45	Canham T657	100 6105 8x10
1 sec	f/22	Canham T657	100 6105 8x10
1 sec	f/32	Canham T657	E100G 8x10
1/2	f/64	Canham T657	E100G 8x10
1/15	f/32	B&J Grover 5x7	64 ASA 6117
1/2	f/32	B&J Grover 5x7	100 ASA 6105
1/4	f/32	B&J Grover 5x7	100 ASA 6105
1/4	f/22	B&J Grover 5x7	100 ASA 6105
1/8	f/32	Canham T657	100 6105 8x10
1/8	f/45	Canham T657	100 6105 8x10
1/2	f/64	Gowland 5x7	100 6105 8x10
1/8	f/32	Gowland 5x7	100 6105 8x10
1/4	f/45	Gowland 5x7	100 6105 8x10
1 sec	f/32	B&J Grover 5x7	100 ASA 6105
1/2	f/45	B&J Grover 5x7	100 ASA 6105
2 sec	f/38	Canham T657	100 6105 8x10
1 sec	f/45	Canham T657	100 6105 8x10
1/30	f/22	Canham T657	100 6105 8x10
1/8	f/32	Canham T657	E100G 8x10
1/30	f/32	Canham T657	E100G 8x10
1/8	f/32	Canham T657	Provia 100F
5 sec	f/128	Canham T657	Provia 100F
1/30	f/27	Canham bag bllws	E100G 8x10
1/15	f/38	Canham bag bllws	E100G 8x10
3 sec	f/32	B&J Grover 5x7	100 ASA 6105
1 sec	f/32	B&J Grover 5x7	100 ASA 6105
1/2	f/32	Canham T657	100 6105 8x10
2 sec	f/128	Canham T657	100 6105 8x10
1/4	f/32	Canham T657	100 6105 8x10
1/2	f/38	Canham T657	100 6105 8x10
1/15	f/38	Canham T657	100 6105 8x10
1/2	f/38	Canham T657	100 6105 8x10
1/2	f/64	Canham T657	100 6105 8x10

no.	serial #		lens	date	place
91	2044	h	240mm f/5.6 Sironar-N	02-Oct-10	MN Highway 210 mp 227 approx
92	2046	h	72mm f/5.6 Super Angulon XL	02-Oct-10	MN Scanlon - Carlton
93	2048	h	135mm f/5.6 Apo-Sironar-S	02-Oct-10	MN Scanlon - Carlton
94	2049	h	90mm f/5.6 Super Angulon XL	04-Oct-10	MN JCSP Silver Creek and River Tr
95	2050	h	135mm f/5.6 Apo-Sironar-S	04-Oct-10	MN JCSP River Trail
96	2053	h	135mm f/5.6 Apo-Sironar-S	07-Oct-10	MN JCSP River Trail
97	2054	h	180mm f/5.6 Symmar Convertible	07-Oct-10	MN JCSP River Trail
98	2059	h	135mm f/5.6 Apo-Sironar-S	19-Oct-10	MN JCSP Forbay Trail
99	2121	v	240mm f/5.6 Sironar-N	01-Oct-11	MN JCSP 210 Little River
100	2126	h	240mm f/5.6 Sironar-N	06-Oct-11	MN JCSP swinging bridge N

time	f/	camera	film
1/8	f/51	Canham T657	Provia 100F
1/4	f/22	Canham T657	Provia 100F
1/8	f/32	Canham T657	Provia 100F
1/2	f/32	Canham T657	Provia 100F
1/2	f/32	Canham T657	Provia 100F
1/2	f/27	Canham bag bllws	Provia 100F
1/2	f/64	Canham bag bllws	Provia 100F
1/4	f/32	Canham T657	Provia 100F
1/4	f/51	Canham T657	E100G 8x10
1/4	f/45	Canham T657	E100G 8x10